INTRODUCTION TO
INFORMATION QUALITY

Craig Fisher, Ph.D., MARIST College,
Eitel Lauría, Ph.D., MARIST College,
Shobha Chengalur-Smith, Ph.D., SUNY Albany,
and Richard Wang, Ph.D., MIT

authorHOUSE®

AuthorHouse™
1663 Liberty Drive
Bloomington, IN 47403
www.authorhouse.com
Phone: 1-800-839-8640

First published by AuthorHouse   12/27/2011

ISBN: 978-1-4685-3028-5 (sc)
ISBN: 978-1-4685-3027-8 (hc)
ISBN: 978-1-4685-3026-1 (ebk)

Library of Congress Control Number: 2011962905

Printed in the United States of America

TABLE OF CONTENTS

Preface

Data and information quality are receiving significantly more attention from the United States government since the terrorist attacks of 2001. The news media reported claims that bad information was, in part, responsible for the inability of the U.S. to prevent the attacks or readily track down the perpetrators. For example, as America was being attacked on September 11, 2001, fi5ghter planes were still searching for the airliner that had already struck the World Trade Center. They obviously did not have timely information. Shoot-down orders did not reach pilots until after the entire scenario was over. On the last day of public hearings, an independent panel revealed that military and aviation officials were inundated by bad information and poor communication. There were numerous reports of terrorist hijackings and suicide missions throughout the 1990s, yet all of that information seemed to be useless. A committee, headed by Eleanor Hill, delivered a 9-11 report to joint congressional and senate defense committees covering these points and others.

There is no doubt that we live in an information age. Ninety-three percent of corporate documents are created electronically. Every year, billions of email messages are sent worldwide. U.S. consumers spend billions of dollars over the Internet, and networked business-to-business (B2B) transactions are in the trillions of dollars. Pierce says, "The motivation for organizations to understand and improve data and information quality is more pressing than ever. Increasingly many organizations no longer maintain face-to-face contact with customers, vendors, government regulators or even employees" [6]. Clearly, there is much more use and dependence on information now than ever before. Hess and Talburt said that "Data quality is an essential element for successful Customer Relationship Management (CRM)" [3] while Strong and Volkoff said that Enterprise Resource Systems demand data of higher quality [7]. While the need for higher quality has increased, such as in customer data integration [3], data quality problems have also increased. Estimates of data quality problems vary widely, but none are small. Information quality problems cost U.S. businesses more than $600 billion annually.

A recent law requires Federal agencies to be responsible for disseminating quality data. The Treasury and General Government Appropriations Act of 2001 directs the Office of Management and Budget

(OMB) to issue government-wide guidelines that "provide policy and procedural guidance to Federal agencies for ensuring and maximizing the quality, objectivity, utility and integrity of information (including statistical information) disseminated by Federal agencies." Unfortunately, compliance is not easy. Not only are the guidelines subject to interpretation, but there is disagreement on the definitions of data quality and their implications. An edict won't make it happen without knowledge and skill.

Researchers have only recently begun to address data quality as a discipline in its own right, and a body of data quality literature has just begun to appear. Researchers at MIT began a total data quality management program and have hosted ten international conferences on information quality aimed at practitioners, academicians, and researchers. In addition, Information Impact International, Inc. has hosted 17 conferences on information quality, primarily aimed at practitioners. This book is built on two primary sources. After an extensive literature review and study, an importance of data quality knowledge and skills survey was completed by 110 data quality researchers and practitioners, all data quality leaders in their own right, at the International Conference on Information Quality held at the Massachusetts Institute of Technology (MIT)[2]. The results of these studies led to a consensus of the most critical skills necessary to begin performing information quality work. An introduction to those critical skills and knowledge areas are the primary topics of this book. The second source is the research into data and information quality of the four authors who collectively have published over 100 articles.

The goal of this book is to provide a foundation of knowledge and skills that, along with guidance, will prepare information systems (IS) and information technology (IT) professionals, systems and business analysts, and anyone who relies on data, to avoid or address data quality problems. Although today's IS and IT curricula require many courses that prepare the students to embark on a career of developing and implementing information systems, data quality problems still plague our systems. A total quality approach is required, which must involve stakeholders related to the data and information. It is much more than learning a few isolated skills and following a simple checklist. One author recently told a business executive that there are lots of data quality problems in the information products produced by IS and IT organizations. If a manufacturing plant had a fraction of the problems that IS has, the general manager would certainly be fired. He thought it was obvious; manufacturing uses statistical process controls, total quality management, and a variety of inspections.

The current IT and IS curricula include computer programming, database analysis and development, systems analysis and systems design, data communications, project management, and various related courses. The IS profession includes the formal application of specific methodologies for developing and implementing systems. Given the well-entrenched IS curriculum, many may ask why we need to focus on data quality. Some would say we cover data quality in data management or in programming. However, there is no denying that even with the education and methodologies, there have been tremendous adverse effects of poor-quality data and information throughout our society. Almost all businesses, government organizations, hospitals, educational institutions, and individuals have been hurt by data quality problems. The authors are convinced an organized discipline for data and information quality is sorely needed. Chapters 1-4 provide a broad basis for understanding the concepts and philosophy of data and information quality. Subsequent chapters build on these concepts by introducing tools and techniques essential for a data quality analyst to make improvements [1, 2, 4]. For people interested in using and applying these new tools and techniques, there are new jobs being formed in the information quality field. Dr. Elizabeth Pierce defined the role of data quality analyst in a paper she presented at the eighth International Conference on Information Quality [5].

Chapter 1 deals with the effects of poor-quality data. We believe that knowledge and awareness of this problem will motivate students to discover and solve the challenges ahead. The breadth, depth, and pervasiveness of data and information quality problems are staggering. We consider exposure and understanding of data and information quality problems to be a major aid to students' full understanding of, and commitment to improving data quality.

Chapter 2 harnesses the principles of total quality management with a heavy reliance on the works of Deming and Woodall. These principles allow IS and IT professionals to learn quality principles resulting from over 100 years of manufacturing experience.

Chapter 3 introduces the current state of research in data and information quality definitions. MIT and Northeastern researchers have defined 16 dimensions of information quality. Their meanings and relationships are explored. The understanding of these dimensions, their interactions and implications, provides a foundation for applying total quality management (TQM) principles to information.

Chapter 4 discusses the need to treat information as a product which opens the doors to the application of experience gained in manufacturing. The combination of treating information as a product and application of TQM leads us to total data quality management (TDQM).

Chapter 5 provides an essential introduction and review of statistics. Statistics is a key discipline that should be well understood in order to properly understand, weigh, and use evaluation and improvement treatments. Although the authors believe that a statistics course should be a prerequisite for an introduction to data quality course, they feel that a chapter dedicated to statistics will help the student make a clear application of statistics to data quality issues.

Chapter 6 summarizes statistical quality process control techniques that provide the foundations for applying statistics to improve the quality of products. One job of researchers and analysts is to make the leap from physical products to information products. Success will allow the tools and techniques used throughout the well-known and time-proven quality control processes in manufacturing to be applied to the management of the quality of information products.

Chapter 7 is an introduction to subjective and objective measurement tools. The subjective tool *Information Quality Assessment* examines all dimensions from the users' perspective while the *Integrity Analyzer* tool assesses the objective measures of data quality as defined by Codd.

Chapter 8 is an introduction to the role that data quality plays in data warehouses and data mining. Approaches and procedures to improve warehouse quality are covered. A good-quality data warehouse may be mined for critical data that provides information for improving an organization's business intelligence.

The primary target for this book is upper-level undergraduate students who are majoring in IS, IT, management information systems, marketing, economics, accounting, or business administration. It can also be used as a text in undergraduate courses such as data/information quality in information systems, or as supplemental reading in a variety of related courses. These include database design, data management, data warehousing, TQM, data mining, decision support systems, and business intelligence. It may also serve as supplemental reading in a graduate course or in a variety of industrial courses and public sector seminars that focus on information quality.

This book is an excellent guide and supplement for students pursuing graduate studies in Information Quality. It is anticipated that many graduate programs in information quality will begin over the next few years. The growth and dependence on information along with the increase in IQ problems supports this opinion. New programs have already started. Dr. John Talburt has pioneered advanced education in information quality through both masters and doctoral programs. He created the world's first graduate program in Information Quality, the Master of Science in Information Quality program, at the University of Arkansas, Little Rock (UALR) [4] and he has also begun the world's first Ph.D. program in Information Quality.

The primary purpose of this book is to help educate people about the critical issues in data and information quality that have been plaguing information systems for many years. Without proper attention, these problems will only get worse. Both the private and public sectors are beginning to take notice, but without focused attention on the processes, there is little hope for change. This book provides a good start.

Many people have contributed to the publication of this book. This book could not have been completed without the productive work environment provided by the MIT information quality program, the MIT TDQM program, and the UALR information quality graduate students who submitted many suggestions for edits and improvements.

We thank all our colleagues who inspired this book through their leadership in the field, especially Don Ballou and Harry Pazer, who pioneered research in this area at the University at Albany. During the Sixth International Conference on Information Quality in 2001, more than 100 researchers and practitioners completed a questionnaire that was used to determine which skills to include in this text. The paper, *What Skills Matter in Data Quality,* presented at the Seventh International Conference on Information Quality in 2002 represents the findings of that survey [2]. At that conference, Diane Strong and David Feinstein, who have long supported improvements in information quality education for our college students, participated in an education panel for that purpose.

Craig Fisher
Poughkeepsie, New York
craig.fisher@marist.edu

Shobha Chengalur-Smith
Albany, New York
shobha@albany.edu

Eitel Lauría
Poughkeepsie, New York
eitel.lauria@marist.edu

Richard Wang
Cambridge, Massachusetts
rwang@mit.edu

REFERENCES

1. Chung, W., C. Fisher, and R.Y. Wang, *Redefining the Scope and Focus of Information-Quality Work*, in *Information Quality*, R.Y. Wang, et al., Editors. 2005, M. E. Sharpe: Armonk, NY. p. 265.
2. Chung, W.Y., C.W. Fisher, and R. Wang. *What Skills Matter in Data Quality*. in *The Seventh International Conference on Information Quality*. 2002. Cambridge, MA: MIT TDQM Program.
3. Hess, K. and J. Talburt. *Applying Name Knowledge to Name Quality Assessment*. in *The Ninth International Conference on Information Quality*. 2004. Cambridge, MA: MIT TDQM Program.
4. Lee, Y.W., E.M. Pierce, J. Talburt, R.Y. Wang, and H. Zhu, *A Curriculum for a Master of Science in Information Quality*. Journal of Information Systems Education, 2007. 18(2): p. 233-242.
5. Pierce, E.M. *Pursuing a Career in Information Quality: The Job of the Data Quality Analyst*. in *Eighth International Conference on Information Quality*. 2003. Cambridge, MA: MIT TDQM.
6. Pierce, E.M., *Introduction to Information Quality*, in *Information Quality*, R.Y. Wang, et al., Editors. 2005, M. E. Sharpe: Armonk, NY. p. 265.
7. Strong, D.M. and O. Volkoff. *Data Quality Issues in Integrated Enterprise Systems*. in *Tenth International Conference on Information Conference*. 2005. Cambridge, MA: MIT TDQM.

Information Systems and Impacts of Poor-Quality Data

*I*nformation systems (IS) help organizations get, process, store, manage and report information so that everyone can do their jobs as efficiently and effectively as possible. IS organizations exist in every large corporation, government entity, and educational institution in the United States. Although these systems have had many names—electronic data processing, data processing, information systems, information services, information processing, data centers, information technology—the key words are *data* and *information*. The purpose of IS has always been to provide data and information to those who need it.

However, even after 40 to 50 years of IS experience, organizations are often less—rather than more—satisfied with the information they are getting. Experience in developing IS includes many years of improving techniques and processes to assure quality results. Some techniques are: structured programming, data validity checks, check digits, test and conversion strategies, inspections, and computer-assisted software engineering tools. Processes include application development methodologies often modeled after engineering development processes, joint application development, various levels of integration tests and user acceptance tests, rapid application development (RAD) methodology, use of various models such as data flow diagrams, and entity relationship diagrams. Object-oriented approaches, including a unified modeling language, are now being used. These can be found in modern textbooks on systems analysis and design or management information systems [26, 34, 36, 54].

Even with all of the improvements in processes and techniques, complaints of poor-quality data and bad information are frequent. Many of the processes and procedures mentioned in the previous paragraph take time and are full of errors. As a result, people bypass what seems to them a bureaucratic, time-consuming process. For example, the rapid development processes called RAD allow the developer to skip many of the bureaucratic steps [1]. Another factor that contributes to poor-quality data is end user computing (EUC). Although one of the primary goals of modern Windows-type facilities is to make it easy for end users to quickly build systems, this does not guarantee quality. Are organizations relying too much on EUC? Compare the training of an end user with an IS student. The IS student takes at least one semester of database development in which normalization and referential integrity are covered in detail. Many end users are not even aware of these data quality (DQ) techniques.

End-user-created databases are generally not easily integrated into the corporate IS. Data definitions, the abbreviations and names of the data, the system architecture, the software, and the interfaces involved vary so much from user to user and department to department, that any attempt to create an integrated database or data warehouse seldom ends satisfactorily. The existence of good development procedures is not effective if people can simply bypass them, whether through ignorance or design. An overall approach which includes treating information as products [51,52], modeling information management systems [3], building information product maps [5, 39, 41, 45], and applying total quality management (TQM) approaches, will be discussed in later chapters.

It could be that modern day information systems are so complex and cumbersome that accidents and errors cannot be avoided. For example, Fleet Bank launched a $38-million customer relations management project to pull together customer information from 66 source systems. The project failed in less than three years because it was too difficult and time consuming to understand, reconcile, and integrate data from so many sources [15].

Home Depot's IS supports over a million products in approximately 2,300 stores with many databases. Home Depot is attempting to tie together thousands of its software applications, stores, and systems [46]. Information systems consist of people, procedures, databases, systems hardware and software, and computer application programs [46]. The complexity of the systems, and of its components, may lead to DQ problems. Clearly, a very comprehensive approach to quality is necessary, and this will be covered in the remaining chapters.

INFORMATION SYSTEMS

This chapter is focused on examples of problems and their effects on people, organizations, the Federal Government, and society in general. We will summarize the effects after we distinguish between data and information.

Data Versus Information

There is an old saying that "one person's data is another person's information." Several textbooks distinguish between data and information. Data is defined as isolated facts devoid of meaning. Information is defined as processed data that has meaning because of relationships established with other data. For example, if a retailer sold 10 dresses, that might be an interesting fact but doesn't have much meaning by itself. However, if that retailer sold 100 dresses yesterday and 10 today, then more meaning can be derived. Meaning is enhanced by establishing relationships with other data. Additional data might include comparisons of this retailer's sales to those of a competitor; or comparisons of sales over intervals, such as sales per month, per quarter, or per year. It might also be important to know how many dresses were sold during a sales promotion or during an employee incentive program to sell, for example, 100 dresses. Another view might be the rate of sales. If sales were very high—10 dresses in 30 minutes—that might make the manager take action that would not be taken if the rate of sales was very low. Depending on the users and their purpose, the previous examples might be indicative of either data or information. The floor manager may want to know how many dresses are on display to determine if more should be brought to the floor. The store manager might want to know average daily sales to compare with the sales goals and competitors' sales.

Here is a manufacturing example. The number of parts in a stock room is a critical piece of information and must be accurate. The shop manager needs to know that detail to determine if he can build a product at 10:00 A.M. The shop manager's information, however, is simply data to an executive, since the executive needs to combine it with many other indicators to determine how well the plant is running overall relative to his goals and his competitors' performance. Since there are many levels and interpretations of the differences between data and information, we will treat data and information interchangeably. The context will make it clear.

The effects of poor-quality data and information are more than just a nuisance; they inhibit people at all levels in all types of organizations from performing their jobs properly. Poor-quality data is prevalent in both the private and public sectors.

Data quality is one of the most critical problems facing organizations today. As executives become more dependent on IS to fulfill their missions, DQ becomes an even bigger issue. Poor-quality data is pervasive and costly [12, 38, 42, 44]. "There is strong evidence that data stored in organizational databases are neither entirely accurate nor complete" ([28] p. 169).

Estimates of DQ problems range widely, but none are small. "Current data quality problems cost U. S. businesses more than 600 billion dollars a year" ([11, 15] p. 99). In industry, error rates as high as 75% are often reported, while error rates to 30% are typical [43]. Of the data in mission-critical databases, 1% to 10% may be inaccurate [29]. More than 60% of surveyed firms had problems with DQ [50]. In one survey, 70% of the respondents reported their jobs had been interrupted at least once by poor-quality data, 32% experienced inaccurate data entry, 25% reported incomplete data entry, 69% described the overall quality of their data as unacceptable, and 44% had no system in place to check the quality of their data [55].

In the summer of 2002, a couple checked into a lodge and were given a room key. When they arrived at their room, they found it was already occupied. The clerk who assigned the room had simply grabbed a key off the row of hooks and assigned that room number. This type of error can also happen to anyone using a computer to enter or extract data. Any interruption, such as a telephone call or someone dropping by the office, could cause a momentary loss of concentration, leading to an error with a costly or sometimes embarrassing effect.

Because of the nature of the system, some incidents of DQ problems may be systemic or unavoidable. Quality problems caused by human error are certainly avoidable, but some data problems fall in between these two extremes. The user may not have made an obvious error, and the system may not have errors due to system design. It is these not-so-obvious problems that lead to many of the undetected problems that plague systems end users. Much of the remainder of this book is dedicated to exploring those errors and how to avoid them, but for now we continue with the problems and effects of poor-quality data.

MANDATING QUALITY INFORMATION

Can We Legislate Good-Quality Information?

As a prelude to providing discussion of the effects of poor-quality data, let us consider the gravity of the situation. The Federal Government has now made poor-quality data illegal. Did you ever believe that the government would have to pass a law requiring its agencies to give out only good-quality data? Just a little reflection makes the situation seem absurd. One would expect that in the course of performing their tasks, those agencies would deliver good-quality information. However, industry and business leaders believed that agencies were disseminating information that forced their organizations to implement actions they weren't really required to take. Therefore, they pressed for "regulation of information."

Section 515 of the Treasury and General Government Appropriations Act of 2001 (PL 106-544, H. R. 5658) directs the Office of Management and Budget (OMB) to issue government-wide guidelines that "provide policy and procedural guidance to Federal agencies for ensuring and maximizing the quality, objectivity, utility and integrity of information (including statistical information) disseminated by Federal agencies." [37].

During 2002, the year following approval of Section 515, generally known as the *information quality act*, federal agencies issued hundreds of pages of agency-specific guidelines that included "administrative mechanisms allowing affected persons to seek and obtain correction of information maintained and disseminated by the agency that does not comply with the OMB guidelines." [37]. So we now live in an age where Federal laws are required to ensure that good-quality information is disseminated. In spite of this, good-quality information has not been achieved. There has been enormous public pressure for improved information because of situations like 9-11, terrorist tracking, the Iraq war, information warfare, downsizing, dependencies on electronic information, errors in everyday databases (such as billing files and credit ratings), corporate databases, NASA programs, and military problems. Bombing the wrong targets, the right targets at the wrong time, and problems such as those that occurred on the USS *Vincennes*[1] are just a few examples of the latter.

Information Warfare

Threat exposure is increasing. Information systems and their databases are becoming more prolific every year, making them a prime target. Digital assets include everything from financial statements to patient records to proprietary algorithms. For example, 93% percent of corporate documents are created electronically. Every year, billions of email messages are sent worldwide. U.S. consumers spend billions of dollars over the Internet, and networked business-to-business (B2B) transactions are in the trillions of dollars.

A growing concern is that we do not know the extent and impact of poor-quality data. The FBI says that approximately 10,000 cyber-crime complaints were filed in the year 2000, in which losses totaled over $265 billion. But reported losses do not begin to tell the story. Most cyber crime goes unreported and undetected [47]. Because of incomplete data, organizations do not know the actual extent of their losses and therefore cannot perform a proper evaluation to determine how much they should invest in security systems. Information is becoming increasingly important, which makes our exposure to poor-quality information even more critical.

Information is now a primary instrument of national power, and information warfare is an emerging area for conflict. Information is our most powerful weapon to secure our nation and combat terrorism. The office of the Assistant Secretary of Defense said that information warfare is "action taken to achieve information superiority by affecting adversary

---

[1]   The USS *Vincennes* is the U.S. Navy battleship that fired upon and destroyed an Iranian passenger airplane in 1988.

information, information-based processes, information systems and computer-based networks while defending one's own . . . ." However, simply gathering huge amounts of information is not the answer. Although law enforcements agencies gather data, they do not always properly manage, analyze, and share information [16].

On November 25, 2002, President Bush signed the "Homeland Security Act of 2002" into law. This law represents a concerted effort by the Federal Government to prevent terrorist attacks in the United States and to reduce vulnerability and minimize damage from attacks should they occur [16]. The newly formed Department of Homeland Security has made information a central element of its mission. One branch of the new department is called the "Information Analysis and Infrastructure Protection Directorate." It focuses on improving access—one dimension of DQ—to information that may help detect and disrupt terrorist activity. The directorate is also responsible for protecting that information [16]. There is a strong need to improve information sharing, and the government has designated $4.5 billion to address interoperability and sharing issues.

Conventional approaches to defensive information warfare focus primarily on physical security, electronic measures, and encryption. These areas control only a small subset of the range of impacts that information warfare attacks can have on information DQ. For example, subtle changes to information timeliness, accuracy, and believability can have significant impact on military command and control, yet pass undetected through standard security safeguards [25].

Compared to physical asset systems, information systems have more layers of abstractions and many interdependencies between nodes. Some attacks on IS may be easily detected. However, many types of attacks are very difficult to detect until the bad effects have already rippled through the system [25].

HEALTHCARE AND MEDICAL PROFESSION

"In recent years, the importance of good data has grown exponentially as most of the industrialized world has adopted data-driven, or evidence-based, health care which uses comparative data methods for clinical treatment methods" ([33] p. 85). Evidence-based decision making relies on consistent classification and reporting of medical information. A national survey of all accredited U.S. medical records managers examined variations in the classification of health care. In the healthcare industry, significant variation in the application of classification rules results in much misreporting of patient data. A recent study indicates that impacts occur in five areas [33].

- Over-reimbursement: errors caused over-reimbursement of billing claims in about 5% of records (p. 86).
- Under-reimbursement: Overall, 16.8% of respondents said that more than 5% of their records had significant under-reimbursement errors (p. 86).
- Billing recoding: Overall, 14% of managers reported that more than 5% of their data classification codes are changed by their billing departments. The data classification codes reflect things like principle diagnosis, and changes make it difficult to reconcile doctors' reports with billing reports. This contributes to the confounding of medical data reporting. "Data is often changed by health care billing departments, often to the financial advantage of organizations" (p. 86).
- Management influences: 43.5% of respondents indicated that senior management sought to "reflect the maximum allowable reimbursement rate" (p. 87).
- Clarity of Guidance: 36% of respondents said that government guidance on how to comply with coding and classification requirements was unclear. Ignorance of the requirements resulted in different interpretations and definitions by the organizations, making information consolidation attempts impossible.

Doctors generally support patients' attempts to recover money from stringent healthcare organizations and insurance companies. The pressure to control healthcare costs causes erroneous data. When doctors, clinics, and hospitals feel that insurance companies do not give fair value for treatment, the medical provider may change the diagnosis to a more serious one. For example, 40% of physicians reported that they exaggerated the severity of patient conditions, changed billing diagnoses, and reported non-existent symptoms to help patients recover medical expenses. The reimbursement for bacterial pneumonia averages $2,500 more than for viral pneumonia. Multiplying this by the thousands of cases in hundreds of hospitals will give you an idea of how big the financial errors in the public health assessment field could be ([33] p. 87).

Insurance companies and Health Maintenance Organizations (HMO) use comparative studies across groups to set their coverage rates. They base them on what treatments for the condition typically costs. "Inaccurately classified medical information in such environments can result in health care decisions that are ineffective or potentially life threatening" ([33] p. 88).

Examples of the impact of poor-quality data in medical situations abound in daily life. One case in point has a nurse stopping at a hospital room on her floor at 11:00 P.M to give medications to a patient. The sleepy patient fortunately asked what the medications were and what purpose they served. During the ensuing conversation it was determined that the patient did not have the maladies that the medication was intended to cure. In addition the patient was allergic to that medicine. Finally he was the wrong patient! It turned out that she had intended to stop in the next room, but after talking to someone in the hall, she accidentally turned the corner too soon and walked into the wrong room. She was embarrassed, but the patient was miffed. The result could have been deadly. It is easy to see how this happened, but not all DQ problems are quite so easy to analyze. One function of this book is to alert information quality analysts to the types of errors that happen and provide techniques for addressing them.

To emphasize the seriousness of so-called simple mistakes, consider

> Why is this accident of walking into the wrong hospital room considered a DQ problem? In what ways is a general mistake something that should concern data quality analysts?

this quote from the Institute of Medicine. "In December 1999, the Institute of Medicine issued a report estimating that 44,000-98,000 Americans die each year from preventable medical errors such as prescription mistakes, mislabeled blood samples, and illegible handwritten patient data on paper forms" [40].

PUBLIC SECTOR

There are examples of the serious negative impacts of poor-quality data in the public sector as well as the private sector. Poor-quality data contributed to the 9-11 disaster. For example, as America was being attacked on September 11, 2001, fighter planes were searching for the airliner that had already struck the World Trade Center. They obviously did not have timely information. Shoot-down orders did not reach pilots until after the entire scenario was over. On the last day of public hearings, an independent panel revealed that military and aviation officials were inundated by bad information and poor communication. There were numerous reports of terrorist hijackings and suicide missions throughout the 1990s, yet that information seemed to be useless. A committee, headed by Eleanor Hill, delivered a 9-11 report to joint congressional and senate defense committees covering these points and others [17, 21, 30].

The pervasiveness of poor-quality data extends into our most advanced technological projects. It can be argued that the USS *Vincennes'* decision to shoot down an Iranian Airbus in 1988 was, in part, based on poor-quality data. Both space shuttle disasters, the *Challenger* in 1986 and the *Columbia* in 2003, can be blamed, in part, on poor-quality data. Incidents of poor-quality data extend far beyond these examples. In chapter 3 we will discuss these incidents in light of the work being done to further define the multiple dimensions of DQ.

Nothing illustrates the *security* and *privacy* problems of modern day government databases as well as the FBI's recent counter-terrorism efforts. Ann Davis of the *Wall Street Journal* reported that the FBI, in response to 9-11, circulated the names of hundreds of people it wanted to question. Counter-terrorism officials gave the list to car-rental companies. FBI field agents and other officials circulated it to banks, travel agents, firms that collect consumer data, and casino operators. Other recipients were businesses thought to be vulnerable to terrorist intrusion, including truckers, chemical companies, and power-plant operators. It was the largest intelligence-sharing experiment the Bureau has ever undertaken with the private sector [13].

A year later, the list took on a life of its own, with (error-filled) versions being passed around like bootleg music. Some companies fed a copy of the list into their databases and used it to screen job applicants and customers.

A trade association used the list in lieu of standard background checks, says the New Jersey group's executive director [13].

This watch list of potential terrorists and contacts—just one part of the FBI's massive counter-terrorism database—quickly became obsolete as the bureau worked its way through the names. The FBI's counter-terrorism division quietly stopped updating it, but never informed most of the companies that had a copy. FBI headquarters doesn't know who is still using the list, because officials never kept track of who got it. "We have now lost control of that list," says Art Cummings, head of the strategic analysis and warning section of the FBI's counter-terrorism division. "We shouldn't have had those problems" [13]. This example is frightening—the FBI could not control a simple tracking database. The reader should want to know how pervasive poor-quality data problems are and what impact they have.

The space shuttle disasters and the USS *Vincennes* attack on Flight 655 portray a variety of data-quality issues. The USS *Vincennes* mistakenly shot down an Iranian Airbus on July 3, 1988. The ship's captain and others stated that their information was ambiguous, and they had less than four minutes to take action. These servicemen argued that with more time, they would have verified their information and might not have shot down the Airbus. They considered the time constraint a major factor in their decision, and acknowledged they did not have time to verify the information according to standard procedure.

The case of the space shuttle *Challenger* also included deficiencies in DQ. The physical cause of the explosion was O-rings that failed to seal properly, but NASA was aware of O-ring problems for many years. It had restudied the problem of O-rings six months before the *Challenger* launch and had a decision process in place that took more than six hours. Yet NASA decided to launch the space shuttle *Challenger*, which exploded 73 seconds later because of those faulty O-rings. The Roger's Commission cited mismanagement; however, the deficiencies in various dimensions of DQ may have contributed to that mismanagement [19]. Deficiencies included errors in databases, such as misclassification of severity levels of O-ring problems, and problems were listed as closed when they were not; these represent the DQ dimension, *accuracy.* Examples of the *completeness* dimension are: there was no list that cross-referenced critical components with detail testing plans, certain launch-constraint waivers were not passed to upper-level managers responsible for final launch decisions, and regression graphs used to analyze the relationship between temperatures and O-ring defects did not contain all the data. Charts were not in a format readily understood by the executives, and thus were not *interpretably relevant* to the problem.

The space shuttle *Columbia* disaster showed deficiencies in several dimensions of information quality. The information was *incomplete, inaccessible, inaccurate, unbelievable,* and *untimely* (the information came too late). These five dimensions are covered in detail in chapter 3, but the subset related to the *Columbia* and *Challenger* is mentioned now. Officials ignored warnings because they didn't believe that foam falling off part of the rockets could damage the heat shield on the shuttle; this is the DQ dimension *believability*. Certain analysis charts omitted problems with the foam, and pictures were not available for analysis; this is the DQ dimension *completeness*. A task force that was working on fixing a ramp problem fell behind and scheduled their report to be completed after the *Columbia* was scheduled to land. One of the meetings of engineers called to analyze the risks of the loss of heat shield tiles was concluded too quickly with the leader saying "Let's wrap it up. We have got to go to Linda Ham's meeting at 8, and we just have got 5 or 10 minutes. Let's speed it up here" ([6] p. 128). These are examples of the DQ dimension *timeliness*. The models that were meant to illustrate where debris would hit the shuttle were not *accurate*. NASA engineers asked the Department of Defense for pictures of the shuttle in flight but were overruled, and the protocol for engaging Department of Defense managers was unclear. The ignorance of the protocol and the strict protocols made the information inaccessible; this is the DQ dimension *accessibility*.

PRIVATE SECTOR

Problems with data quality cause real losses, both business and social [22]. Although we know that poor-quality data is responsible for these losses, it is difficult to measure the extent of these losses. Davenport states, "no one can deny that decisions made based on useless information have cost companies billions of dollars" ([12] p. 221).

Costs may involve reduced customer satisfaction, increased expenses, reduced job satisfaction, impeded re-engineering, hindered business strategy, and hindered decision making [43, 55]. Poor-quality data also affects operational, tactical, and strategic decision making [44]. Davenport describes a manufacturing problem in which managers needed more scheduling information, and so implemented an expensive IS. However, because line managers supplied inaccurate data to the new system, its implementation did not improve production scheduling [12].

Because of their economic situation, many companies have raced toward downsizing. Management has often chosen to maximize automation to reduce people costs. Although these automation projects have reduced labor costs, they have backfired because of DQ problems and actually cost companies billions of dollars, according to the *Wall Street Journal* [4]. .

In 1995, the Niagara Mohawk Power Corporation in upstate New York automated its accounts payable and reduced its accounts payable staff by 50%, only to find that it was now overpaying vendors by hundreds of thousands of dollars. For example, Niagara Mohawk paid $10,680 twice to a maintenance company because two different purchase orders were issued for the same service, and the system did not detect the discrepancy. "An accounts payable clerk with long experience would have spotted the error but a computer only spots an error if it is programmed specifically to catch the exact mistake" ([4], p. 1). "Niagara Mohawk receives approximately 200,000 invoices per year. Their system can check purchase orders against invoices to spot duplicate payments but fail to kick out such payments if the order and invoice didn't have the exact same identification number" ([4], p.1). These problems are analogous to duplicate records found in many large databases and warehouses in which data has been combined from smaller databases. Techniques such as *record matching* detect duplicates; these are discussed in the chapter on tools and techniques.

Data quality problems allow unscrupulous people to commit fraud. "Computers don't always catch payables fraud, Mr. Arnold finds. He recalls a Midwestern manufacturer that reduced its payables staff and later paid $175,000 to a so-called plastic-molding business. After it sent the check, it learned that the vendor doesn't exist. The computer didn't spot a dead giveaway: 'The "vendor's" initials matched those of the company official who signed the invoice, Mr. Arnold says. A curious employee checking the invoice would surely have spotted the duplicate initials'" ([4], p. 1). "At one company a clerk stole thousands of dollars by changing a vendor's name to his own, writing checks to himself and reprogramming the computer to conceal the theft" ([4], p. 1).

In the cases cited, people can judge and sense discrepancies that software cannot. However, humans do not detect some errors as well as computers. Humans get tired and bored and make oversights when looking at thousands of transactions. Humans need special instructions, motivation, and rewards to be effective at detecting errors [28, 29].

Despite the pervasiveness of poor-quality data, users are generally ineffective in detecting errors. MIS researchers need to develop better theories of human error detection [29]. It is well known that using certain behavior theories improves performance [32, 49]. For example, Locke and Latham have shown that specific and demanding goals significantly improve performance compared to vague and easy goals [31]. Taylor demonstrated the critical role of specific feedback [49]. Klein (1997, 1998) has shown that the judicious application of measurements and goals can improve human performance in catching data errors. These studies show that people need specific measurements and goals to detect errors and correct data. However, companies rarely have measures of the quality of their information [12]. Measurement is a key subject in chapter 5 of this text.

An organization wants to know if its employees are conscious of the importance of DQ. However, it is not enough to ask people for self-reports, since people generally report what they think upper management wants to hear [35]. One possible approach is to give randomly selected members of an organization a task that includes data quality information (DQI). If the DQI was used to influence the task outcomes, then members were sensitive to it. Conversely, if the DQI did not influence the task outcomes, then people were not sensitive to it. Fisher, Chengalur-Smith, Ballou, and Pazer have been exploring the usefulness of providing information that describes the reliability of data to the decision makers [8, 18]. There are moderating variables: general experience, specific experience, managerial role or technical role, time constraints, and time pressure [18].

Exactly how poor-quality data affects decision makers is not completely known [9]. However, it is clear that if data is wrong, decisions based upon that data might be wrong. When doctors, lawyers, weather forecasters, and mechanics make decisions based on poor-quality information, there is a greater risk that their conclusions are wrong. Conversely, if data is 100% reliable, conclusions are much more likely to be correct. If a decision maker was certain of having wrong data, then the decision maker would not rely on the data. However, *certainty* is an elusive component in our everyday lives. Kingma said that even a suspicion of poor-quality data influences decision making [27]. For example, a used car salesperson may have a good-quality car worth several thousand dollars, but because of the poor credibility of used car salespeople, no one will pay what the car is worth. The consumer just doesn't believe it. We will later see that believability and reputation are key dimensions of information quality. It is interesting that Kingma arrived at his finding—believability—by following laws of economics.

Poor-quality data spreads beyond the organizational database. The problem is prevalent in many, if not all, markets to varying degrees [27]. Whenever information is bought or sold, there is a possibility that imperfections in the information could cause market failure [27]. The interaction of quality differences and uncertainty may account for the existence of important institutions in the labor market [1]. The economy is so universally affected, that whole new markets (legal guides, consumer magazines, credit reporting agencies, seals of approval, endorsements) have evolved specifically to correct problems with poor-quality information [1, 27].

Every day, poor-quality data affects decisions made by people in all walks of life, people who are not always aware of the poor quality of the data on which they rely. Selling a used car is a good example of the effect that a suspicion of poor-quality data can have on decision making. A very good used car is almost never sold at its true value. Buyers are seldom willing to pay the price because of their suspicions of the quality of the seller's information. Poor-quality data reduces the average quality of goods and shrinks the market [1, 27].

Poor-quality data has many impacts on decision making. Choices are made among various alternatives, each with their own strengths and weaknesses. Analysis of the alternatives and their attributes are highly dependent upon quality information. People make choices based on limited resources (data), and misinformed people tend to make poor decisions [27].

ONE COLLEGE EXAMPLE—STUDENT EVALUATIONS

At most colleges today, students evaluate classes during the last few weeks of the semester, and the evaluations are forwarded to the professors within a month or so. The evaluations are completed in class on optical mark-sense forms. One hallmark of the evaluations is that they are anonymous, so a student can be completely honest without fear of retribution from the teacher.

Although it is said that these evaluations are only one indication of the teacher's performance and must be included in a bigger picture in order to make a formal assessment of the teacher, most feel that a lot of weight is placed on them. For example, when a teacher applies for tenure or promotion, one of the first few questions asked is "How were the evaluations?" If the evaluations were weak, then the teacher has little chance of success. More importantly, teachers use these evaluations to determine what did or didn't work for that class. If a teacher added a new grading procedure, then a question about clarity of grading policies might show if the teacher should keep using the new procedure or switch to a different one. Over time, teachers can make use of the evaluations to improve their courses. Therefore, the quality of these evaluations is important.

One college recently switched procedures for producing the evaluation reports. Historically, the employees in the office of the dean of faculty were responsible for scanning and running the evaluations. In the fall of 2004, this responsibility was moved to another department. Simultaneously, a new system was installed, and a new reporting format was used. The new department used the semester registration course/class call number[2] as a control number for identifying which set of evaluations went with which teacher. In effect, they decided that "call number" would be a good primary key. On the surface, this had merit, but it was not researched very well. The call number is short, clear, and is used easily by students and the registrar for registration. There is no ambiguity; each class has one—and only one—call number. What could possibly go wrong?

In June of 2005 the evaluations for the spring 2005 semester were mailed to faculty. A few faculty members immediately recognized that their evaluations were wrong. An evaluation for a teacher who taught an independent study course to one student received a report indicating 32 students completed the evaluation. The teacher thought that perhaps when only a few students completed the evaluation, a dummy number was substituted. That idea was soon rejected, since the teacher would

---

[2]   "Call number" is the number used by the registrar during the registration process to control registrations for a particular semester.

still be able to immediately identify the author of the evaluation, thus nullifying the anonymity requirement. The teacher also wondered how the student could have done an evaluation, since the student was never given an evaluation form. The teacher discussed it briefly with another teacher who explained that students had been known to go directly to the dean for evaluation forms. But the teacher's dean said "No, that is not possible. It is only possible if a particular class was established to get evaluated that semester." Another teacher had a course with 14 students, but her evaluation form listed the student count at 22, so she is investigating that evaluation. Several other teachers reported problems as well. However, an administrative assistant said that since it looked like only a few reports were wrong, the process worked pretty well.

> **Food for Thought:** *What roles do opinions like those of the administrative assistant play in the quest for improving information quality? Should the college assume that there were only a few errors, or should it undertake a review? Explain your views.*

The potential impact of this DQ problem was high and annoyed many teachers in spite of the administrative assistant's assessment. Even when such a problem is corrected, there is lingering doubt that someone, perhaps a dean, received a printed copy of the evaluation and didn't discard it. The reputation of the system is jeopardized, and the believability of the information is at stake. There is some fear that the report might show up again.

So what was the problem? Unbeknownst to the department running the evaluation reports, the registrar regularly reuses call numbers. Every faculty member who taught a course that was not scheduled for evaluation became subject to the current error. The system scanned the current semester call numbers for a match; if a match was not found, it scanned prior semesters. However, the call number for a prior semester might be for any of approximately 600 teachers, including adjuncts. Interestingly, this type of problem occurred in the USS *Vincennes* example discussed in the text. There were several aspects of the problem starting with the reuse of a primary key field. Entity identifiers should only be reused with the greatest of awareness and caution. *We do not recommend it!* Target identifiers were reused in the AEGIS Weapons system onboard the USS *Vincennes*.

Another aspect is that there was not much of a TQM understanding and commitment demonstrated by the administrative assistant's comments: the system ran well, since there were only a few errors.

IMPACT OF TOTAL QUALITY MANAGEMENT (TQM) IN THE MANUFACTURING WORLD

This book is being written because the skills and techniques covered and stressed throughout the IS curriculum still do not guarantee good-quality databases. Since the mid-1980s, there have been numerous articles calling for IS managers to become part of the corporate strategic management team. But would the corporate information officer (CIO) really be accepted in that company? Suppose a manufacturing plant had a 30-70% error rate in its main product. Would the general manager survive in the executive position? Not likely. Why would the other top managers want the CIO as part of their team if the CIO's primary responsibility of creating information produced information with 30-70% errors? Driving home this point, please consider what would happen to a manufacturing manager who delivered products with 30-70% defects.

Many books and journal articles note the positive success of TQM techniques in the manufacturing environment. Deming, Juran, and Crosby, among others, have pioneered TQM techniques as they apply to reaching the best-quality production of the manufactured product. One basic concept of TQM is an attitude that good quality is achievable, and that the total organization should be involved in making it happen. Compromises that lessen quality simply do not pay off [10, 14, 24].

As an IS development manager in a large corporation, one author had the privilege of meeting Phil Crosby at a meeting in which he was telling a group of manufacturing managers the necessity of achieving zero defects. The managers thought this was unobtainable. They complained that their vendors could never deliver the best-quality parts in order to make this a reality. Mr. Crosby said the managers should reject the poor-quality parts and demand 100% quality. He told them they have to start somewhere. The managers again lamented the foolishness of this idea. But Mr. Crosby patiently explained that the vendors knew their quality and knew which customers would accept poor-quality parts. So, if they continued to accept poor-quality parts, the vendor would probably be sending their best-quality parts to their competitors.

The Data Warehousing Institute (TDWI) doesn't agree that the goal should be error-free data. It reports that ". . . it is nearly impossible to ensure that all data meet the above criteria [accuracy, integrity, consistency, completeness, validity, timeliness and accessibility] 100 percent" ([15] p. 11). At first this statement seems counterproductive, but TDWI reported that different workers and different types of workers require different levels of quality. The goal is to meet the required needs for the various users. As shown earlier, an executive has different needs than a line manager. We will follow the theme that the data must be fit for the use of a specific user and, therefore, can vary in degree of quality. However, this is a fine line, because once the users see and use the data, the data must function as 100% quality for the users' purposes [15].

AN EXAMPLE OF AN INFORMATION QUALITY PROBLEM IN AN ENGINEERING LABORATORY

The engineering division of a company consisted of over 30 departments of engineers. Because of the demand for EUC to relieve the backlog of IS and eliminate the middleman between IS and the user, the engineering departments were encouraged to develop their own application systems. The engineers were, of course, intelligent people and could improve their productivity by bypassing the IS personnel. The departments worked together in groups of two, three, or four on similar aspects of their end products. For example, engineers working on power and electrical problems worked closely with those working on mechanical and thermal problems. Certain components needed to be cooled, and cables needed to be run through a product bypassing other wires and components. An engineering records organization worked closely with a product and systems assurance organization. Also involved in the overall process was an engineering model room, an engineering change coordinator, and the logic engineers. The EUC philosophy led to a total of 15 standalone systems for project management, problem management, change management, and tracking. When an executive inquired as to where they were in the process, it often took over a week to get the answer.

Because of differing definitions, the engineering organization could not tell the executive the exact number of open problems. Some departments reported a problem as closed if they solved it. Some said a problem was closed only if an official engineering change had been built and implemented on the engineering model. Others considered it closed if it had simply been rejected by that department, and some said it could only be closed if the person who opened the problem was satisfied.

The real problem was that the 15 standalone systems were just that, sand alone systems. Each of these systems had their own architectures, their own definitions, different concepts of problem status, and contained redundant data. The problem with redundant data is not just the disk space it takes, but also the asynchronous updating. One group might update in real time, another might update nightly, while yet another might update only at the end of the week. What were the DQ problems here? The information requested was unavailable when it was needed, information was inconsistent from one file to another, it was not timely, and no one knew for certain what files to believe.

SUMMARY

As data becomes a corporate resource, more sharing occurs, especially in data warehouses [20, 23]. Users and uses of data have varying quality demands; what is adequate for one user may be inadequate for another [38, 48]. Accuracy levels may be fine for one group, whereas the timeliness may make it useless for another group. In addition, local files may be incompatible, making it difficult and costly to aggregate databases. Another problem is the increasing use of unverifiable or soft data in corporate databases [48]; 60% of the data entered into a data warehouse may contain errors [38]. Up to half of the cost of creating a data warehouse is attributable to poor-quality data and the cleansing activities [2, 7].

The Federal Government's ability to track terrorist suspects has been hampered by inadequate information. Our ability to predict potential terrorist activities depends on good-quality information. The ability of Federal agencies to share information has been highly criticized. Social programs, such as food stamps, are fraught with fraud. Huang and others commented that "dead people eat." This illustrates the DQ problems that allow fraud in the food stamp chain [22].

If businesses and government don't make drastic changes, the situation will worsen. "Most organizations do not fund programs designed to build quality into data in a proactive, systematic and sustained manner. According to The Data Warehousing Institute (TDWI) Data Quality Survey, almost half of all companies have no plan for managing data quality" [15].

In the next chapter, we'll discuss TQM in detail and how it can be applied to information systems. Largely because of the efforts of Dr. Richard Wang and Dr. Stuart Madnick, both of MIT, researchers and practitioners gather at the International Conference on Information Quality [53] every year to share successes and failures of techniques. Finally, real progress is being made in improving data and information quality.

CHAPTER ONE QUESTIONS

Review Questions

1. Explain the phrase, "one person's data is another person's information."
2. What five actions are performed on information by information systems?
3. Why are organizations becoming increasingly disappointed with their information?
4. What are the business impacts of poor-quality data?
5. Agree or disagree with the following statement and explain why: Poor accuracy of data can adversely affect decisions, but suspicions of low accuracy do not affect decisions.
6. Agree or disagree with the following statement and explain why: Poor-quality data might affect a business's accounting database but cannot affect something as advanced as NASA's Space Shuttle Program.
7. What is the issue of redundancy in a database from an information quality perspective?
8. Compare the seriousness of defects in a manufacturing line to the errors in an information system.
9. What is Total Quality Management (TQM)?

10. Agree or disagree with the following statement and explain why: Once data has been declared to be accurate, it will always be accurate.

Discussion Questions

1. Discuss DQ in the healthcare industry.
2. Argue for and against End User Computing (EUC).
3. Explain two types of poor-quality data that have directly affected you.
4. Should private companies be given the names of people the FBI wants to interview in its counter-terrorism efforts? What are the risks of doing so? Explain in depth how you would feel if your name appeared on such a list.
5. For Question 4, what approaches might minimize the risks?
6. Discuss the issues of reusing entity identifiers.
7. Why do you think that the problems with poor-quality data are getting worse?
8. Argue whether or not a corporation's goal should be to have error-free data.
9. Given the 40+ years of experience in IS development, why are there still information quality problems? What is missing in current approaches?
10. Explain why the actual value of a good used vehicle is rarely realized by the seller.

REFERENCES

1. Akerlof, G.A., *The Market for 'Lemons': Quality Uncertainty and the Market Mechanism.* Quarterly Journal of Economics, 1970. 84(3): p. 488-500.
2. Atre, S., *Rules for Cleansing*, in *ComputerWorld.* 1998.
3. Ballou, D.P., R. Wang, H. Pazer, and G.K. Tayi, *Modeling Information Manufacturing Systems to Determine Information Product Quality.* Management Science, 1998. 44(4): p. 462-484.

4. Berton, L., *Downsize Danger: Many Firms Cut Staff In Accounts Payable and Pay a Steep Price*, in *Wall Street Journal*. 1996: New York.

5. Bovee, M., R.P. Srivastava, and B. Mak. *A Conceptual Framework and Belief-Function Approach to Assessing Overall Information Quality*. in *Sixth International Conference on Information Quality*. 2001. Cambridge, MA.

6. Cabbage, M. and W. Harwood, *COMM CHECK . . . The Final Flight of Shuttle Columbia*. 2004, NY: Free Press. 320.

7. Celko, J., and McDonald, J., *Don't Warehouse Dirty Data*. Datamation, 1995. Oct. 15: p. 42-53.

8. Chengalur-Smith, I., D.P. Ballou, and H. Pazer, *The Impact of Data Quality Information on Decision Making: an Exploratory Analysis*. IEEE Transactions on Knowledge and Data Engineering, 1999. 11(6): p. 853-864.

9. Chengalur-Smith, I. and H. Pazer. *Decision Complacency, Consensus and Consistency in the Presence of Data Quality Information*. in *Conference on Information Quality*. 1998. Cambridge, MA.

10. Crosby, P.B., *Quality Without Tears: The Art of Hassle-free Management*. 1984, New York, NY: McGraw-Hill.

11. Dasu, T. and T. Johnson, *Exploratory Data Mining and Data Cleaning*. 2003, Hoboken, NJ: John Wiley & Sons, Inc. 203.

12. Davenport, T.H., *Information Ecology*. 1997, New York, NY: Oxford university Press. 255.

13. Davis, A., *September 11 Watch List Acquires Life of Its Own*, in *Wall Street Journal*. 2002: New York.

14. Deming, W.E., *Out of the Crisis*. 1986, Cambridge, MA: MIT, Center for Advanced Engineering Study.

15. Eckerson, W.W., *Data Quality and the Bottom Line*. 2002, The Data Warehousing Institute.

16. EMC, *Implications of Homeland Security on Information Technology Infrastructure*. 2003, www.BitPipe.com/data.

17. Ensor, D., *Report cites warnings before 9/11*, in *CNN*. 2002: USA.

18. Fisher, C.W., I. Chengalur-Smith, and D.P. Ballou, *The Impact of Experience and Time on the Use of Data Quality Information in*

Decision Making. Information Systems Research, 2003. 14(2): p. 170-188.

19. Fisher, C.W. and B.R. Kingma, *Criticality of Data Quality as Exemplified in Two Disasters.* Information & Management, 2001. 39(2): p. 109-116.

20. Haisten, M., *Planning for a Data Warehouse.* InfoDB, 1995. Feb.

21. Hill, E., *Joint Inquiry Staff Statement, Part I.* 2002, U.S. Federal Government: Washington DC. p. 31.

22. Huang, K.-T., Y.W. Lee, and R.Y. Wang, *Quality Information and Knowledge.* 1999, Englewood Cliffs, NJ: Prentice Hall. 209.

23. Inmon, W., *What is a Data Warehouse?* Tech Topic Prism Solutions, Inc, 1995. 1(1).

24. Juran, J.M., *How To Think About Quality*, in *Juran's Quality Handbook*, J.M. Juran and A.B. Godfrey, Editors. 1999, McGraw-Hill: New York, NY. p. 2.1-2.18.

25. Kaomea, P., S. Hearold, and W. Page, *Beyond Security: A Data Quality Perspective on Defensive Information Warfare.* 2003, www.iqconference.org/documents.

26. Kendall, K.E. and J.E. Kendall, *Systems Analysis and Design.* 5 ed. 2004, Englewood Cliffs, NJ: Prentice Hall. 914.

27. Kingma, B.R., *The Economics of Information: A Guide to Economic and Cost-Benefit Analysis for Information Professionals.* 1996, Englewood, CO: Libraries Unlimited. 200.

28. Klein, B.D. *User Detection of Errors in Data: Learning through Direct and Indirect Experience.* in *AIS98.* 1998.

29. Klein, B.D., D.L. Goodhue, and G.B. Davis, *Can Humans Detect Errors in Data? Impact of Base Rates, Incentives and Goals.* MIS Quarterly, 1997. 21(2, June): p. 169-194.

30. Lichtblau, E., *9/11 Report Cites Many Warnings About Hijackings*, in *The New York Times.* 2005: New York City.

31. Locke, E.A. and G.P. Latham, *Goal Setting: A Motivational Technique That Works.* 1984, Englewood Cliffs, NJ: Prentice Hall.

32. Locke, E.A., K.N. Shaw, L.M. Saari, and G.P. Latham, *Goal Setting and Task Performance.* Psychological Bulletin, 1981. 90: p. 125-152.

33. Lorence, D.P., *The Perils of Data Misreporting.* Communications of the ACM, 2003. 46(11): p. 85-89.

34. McLeod Jr., R. and G.P. Schell, *Management Information Systems*. 9 ed. 2004, Upper Saddle River, NJ: Pearson Prentice Hall. 420.

35. Northcraft, G.B. and M.A. Neale, *Organizational Behavior: A Management Challenge*. 1994, Fort Worth, TX: The Dryden Press. 117.

36. O'Brien, J.A., *Management Information Systems: A Managerial End User Perspective*. 2 ed. 1993, Homewood, IL: Irwin. 571.

37. OMB, *Information and Quality Act*, in *Section 515*. 2001, Office of Management and Budget; The Executive Office of the President. p. 17.

38. Orr, K., *Data Quality and Systems Theory*. Communications of the ACM, 1998. 41(2): p. 66-71.

39. Pierce, E. *Developing, Implementing and Monitoring an Information Product Quality Strategy*. in *Ninth International Conference on Information Quality*. 2004. Cambridge, MA: MIT TDQM Program.

40. Pierce, E.M., *Introduction to Information Quality*, in *Information Quality*, R.Y. Wang, et al., Editors. 2005, M. E. Sharpe: Armonk, NY. p. 265.

41. Pierce, E.M., *What's in your Information Product Inventory?*, in *Information Quality*, R.Y. Wang, et al., Editors. 2005, M. E. Sharpe: Armonk, NY. p. 265.

42. Redman, T., *On the Cost of Poor Data Quality*. www. dataqualitysolutions.com, 2003.

43. Redman, T.C., *Data Quality for the Information Age*. 1996, Norwood, MA: Artech House, Inc.

44. Redman, T.C., *The Impact of Poor Data Quality on the Typical Enterprise*. Communications of the ACM, 1998. 41(2): p. 79-82.

45. Scannapieco, M., B. Pernici, and E.M. Pierce, *IP-UML: A Methodology for Quality Improvement Based on Information Product Maps and Unified*

46. Stair, R.M. and G.W. Reynolds, Principles of Information Systems. 6 ed. 2003, Boston, MA: Course Technology. 692.

47. Symmetricom, Time: The Currency of Computer Crime. 2003, www.BitPipe.com/Data.

48. Tayi, G. and D.P. Ballou, Examining Data Quality. Communications of the ACM, 1998. 41(2): p. 54-57.

49. Taylor, M.S., C.D. Fisher, and D.R. Ilgen, Individual's Reactions to Performance Feedback in Organizations: A Control Theory Perspective. Research in Personnel and Human Resources Management, 1984. 2.

50. Wand, Y. and R.Y. Wang, Anchoring Data Quality Dimensions in Ontological Foundations. Communications of the ACM, 1996. 39(11): p. 86-95.

51. Wang, R.Y., A Product Perspective on Total Data Quality Management. Communications of the ACM, 1998. 41(2): p. 58-65.

52. Wang, R.Y., Y.W. Lee, L.L. Pipino, and D.M. Strong, Manage Your Information as a Product. Sloan Management Review, 1998(Summer): p. 95-105.

53. Wang, R.Y. and S.E. Madnick, International Conference on Information Quality. 2005, MIT Total Data Quality Management Program: Cambridge, MA.

54. Whitten, J.L., L.D. Bentley, and K.C. Dittman, Systems Analysis and Design Methods. 6 ed. 2004, Boston, MA: McGraw Hill. 780.

55. Wilson, L., Devil in your data, in InformationWeek. 1992. p. 48-54.

Total Quality Management

*W*oodall and colleagues describe the history and development of the total quality concept as management adjusting to the rigors and challenges of manufacturing more products, of demands for better quality products, shorter cycle times and faster production [19].

BACKGROUND

Eli Whitney sparked the industrial revolution in the late 1700s when he invented interchangeable parts. Before this innovation, industry was a loose coalition of craftsmen [1]. One craftsman built an entire product—a musket, for example—from start to finish. As a result, a part made by one craftsman could seldom be used by another, and often could not even be used by the same craftsman in his other products. A single worker made the entire product, since there was no way to divide the labor. Simply put, there were no product standards.

Whitney's innovation had advantages for both production and repair. Instead of one person making all the parts for a one musket, many workers were employed, each making standard parts that were later assembled into muskets by other workers. Each part was produced by a person who became an expert at building that particular part. Because each worker made only one part, the workers could improve their techniques and eventually optimize the process for making each part. Interchangeable parts, standards for those parts, division of labor, and specialization greatly decreased production time.

Another benefit of interchangeable parts was that if a musket broke in the field, it could be easily and quickly repaired. Before standard parts, the musket had to be repaired by a craftsman, usually the one who made it.

Although division of labor was a great concept, it was not easily put into practice. Whitney promised to deliver 10,000 muskets in two years, but it actually took him ten [19]. He faced problems very similar to those faced today. There weren't enough skilled people, since it took time to develop specializations, and the craftsmen resisted change. It was more satisfying and took greater skill to build a complete product than it did to make many copies of one part.

Whitney's initial solution was to develop machine tools to make the parts, allowing him to hire less-skilled workers. It took him about a year to build and organize his factory. This included planning the flow of work from one machine to the next and the assembly of parts. It would be useless to have many of one part if others were unavailable. Whitney also found that raw materials could be defective and metal ores inconsistent [1].

Given these variables, it was clear that his concept of perfectly standard parts was unrealistic. It was too time consuming and costly. Whitney solved this problem by introducing *tolerance limits*—measures of allowable deviation. But nothing is free. A new breed of employee was introduced: inspectors. They examined a sampling of the parts to make sure they were within tolerance limits.

With the introduction of inspectors, additional management decisions had to be made, such as what to do with defective parts. They could be discarded, or they could be reused as raw material. While the latter might appear to save money, it also added a step. It would have to be determined whether a faulty part was caused by defective raw materials, bad machine tools, or a mistake by the operator. If the raw materials were at fault, then it probably would be better to discard them. But a cause analysis might cost much more than discarding the part.

Analysis was needed to determine if some parts had more defects than others, or if defects varied depending on which machine tool was making the part. Because these issues were factors in some defective parts, more analysis was needed. Once the problems were identified, they had to be fixed. It was sometimes more cost-effective to continue making the part and simply discard the defective ones, so someone had to determine whether it was better to discard defective parts or find the cause and correct it. Money was being saved by specialization, but analysis and accounting created additional expense [1]. The analysis relied heavily on statistics and probability techniques.

The Need for Better Techniques

By the early 1900s, the factors of the industrial revolution—standard and replaceable parts and specialization of labor—led to a need for better evaluative techniques. The craftsman who preceded the industrial revolution was his own boss and inspected all of his own work, but this was no longer an option. More management review and decisions became necessary. Some key factors and questions that the analysis techniques had to address included:

1. What should the tolerance limits be?
    - If set too high, there might be a lot of waste and time lost.
    - If set too low, the parts might not work.

2. Did parts meet the tolerance limits?
    - Who would perform the examination and testing? A new job would need to be created to fill the role previously performed by the craftsman.

3. Should all parts be examined?
    - If there are hundreds of thousands of parts, how many should be examined?

4. Are all examinations feasible?
    - Some tests could be destructive; to see if a part was strong enough or would last might break the part or wear it out.

5. If a subset of all the parts is examined, then how big should that subset be?
    - What percentage of parts should be examined?

6. How should the subset be determined?
   - Once the sample size is determined, then a method for choosing which parts to test must be established. For example, should the first 100 parts be chosen or every 10th part? Should the choices be random?

7. What should be done if a few problems are found in a tested sample?
   - How many defects per sample size are needed to determine if the batch meets quality standards?

8. How would you know if a proposed improvement actually helped?
   - If it is believed that a cause of defects is identified, and a corrective action is taken, how can we be sure it is an improvement?

These questions, and others, are addressed with probability and statistics. Although most readers of this book have had an introduction to statistics course, we have included a refresher chapter in this text.

Interchangeable Parts Summary

Whitney introduced interchangeable parts built to specification standards that enabled division of labor and specialization. By the early 1900s, these were combined into the process of mass production and used in assembly lines. Henry Ford is the best-known pioneer of mass production. His car company made thousands of parts and assembled them into a finished product faster than ever before. With this series of innovations came new tasks and costs: inspections, root cause analysis, tradeoff evaluations through balancing costs, and statistical tools. These factors laid the foundation for Total Quality Management (TQM).

Proactive Approaches

The next major focus was a shift from the reactive, costly correction after an inspection to the proactive systems approach. Correcting errors after they occur costs much more than preventing them in the first place [[9, 10]. By treating everything like a complete system, the emphasis could be placed on avoidance of problems through improvement of processes [19]. The elements of this complete system include an organization-wide context. The context of quality has broadened over the years to go beyond a purely production approach. Within this context, the components of customer focus, strategic planning, leadership, continuous process improvement, and teamwork unite to make real and substantial improvements [9, 10]. But this TQ approach did not come easily to the United States.

Right after World War II, most people believed that products developed and produced in Japan were inferior. During the next few years, quality experts from the U.S. visited Japan to provide assistance. Two such experts were Edwards Deming and Joseph Juran. In addition, General Douglas MacArthur recruited Genichi Taguchi to deal with quality improvement in Japan [20]. Taguchi developed the following quality philosophy [17]:

- Quality must be designed into the products, not simply inspected after production.

- Quality means minimizing deviation (from standards and specifications) and variability in the product.

- Products must be robust to withstand hostile environments.

- Cost of quality must be measured as a deviation from the standard.

- Loss because of low quality must be measured system wide.

Early quality programs focused on quality control to determine if job quality met product standards [1]. They were clear cases of: build the product and hope it meets specifications; then measure it through judicious use of inspections and statistics [7]. A number of defects were accepted as part of business. Corrective action was taken to fix defects only when the number of defects increased to the point where it was obvious that the defects were not a result of chance. All action was taken after production and was simply patchwork. Measured loss was the time and effort it took to identify, design, develop, and implement required patches. Woodall states that the goal was to produce uniform products and prevent defects [1]. This goal gradually expanded beyond defects on the manufacturing line to include various human and social processes. The next major step was to begin applying quality techniques to non-production areas such as purchasing, distribution, and finance [19].

Even with this expansion of the quality concept, the vision was relatively narrow until the Japanese—inspired by Deming and Juran—began looking at quality problems in the broadest possible scope. A strong motivator to look beyond the immediate problem is cost of quality. For example, is the cost to fix an erroneous process in the manufacturing line the true cost of the quality problem?

Loss Function

Dr. Taguchi introduced the concept that the total loss to society generated by poor quality products should be included in the measurement of the cost of poor quality. Taguchi's loss function measured all losses to the system and society caused by poor quality [3, 13]. Previously, people only measured the immediate cost to fix the problem, but Taguchi expanded the analysis to be system wide. For example, a product may be manufactured and distributed to thousands of customers. If a problem occurred in the product, the early technique was to calculate loss based on what it cost to fix the problem—perhaps two people working for three days. But Taguchi said that losses because of poor quality were far greater. The losses may be in the form of poor fit, poor finish, undersize, oversize, scrap, rework, and loss of good will [16]. In the case of information rather than physical products, the losses may include the effects of bad decisions made because the data was in error. Examples might include incorrectly lowering prices due to errors in a model or investing in a business venture when the information in a business forecast was in error.

Customers who purchased the product depended on it to perform tasks or build other products. If the product was defective, each customer would incur losses. There may be other companies and organizations that were dependent, in turn, upon the secondary products from the original customers. This effect might be repeated, creating a domino effect. Compare the potential cost of poor quality using Taguchi's loss function to the cost-to-fix-it method. The difference is astronomical. Fixing it may only cost a few thousand dollars, while the loss function says it might cost millions. The astute information professional recognizes that it is not only the poor-quality data that is so damaging and costly, but the decisions that are made upon it. All subsequent decisions flowing from the first poor decision add to the losses, and even potential bankruptcy, for a company. Phil Crosby pointed out that management too often thought about the *cost of quality[2]*. Management was very concerned about the amount of money spent on quality techniques and personnel. For example the company has to hire and pay inspectors. Crosby demonstrated that the savings brought about by quality improvements more than countered the expenses of implementing the improvements. He coined the phrase, Quality is Free to illustrate his point[2].

Taguchi made improvement of quality a national priority in Japan. The result was that Japanese products became known for their excellent quality. You only have to look at automobiles, cameras, and VCRs to recognize the quality achieved by Japan.

The main focus of this broader quality, from an overall process point of view, is on the *why*. It goes beyond the immediate *how* to fix it, and focuses on all of the integrated processes that must come together to build the product ([19], p. 107). The organization must begin by looking at the total set of processes, then continually reviewing and improving them. One view is that there are many processes involved, and each process may be considered the customer of an earlier process.

It is ironic that Deming and Juran were early pioneers in the United States, but were most listened to in Japan. General Douglas MacArthur recruited Taguchi to improve quality in Japan, but the U.S. and many countries in Europe were still resisting change. Japanese businesses started taking business away from the United States, largely based on quality. The world began to recognize that a customer was willing to pay a higher price for a product if it met requirements and worked without breaking.

"The Japanese notion of *control* differs from that of the U.S. and that difference does much to explain why it took so long for U.S. firms to adopt TQM" ([19], p. 108). In Japan, "... *control* means all necessary activities for achieving objectives in the long-term, efficiently and economically." This philosophy of control leads to following the now famous plan-do-check-act cycle of quality improvements [3, 6, 19]. It starts with planning, continues with doing the plan, is followed by measuring the results, and finishes by applying corrective action. The cycle then restarts with plans to implement the corrective action.

In the U.S., *control* often involves lengthy debates over who was at fault. This time could be better spent working together to solve the problems, but corporations do not always want to hear about problems. For example, a systems assurance analyst at a large corporation is responsible for testing software before it is released to customers. These releases may include many integrated packages of software. When he reported over 50 problems in less than six weeks, he was accused of being negative and slowing the process.

CONTROL SYSTEMS APPROACH

Woodall points out the value of contributions by Walter A. Shewhart, who is given credit for devising the control systems approach. His treatment of variations was unique. He knew that variation in a system could be pervasive, and he determined that certain variations were predictable, based upon probability theory. His insights allowed management to begin forecasting production results [14, 19]. Today's quality control (QC) techniques are largely based on these principles [7, 14]. A brief description of the QC techniques appears in a later chapter.

One successful manager had a simple rule of thumb: decide what to do, do it, then check that it is done. That theory is very close to the plan-do-check-act cycle. This theory also follows the systems approach [11], or the scientific method to problem solving [15], that says: collect the facts, define the problem, analyze various solutions, pick the best solution, implement it, monitor the effectiveness of that solution, and make modifications as appropriate. Once management recognizes the plan-do-check-act system and follows it, total quality may be achieved.

Deming said that people are part of a bigger system. In chapter 1 we identified the components of an IS: people, procedures, databases, systems hardware and software, and computer application programs. One of the key jobs of the manager is, with the people's help, to continuously improve the system [3]. Recognizing the need to continuously improve a complete system, while totally involving the people, is a major step toward understanding total quality management (TQM). A brief history of the evolution of TQM helps to clarify the value of TQM when producing services, products, or information.

Evolution of Total Quality Management

Total quality management is not a new idea; there has been a century of management developments. Tichy and Devanna say that TQM is not a quick fix, a management fad, or a simple recipe. It is a collection of ideas, concepts, and tools designed to promote quality throughout an organization in all its functions and aspects. This definition implies the all-encompassing nature of quality. Quality is not a purely technical concept; it also includes organizational and behavioral components of the organization [18].

"Total quality is an overall management framework through which to integrate the various elements of a successful organization: strategy, policy, planning, [use of] information systems, project management—all the activities required to run today's large complex organizations" [19]. Hence, TQM integrates the many facets of management in order to focus on improving overall quality. This may require integrating hundreds of otherwise fragmented organizational sections and functions, as well as controlling the processes and outputs along the value-added chain [19].

Deming, one of the best-known quality gurus, identified a number of deadly diseases in the U.S. quality crisis of the 1940s ([3], p. 97).

1. Lack of constancy of purpose.
   - Protect investments by working continuously toward improvement of processes and services to retain customers.

2. Emphasis on short-term profits.
   - Once a company begins to offer quality products, profits follow, whereas a short-term focus on profits may lead to poor quality and no long-term improvement.

3. Evaluations of people by rating and annual reviews.
   - Destroys teamwork, creates rivalry and fear, and annihilates long-term planning.

4. Management mobility.
   - Leads to inadequate understanding of how the organization works, lack of incentive for long-range planning, and inhibits teamwork.

5. Managing the organization by visible numbers only.
   - Focus on creating happy customers instead of adding numbers. A happy customer will buy many more products and tell his friends and neighbors, but an unhappy one will sing the blues to everyone he meets.

6. Excessive medical costs.
   - Medical costs are expenses to industry and increase the costs of products.

7. Excessive costs of liabilities.
   - Exacerbated by attorneys working on contingency fees.

Deming didn't simply list problems; he is also known for his 14-point solution. The 14 points apply to all organizations, small as well as large, and to service as well as manufacturing industries. A key characteristic of the points is that they require action rather than platitudes ([3], p. 24).

1. Create constancy of purpose toward improvement of product and services.
   - Allocate resources for long-term planning.
   - Put resources into research and education.
   - Constantly improve design of product.

2. Adopt the new philosophy.
   - Quality orientation.
   - Customer orientation.

3. Cease dependence on massive inspections.
   - Inspection to improve quality is too late.
   - Focus on improvement of production processes.

4. End the practice of awarding business on the basis of price tag.
   - Without adequate measures of quality, business drifts to the lowest bidder.

5. Improve constantly and forever the system of production and service.
   - Quality must be designed in.
   - Root cause analysis of problems must be done within the context of the overall system process.

6. Institute training.
   - Management must be trained on all steps in the process, from incoming materials to customer receipt of the finished product.

7. Institute leadership.
   - Management must become coaching, supportive leaders who remove production obstacles.
   - A focus on outcomes and administrative measures that are often punitive must be abolished.

8. Drive out fear so that everyone can work effectively for the company.
   - No one can perform at their best unless they feel secure.
   - People should be willing to take a risk to make improvements.

9. Break down barriers between departments.
   - Teams of people in design, engineering, production, and sales could contribute to designs for the future.
   - People might be told to work harder in each department, but the real problem could be bottlenecks between departments. An analysis of information flow across and through all departments might greatly improve a process.

10. Eliminate slogans, exhortations, and arbitrary numerical goals and targets for the workforce.
    - Urging workers to achieve new levels of productivity and quality assumes the workers are not doing their best.
    - They do not remove any obstacles nor make any inter-department improvements.

11. Eliminate quotas.
  - These rates are set for the average worker, but half the workers are above average and half are below.
  - Peer pressure keeps the upper half from achieving to their capabilities.
  - Below-average people cannot achieve quotas, resulting in chaos and dissatisfaction.

12. Remove barriers that rob employees of their pride of workmanship.
  - Management must eliminate all obstacles to production.
  - Provide the best work environment possible, including quality tools.
  - Provide well-thought-out processes that managers understand and can teach the employees.

13. Institute a vigorous program of education and self-improvement.
  - Organizations need people who are improving with education.
  - The study should not be restricted to immediate needs.
  - People require ever-broadening opportunities to add to society.

14. Take action to accomplish the transformation.
  - Management should agree on the 13 solutions listed.
  - Management should take pride in their adoption of the solutions.
  - Management should educate their organizations on all aspects.
  - Management should recognize that every job is part of a process.
  - Management should start as soon as possible.
  - Everyone is part of a team.
  - Organize for quality.

Other pioneers in the push for total quality commitment included: Joseph Juran [8], Philip Crosby [2], Armand Feigenbaum [4], and Genichi Taguchi [17]. Students who wish to pursue a career in the information quality (IQ) field are encouraged to study the works of these pioneers who laid the groundwork for today's TQM practices.

Total Quality Management Awards

To increase awareness of quality in many companies across the world, some agencies have initiated awards, standards, and certificates for incorporating quality in production processes of goods and services ([20], p. 12). We will review two motivational prizes and one set of standards that have helped the acceptance and active use of TQM. "In 1951, the Japanese Union of Scientists and Engineers (JUSE) created the Deming Prize for companies wishing to improve quality in their products. Later, JUSE revised its Deming Prize guidelines to require that quality efforts be organization-wide" ([20], p. 13).

For a variety of reasons, the Deming award was not popular in the U.S. Thirty-eight years after the inception of the award in Japan; Florida Power & Light became the first non-Japanese organization to win it. However, the CEO who pushed for the award was shunted aside, and the newly-formed quality improvement department was dismantled. The effort required to win the award was thought to outweigh the advantages of the award. The award application was around 1,000 pages, required many years of work, and was very bureaucratic [20]. Yet, proponents of the award believed that the detailed self-analysis was beneficial. Also the "prestige and recognition generated by winning the award make the award an effective quality incentive" ([20], p 13).

Malcolm Baldrige Award

Another well-known award is the Malcolm Baldrige Award, which was instituted to raise the U.S. industry's awareness of the importance of quality in global competition. The application was only 75 pages, a major improvement. However, the award is criticized because it doesn't include productivity, companies with little reputation for quality have won it, and some winners do not produce world-class quality products [20]. To obtain profiles of award winners please visit the web site http://www.quality.nist. gov/Contacts_Profiles.htm.

The Malcolm Baldrige National Quality Improvement Act of 1987 (Public Law 100-107, 1987) was designed to recognize companies that excel in quality achievement. The winners are determined by an award examination that requires companies to document achievement toward quality excellence criteria. The applicants submit information on quality processes and improvements. Guidelines call for the documentation to be thorough enough so that other companies can replicate the processes; the application should focus on results, as well as the conditions and processes that lead to results. There are ten key concepts that form the foundation of the Malcolm Baldrige Award.

Ten key concepts

1. Quality is defined by the customer.
   - Customer-driven quality is a strategic concept that demands constant sensitivity and rapid response to customer requirements. This concept includes defect and error reduction, meeting specifications, and complaint reduction. It recognizes that customer dissatisfaction contributes significantly to the customer's view of quality and must be thoroughly addressed.

2. Executives create clear quality values.
   - The senior leadership of businesses needs to create clear quality values and institutionalize those values into the company culture. The senior leaders must reinforce the values of quality and encourage quality leadership at all levels of management.

3. Well designed/executed systems/processes.
   - Quality excellence derives from well-designed and well-executed systems and processes.

4. Continuous improvement must be part of all systems.
   - Once the systems and processes are in place, there must be a clearly-defined process for enhancing and improving all existing processes. This includes all operations and work unit activities of the company.

5. Goals, strategic and operational plans.
   - The leadership must develop strategy and define specific goals, as well as systems for achieving the strategy and goals.

6. Shorten response time.
   - Shortening the response time of all operations and processes of the company needs to be part of the total quality improvement effort. Fast response itself is a major component of customer satisfaction. It is believed that major gains in response occur when work processes are simplified.

7. Operations and decisions must be based on facts.
   - Meeting quality improvement goals of the company requires that actions in setting, controlling, and changing systems be based upon reliable information, data, and analysis.

8. All employees trained, developed, and involved.
   - Meeting the company's quality objectives requires a fully-committed well-trained work force that is encouraged to participate in the company's improvement activities.

9. Quality should be a design task, not an afterthought.
   - Design quality as well as defect and error prevention into every system at the beginning of a project. There should be documented product development procedures that indicate the need to meet quality considerations as the product is being designed.

10. Demand quality from suppliers.
    - Companies must communicate their quality requirements to vendors and then measure the quality they get. Relationships should be established in order to acquire good-quality supplies from their vendors.

Even if a company doesn't apply for the award, the examination is extremely useful as a self-assessment tool. The applicant reviews training, quality system development, and strategic planning. There are seven areas in which an organization must demonstrate high performance in order to qualify for the award. The performance criteria follow[3].

Performance criteria[4] [12]

1. Leadership
   - Describe how an organization's senior leaders guide and sustain the organization. Include how senior leaders communicate with the workforce and encourage high performance.
   - Describe the organization's governance system including how it addresses its responsibilities to the public, ensures ethical behavior and practices good citizenship.

2. Strategic Planning
   - Describe how the organization determines its strategic challenges and advantages, establishes strategic objectives, plans and goals.
   - Describe the process for converting strategies into action plans, summarize those action plans including key performance measures and project future performance based upon those measurements.

3. Customer and Market Focus
   - Describe how the organization obtains and uses customer and market knowledge.
   - Describe how the organization builds customer relationships, grows customer satisfaction and loyalty.

4. Measurement, Analysis and Knowledge Management
   - Describe how the organization measures, analyzes and improves organizational performance.
   - Describe how the organization manages its information, information technology and organizational knowledge.

---

[3]   The law is public record, but more information can be found at the following web site. http://www.quality.nist.gov/

[4]   The entire section on performance criteria is taken from NIST, *Criteria for Performance Excellence*, in *Baldrige National Quality Program*. 2008, U.S. Department of Commerce: Gaithersburg, MD.

5. Workforce focus
   - Describe processes to engage workforce to achieve organizational and personal success.
   - Describe how the organization builds and effective and supporti9ve workforce environment.

6. Process Management
   - How does the organization design its work systems?
   - How does the organization manage and improve work processes?

7. Business Results.
   - Describe (using previously given measurements) product and service performance results.
   - Describe the customer focused performance results.
   - Describe the financial and marketplace performance results.
   - Describe the workforce-focused performance results.
   - Describe the process effectiveness results.
   - Describe the leadership results.

As TQM became a key factor in U.S. industry, there were still big holes that allowed problems in data and information quality. Management clearly recognized the importance of IS to contribute information to management for control processes. Woodall describes the unique synergy between total quality and IT. Total quality and IS work together to reduce defects, decrease cycle times, improve safety, improve delivery, increase reliability, and increase customer service and satisfaction [19]. However important this philosophy is, it makes a basic assumption that we have seen to be false, the assumption that data and information are of good quality. If the data is not of good quality, the IS will be a bad partner to work with to remove product defects. TQM practices have recently been brought to bear on data and information quality.

TQM Needed within Information Systems

Modern systems analysis and design textbooks used throughout the IS and management information systems curricula stress quality through software assurance techniques. Current views contain a broader view of quality than earlier programming centric views, which stressed the need to catch and fix bugs. Management evaluated programmers according to how much code they produced and their error rate (errors per line of code). They were correct regarding the importance of catching bugs early, since it is cheaper to repair the specifications than it is to fix a program that has been released to the user for production. It is not just the cost of fixing a bug that went to a user, but the fact that they may have used the bad information in their decisions.

The cost of fixing errors can be far greater than the cost of the programming itself. Kendall and Kendall stress that TQM is essential throughout all the steps in the systems development life cycle [3]. Dean and Evans raise the focus to the organization level—quality principles must be in the context of a comprehensive focus on quality by the organization [17]. Quality is not simply removing bugs from a program; it is a continuous process to ensure that all aspects of systems and their outputs meet user needs. The emphasis is on achieving organizational support for total quality [9, 10]. They stated that "Organizational support for quality in management information systems can be achieved by providing on-the-job time for IS quality circles, which consist of six to eight organizational peers specifically charged with considering both how to improve information systems and how to implement improvements" [9, 10]. Kendall & Kendall suggest that the quality circles are where management and users can work together to develop guidelines for quality standards of IS [10]. Hess and Talburt illustrate that effort to consolidate identification of best practices for data validation takes considerable effort but pays off for the entire corporation [5]. Again, the emphasis on total quality management rather than individual departments provides the biggest benefit to the corporation.

Questions remain. Who are the members of the IS quality circles? Standards are important, but exactly what standards are being discussed? What standards are being developed? When Kendall and Kendall say, "Departmental quality standards must then be communicated through feedback to the systems analysis team," what do they mean? A TQM focus is necessary to address these issues and similar ones. Information systems organizations are beginning to follow International Standards Organization (ISO) Standards. The following of these standards is intended to provide a uniform basis for quality.

"The U.S. air force in World War II recognized the necessity of quality standards for manufacturing and initiated quality assurance programs, which led to the development of the military quality assurance standards in 1959. The U.S. military standard was adopted by NATO in 1968." "The European Committee for Standardization, Europe's standard-setting body, commissioned the International Standards Organization (ISO), a private organization, to develop quality assurance standards. These standards were called ISO 9000 and were adopted by the European Committee for Standardization in 1987 as the norms for quality assurance" ([20], p 14). The U.S. adopted the ISO 9000 series, with minor language changes, as a Q90 series. The ISO 9000 series is used for certification purposes, whereas the Q90 series is a voluntary standard of quality assurance in the United States [20]. The European position is much stronger than the U.S. position, since companies dealing with the European Common Market countries must have ISO 9000 certification.

Quality Function Deployment (QFD), a technique found in many firms practicing TQM, helps information systems planners make choices that will enhance customer satisfaction [4]. QFD focuses on removing ambiguity from terms used in describing various business functions and processes. QFD provides a structured approach to defining the parameters and tolerances for the terms such as quick, accurate, accessibility, and so forth. It is a major step toward writing clear specifications. Future data quality analysts and researchers are advised to apply the QFD technique using all dimensions of data quality.

SUMMARY

The field of quality has advanced a long way since the start of the industrial revolution. Application of TQM principles to the IS field appears to be a step in the right direction to fix many data quality problems. In chapter 4 we will discuss total data quality management, or how TQM can be applied to information systems. Researchers from MIT, Berkeley, SUNY, Albany, Indiana University of PA, Boston University, University of Arkansas at Little Rock and Worcester Polytechnic University have been working on this concept over the last few years, with excellent results. A keynote of their research is that it has not been purely academic. Largely due to the efforts of Dr. Richard Wang of MIT, researchers and practitioners gather at a conference every year to share advances in IQ theories and techniques. Finally, real progress is being made in improving data and information quality.

CHAPTER TWO QUESTIONS

Review Questions

1. Is TQM an effective approach to improving quality? Why?
2. In what ways does the idea of interchangeable parts provide potential for productivity improvement?
3. In what ways did the innovation of interchangeable parts introduce quality problems?
4. If TQM applies to manufactured products, how could it apply to IS and information? Explain.
5. What are the ten key concepts of the Baldrige Award for TQM?
6. What are the seven performance criteria that a company must report on when applying for the Baldrige Award?
7. What is a tolerance limit?
8. What was new in Taguchi's loss function compared to previous views on the cost of quality?
9. Define each of Deming's seven deadly diseases.
10. List Deming's 14-point solution.

Discussion Questions

1. It has been said that Eli Whitney's standard interchangeable parts led to the industrial revolution. Discuss the new techniques that were needed for evaluating product quality within the industrial revolution as compared to the techniques used by craftsmen.
2. Do you believe that craftsmen were worried about quality in the same way that industry is today? Why or why not?
3. How can a company deal with information proactively rather than reactively?
4. Discuss whether you believe that TQM is an effective approach to improving quality.

5. How does the TQM "plan-do-check-act" cycle compare to the scientific method of problem solving?
6. Investigate Quality Function Deployment (QFD) and report the pros and cons of QFD.
7. In what ways do you think management can show organizational support for quality?
8. What does it mean to say that "quality is defined by the customer?" Can you give an example from your own experience as a customer of an information system of receiving information that did not meet your quality expectations? Were you ever asked what your quality expectations were related to that information?
9. Phil Crosby is known for his book, *Quality is Free*. What do you believe the author means by the expression, *quality is free*?
10. If the cost of losses because of poor quality is so high, why would companies resist applying the latest theories about TQM in their day-to-day business?

Research Project

Read the theories of two quality researchers, then compare and contrast their theories and practices. Identify the factors in each theory, and state the relationship of those factors and the conclusions drawn. Where do the authors agree, and where do they contradict each other? Which theory is most convincing? Illustrate with examples where they provide the same degree of empirical evidence.

REFERENCES

1. Cox, B.J. and A.J. Novobilski, *Object-Oriented Programming: An Evolutionary Approach*. 2 ed. 1991, Reading, MA: Addison-Wesley Publishing Company. 270.
2. Crosby, P.B., *Quality is Free*. 1979, New York: McGraw-Hill. 270.
3. Deming, W.E., *Out of the Crisis*. 1986, Cambridge, MA: MIT, Center for Advanced Engineering Study.
4. Feigenbaum, A., *Total Quality Control*. 3 ed. 1991, New York: McGraw-Hill.

5. Hess, K. and J. Talburt. *Applying Name Knowledge to Name Quality Assessment*. in *The Ninth International Conference on Information Quality*. 2004. Cambridge, MA: MIT TDQM Program.

6. Huang, K.-T., Y.W. Lee, and R.Y. Wang, *Quality Information and Knowledge*. 1999, Englewood Cliffs, NJ: Prentice Hall. 209.

7. Ishikawa, K., *Guide to Quality Control*. Second ed. 1982, Tokyo, Japan: JUSE Publishing Company. 226.

8. Juran, J.M.J., *On Quality by Design*. 1992, New York: The Free Press.

9. Kendall, K.E. and J.E. Kendall, *Systems Analysis and Design*. 5 ed. 2001, Englewood Cliffs, NJ: Prentice Hall. 914.

10. Kendall, K.E. and J.E. Kendall, *Systems Analysis and Design*. 5 ed. 2004, Englewood Cliffs, NJ: Prentice Hall. 914.

11. McLeod Jr., R. and G.P. Schell, *Management Information Systems*. 9 ed. 2004, Upper Saddle River, NJ: Pearson Prentice Hall. 420.

12. NIST, *Criteria for Performance Excellence*, in *Baldrige National Quality Program*. 2008, U.S. Department of Commerce: Gaithersburg, MD.

13. Reeves, C.A. and D.A. Bednar, *Defining Quality: Alternatives and Implications*. Academy of Management Review, 1994. 19(3): p. 319-445.

14. Shewhart, W.A., *Economic Control of Quality of Manufactured Product*. 1931, NY: Van Nostrand.

15. Simon, H.A., *A Behavioral Model of Rational Choice*. Quarterly Journal of Economics, 1955. 69: p. 99-118.

16. Summers, D.C.S., *Quality*. 2006, Upper Saddle River, NJ: Pearson/ Prentice Hall. 819.

17. Taguchi, G., *Taguchi Methods*. 1989, Tokyo, Japan: American Supplier Institute.

18. Tichy, N.M. and M.A. Devanna, *Transformational Leader*. 1986, New York: Wiley & Sons.

19. Woodall, J., D.K. Rebuck, and F. Voehl, *Total Quality in Information Systems and Technology*. 1997, Delray Beach, FL: St. Lucie Press.

20. Zahedi, F., *Quality Information Systems*. 1995, Danvers, MA: boyd & fraser publishing co. 420.

The Multiple Dimensions of Information Quality

*A*lthough we have discussed data quality (DQ) and information quality (IQ) in chapters 1 and 2, it is now time to begin a serious attempt at defining them.

INTRODUCTION

We place data and information in the context of IS. Data is collected from multiple sources, massaged, edited, validated, and stored in databases. IS professionals develop or buy programs and systems that either generate useful information, or provide facilities to do so for the members of the organization. DQ issues can occur throughout the entire process, starting from the collection of data to the final distribution of information [37].

Just as organizations want to measure the quality of their products, we want to measure DQ and IQ. We have stated, through introductory discussions on quality and TQM, that we need measurements and monitoring in order to improve the quality of our information. As a review, the student should note a few critical reasons for measurement. It is necessary to identify that a problem exists by showing a deviation to a norm. Measurement is needed to determine if a given improvement plan really worked. Most IS and IT professionals recognize the concept of *benchmarks*. These are measurements taken at a starting point, sometimes called *current state*. Then, some change or improvement is implemented and the measurements are retaken at the new or final state. The comparison allows the analyst to determine the degree of improvement attributable to the change. Therefore, measurements are very important, but they cannot be made without definitions.

The need for measurement is one of the reasons we spend so much time on definitions. How easy is it to define DQ and IQ? As mentioned in the preface, people disagree on the definitions [14]. Instead of arguing about it, researchers from MIT and Northeastern University explored what DQ means to consumers. In one study they identified over 100 definitions of DQ [45]. Fortunately, they continued to analyze the definitions, using advanced statistical techniques and follow-up surveys, reducing the number to 15. Currently, 16 dimensions of DQ are recognized. The remainder of this chapter deals with the definitions of dimensions of DQ and IQ.

Food for thought: *Before reading this chapter, write your definitions of quality and data quality. Save them and review them at the end of the chapter.*

DEFINITIONS OF QUALITY

Few would disagree that the user of the MIS is the single most important factor to consider in establishing and evaluating its quality [8, 18]. Recently (1999), Tayi and Ballou stated that DQ would be best defined as fitness for use [41]. Data must be presented in a format that serves the user's purpose, and must be stated in terminology familiar to that user. One of the most recognized people in the field of quality, W. E. Deming, said, "Quality can be defined only in terms of the agent ([8], p. 168)." Leaving it there would be of little help. If the definitions are that simple, why is there so much disagreement?

Fitness for use is relative and varies by job type, level in the organization, organizational culture, and personal preference. What may be useful to engineers may not be useful to administrators. Charts that engineers used to describe the O-ring problem on the space shuttle *Challenger* did little to convince executives of the dangers [13]. Yet, once the data was organized using statistical regression techniques with a complete set of data, the director of the NASA Marshall Space Center said the data jumped right off the page [13, 40]. Most analysts recognize the importance of detailed information for operational level managers and summary data for upper-level managers and executives. Some people prefer visual charts, while others like to see columns of data. The analyst must study all aspects of the uses and the users in attempting to specify the quality requirements.

How information is presented influences the choice processes of decision makers and can change how the user makes decisions, as well as the results. For example, the user may have been making decisions using one process, but information presented in a different format could influence the user to make different decisions, which, in turn, might lead to different conclusions. Numbers are easier to calculate than words, and lead to *compensatory* decision techniques, such as weighted average approaches, instead of *hurdle* (cutoff) approaches [17, 36].

An example of the difference between compensatory and hurdle techniques of decision making will illustrate this point. When a person applies for a job, the employer's hiring process might include several steps: reviewing resumes, telephone interviews, multiple interviews, skill exercises, and reference checks. A compensatory technique would require that all the steps be completed and scores calculated. Presumably, the applicant with the highest score would get the job. A hurdle technique would require each applicant to complete the first step, and then the company would eliminate a number of applicants before the second step. Clearly, there are advantages and disadvantages of each technique. One example is the candidacy for pilots in the airline industry. The vision requirement would eliminate many applicants before going through many steps. Conceivably, a blind person could score higher on all the other tests. While this seems like a digression, the student should note that the format of the data can influence which decision technique is used [31]. It is imperative that the analyst thoroughly understand the user's purposes and decision—making processes. Some IS programs teach analysts to develop reports in multiple formats, and then see what decisions the user makes based on each decision.

It is time that we delved into a more thorough definition of DQ. It can safely be said that the largest group of people believe DQ is based on the accuracy or reliability of the data. The second largest group believe DQ is based on what the user says it should be (quality is in the eye of the beholder). Perhaps there is a way to go beyond accuracy and delineate enough concerns to typical beholders that we can form a multidimensional concept of DQ. Fortunately, some researchers have already tackled this issue.

WANG AND STRONG QUALITY FRAMEWORK

Dr. Richard Wang, co-director of MIT's Total Data Quality Management (TDQM) program and Dr. Diane Strong of Worcester Polytechnic Institute, along with their colleagues, set out to determine how users of data conceptualize DQ [43, 45]. One of the most important features of their work is that quality attributes of data are collected from users, rather than abstract or theoretical definitions by the researcher. Wang and Strong noted the existence of TQM-like approaches to DQ, along with a variety of systems and tools to ensure DQ, but also noted that all of these approaches and tools were tailored toward a single dimension—accuracy. They found that there was not a clear understanding of what DQ means to data consumers. Therefore, they set out to develop a framework that captures the aspects of DQ that are important to data consumers [45].

This goal was accomplished using a two-stage survey. The first stage determined the list of possible DQ attributes that a user might think of, and the second stage assessed the importance of those attributes to the users. The first survey yielded 179 attributes, 178 more attributes than just accuracy! Regardless of the final conclusion, the fact that 179 attributes were identified should open the eyes of the IS and IT professional; DQ means a lot more to users than just accuracy. If the systems analysts are inspecting accuracy but not the other attributes, then it can be assumed that users will not feel that their concerns for quality are being addressed. Instead of a simple cliché—quality is in the eye of the beholder—we now have evidence.

The 179 attributes of DQ were too many to be of much practical use. The research team continued by performing a test with another group of individuals to clarify attributes, as well as look for direct synonyms. Through this process, the 179 attributes were consolidated to 118 DQ attributes, and their importance assessed by a second survey of 355 people [45].

The researchers applied advanced statistical techniques (factor analysis) to uncover correlations between attributes. Factor analysis explores the interrelationships among variables to discover patterns that can be used to reduce the number of variables. More simply put, if multiple variables are highly correlated, then there may be one factor that can be used to represent them all. For example, the users defined five DQ attributes: retrievable, accessible, speed of access, available, and up-to-date. These five may be grouped tightly around a common factor that can be called a *dimension*. The name chosen for that factor will represent the five attributes. Hence, we have reduced five attributes to one factor or dimension. The initial findings identified 20 dimensions of DQ which, through further statistical analysis, was reduced to 15 [45]. Later one of the deleted dimensions, "ease of operations" was added as the manipulability dimension bringing the final total to 16. As a final step they built a clear hierarchy of DQ attributes that includes four categories of dimensions.

Categories

The categories provide a framework for understanding and solving DQ problems. Wang and Strong used statistical factor analysis to define the dimensions and to form categories [45]. We will now review the rationale surrounding the four categories: intrinsic, contextual, representational and accessibility.

The word *intrinsic* means belonging to the essential nature of an item [1]. The researchers found that four dimensions—accuracy, believability, objectivity, and reputation—were highly correlated. This high correlation indicates that the data consumers considers these four dimensions to be intrinsic in nature [45]. They grouped these four dimensions into a common category called *intrinsic* DQ. In this category the context does not determine the quality. For example, it is either accurate or it is not. If the data in the information system indicates that there is ten of a given item in the stock room, then a stock clerk should be able to walk through the stock room and count exactly ten. When the quality of the data is directly knowable from the data, then the quality is said to be *intrinsic*.

The second category of DQ is *contextual* DQ. The contextual category is dependent on the organizational context and includes value-added, relevancy, timeliness, completeness, and quantity of data. In these cases, the DQ may be known only in context of other data items or by the use of the data. For example, the data item may be accurate, but if it is not received on time or is irrelevant, it is of little good to the user.

The *representation* category reflects the importance of the presentation of data and includes four dimensions—interpretability, ease of understanding, representational consistency, and conciseness of representation. This third category of DQ is based on the direct usability of the data. Some data is accurate but may be codified in such a way as to make the data very difficult to use. If the data is not in a form that represents what the user can easily work with, then it has representational DQ problems.

Finally, the *accessibility* category includes two dimensions, access and security, that deal with availability of the data and how well-protected the data is from unauthorized use. If the user who needs the data cannot readily retrieve the data, or if people who are not supposed to retrieve the data do retrieve it, then we have accessibility problems. The accessibility category includes access and security. Figure 3.1 provides a pictorial representation of the categories and dimensions.

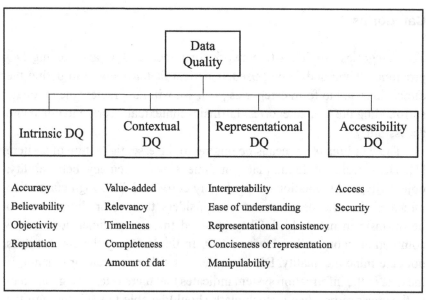

Figure 3.1 Data Quality Hierarchy of 4 Categories and 16 Dimensions[5]

---

5   Manipulability was included in the original list of 20 dimensions in the Beyond Accuracy paper but as the topic of "Ease of Operation"

45. Wang, R.Y. and D. Strong, *Beyond Accuracy: What Data Quality Means to Data Consumers.* Journal of Management Information Systems, 1996. 12(4): p. 5 - 34. Ease of Operation along with 4 other dimensions was statistically dropped from the list but later added as "manipulability"

44. Wang, R.Y., Y.W. Lee, L.L. Pipino, and D.M. Strong, *Manage Your Information as a Product.* Sloan Management Review, 1998(Summer): p. 95 - 105.

The importance of using correct terminology cannot be overstated. Research has shown that the use of common terms can dramatically improve the problem-solving process, especially when multiple parties with different backgrounds are involved [12]. It is with this in mind that we explore these definitions and dimensions in detail. It is safe to say that prior to Dr. Wang, Dr. Strong and their colleagues' research on the dimensions, there was limited understanding of the totality of the definitions and factors employed by the general user to reach their assessment of quality. Using the theme that quality is in the eye of the user we continue with some elaboration of the dimensions of data quality.

Dimensions

The intrinsic category has four dimensions: accuracy, believability, objectivity, and reputation. *Accuracy* refers to how closely the data specifically represents the real world. Accuracy generally means that the recorded value conforms to the real-world value, and refers to lack of errors [7] or free of errors [45]. It is considered by many consumers of data to be the most important characteristic of DQ [45]. It is also the term most commonly put forward by individuals when asked "What is data quality?"

One of the most common examples is inventory. If an inventory database indicates there are 79 parts in the stock room, then you should be able to go to the stockroom and find exactly 79 parts. Accuracy and reliability are often used interchangeably. That is, if the number of parts is correct, then the database is reliable in reference to that part. Finance and accounting have long been aware of the importance of accuracy, but it is not easy to go to the bank and count every dollar and cent. Therefore, accountants use safeguards such as cross-footing totals and double-entry accounting. The numerous checks and balances built into the accounting system are meant to ensure accuracy.

A data item may be accurate, but is not useful if the user does not *believe* the data is accurate. Think about it. Has anyone ever told you something to be a fact and you responded, "I don't believe that!" In a casual discussion, there is no real damage, but in the world of high finance, such a statement could be disastrous. NASA officials missed warning signs because they didn't believe that pieces of foam falling off the rockets could damage the heat shield on the shuttle [6]; this is the DQ dimension, *believability*. Some researchers have argued that *believability* is even more important than accuracy as a dimension and is more complex than a simple intrinsic dimension [26]. *Believability* could be more important because people may act on their beliefs rather than determining the exact accuracy. Some say *believability* is contextual since it depends upon multiple factors such as source of the data, the user's experience, the user's knowledge, and degree of uncertainty in related data. Perhaps *believability* is dependent upon the user. For example, a field could be *believable* by one user but another user based upon their past experience and current knowledge of other factors. Philosophers distinguish two aspects of *believability* [26]. *Content believability* is the sum of the evidence for and against the truth while *procedural believability* is consideration of the processes that created the information. If the process for creating the data is known and correct, then one can believe the data. While these are exciting topics for research we will stick with Wang and Strong's definition that *believability* is an intrinsic dimension [45]. This is an introductory text but this topic, along with further study on all dimensions, is a good one for further research.

If there is judgment in the process of creating the data, then people may not have as much confidence in it as they would if it was built through totally *objective* means. Objective data is unbiased and impartial. Objectivity influences the dimension of believability, but also stands as a dimension in its own right. Users measure the quality of their data based on the degree of objectivity versus the degree of judgment used in creating it.

Over time, data builds a *reputation* that the users consider in evaluating the quality of their databases and information. Regardless of the exact measurement of accuracy, the reputation of a database might deter users from using that data in their decision making.

The contextual category has five dimensions: value-added, relevancy, timeliness, completeness, and amount of data. The meaning of DQ is closely tied to its context. Without a data dictionary to give the data meaning and context, the data is not fit for use. It doesn't matter if the data is accurate, timely, consistent, and complete. The lack of sufficient data descriptions is a leading cause of poor-quality data. But suppose we are given definitions of fields to be name, phone number, revenue, indicator, gender, state, and usage; do we have enough information to determine quality? The answer is: not necessarily. The fields still need standards in order to assure consistency.

The *value-added* dimension measures the "extent to which data is beneficial and provide advantages from their use" ([45], p 14).

Relevancy refers to the degree that data is appropriate and useful to a particular task. Data relevance refers to the applicability of data to a particular issue by a particular user [25, 27, 41]. Relevant data can be used directly to solve a problem [7]. Users find relevancy to be a significant measure of DQ. You may be familiar with the old cliché: that's a good answer to the wrong question. Indeed, one of the main jobs of systems analysts in the IS profession is to be able to ask and obtain answers to the right questions. In other words, is the data useful for the problem the user is trying to solve?

The *timeliness* dimension refers to the age of the data [45]. Timeliness means that the recorded value is not out-of-date [4, 19, 45]. Timeliness can vary based upon the decision maker and circumstance; a strategic planner may use information that is several years old, but a production manager must have data within the hour. Colloquially, people often state that the data wasn't timely because it was too late. However, data that is late is really inaccessible at the time it was needed, and it is therefore measured in the accessibility category. Some data is unaffected by age; for example, the first president of the United States was George Washington; that will not change no matter how much time passes. There are cases where management needs data that is up-to-date in order to take corrective action, such as in a manufacturing process where thousands of parts are being assembled hourly.

If a tool was creating defective parts that were being assembled into products on an automated assembly line, then a report that contains yesterday's defects would contain data that is too old for the problem at hand. There are many cases of financial decisions being based upon old data, resulting in incorrect decisions.

The *completeness* dimension is as it sounds; are there holes in the data? Completeness refers to "the degree to which values are present in a data collection" [4]. Completeness focuses on whether all values for all variables are recorded, and all records for all files are accounted for.

Dr. Wang and his colleagues defined completeness as "the extent to which the data are of sufficient breadth, depth, and scope for the task at hand" ([45], p. 14). Completeness focuses on whether all values for all database variables are recorded, retained, and presented. More recently, Ballou and Pazer explored the dimension of completeness further by breaking it down into two components: structural completeness versus content completeness [3].

Unfortunately, NASA's space shuttle program has provided two dramatic examples of poor-quality data. The *Columbia* (2003) [6] and *Challenger* (1986) disasters illustrate the completeness dimension in several ways. In the *Columbia* disaster, errors of incompleteness were highlighted by a report that did not contain the status of the foam problem ([6], p. 66). The seriousness of the foam strike could not be determined because there was no visual information. There was no picture of the spot where the foam struck the shuttle. Also, real-time diagnosis of what was happening was inhibited by *loss of information*—various sensors and indicators stopped functioning because of the heat.

In the *Challenger* case, a statistical analysis of previous O-ring problems showed no correlation between temperature and O-ring charring. However, a clear regression line, illustrating a strong correlation, was found when all data, containing both good and bad O-ring results, was considered ([40] p. 423). For example, no flight took place below 60°F/16°C in which there wasn't at least one incident of O-ring charring. While numerous theories have been put forth as to why the managers allowed the *Challenger* to launch, it can be stated that the managers did not have complete data—a serious DQ problem [13].

Another completeness problem was that lower-level NASA managers did not inform upper-level managers of the debates that took place the night before the launch. These were debates about potential problems caused by O-ring failure during a launch in colder temperatures. Since the O-rings were considered critical parts, any potential problems were to be reviewed by an outside audit agency and upper management. However, the problems were not reported as required; therefore, upper management had incomplete information about the issues surrounding the launch decision process [13].

One popular service company handles 350,000 phone calls per day. About 35,000 of those calls are customers making a second call because complete information was unavailable at the time of the first call. This company realized that failures in delivery of information affect client satisfaction and often lead to more work.

Amount of data refers to the quantity of data. Information overload occurs when there is too much information for an individual to process. The electronic society is supposed to make information processes more efficient. However, people complain they receive too much information. Some receive hundreds of emails per day. When too much information is received, it becomes difficult to properly filter and prioritize that information, which can lead to errors of omission, delay, and meaning. When faced with a plethora of written data, the probability of omitting words becomes higher. The omission of one small word can easily reverse a meaning. Thus, quantity of information can be a serious DQ problem.

The third category refers to representation of the data. This category covers a lot of critical points not covered in the other categories. One might conclude that if relevant data is accurate, well protected, and still accessible, it would receive a high good rating from the user, but this is not necessarily the case. The user rates the quality based on its interpretability, ease of understanding, consistency, and conciseness. The four dimensions in this category highlight and solve this problem.

In 1998, NASA's *Mars Climate Orbiter* was lost. The spacecraft flew too close to the planet and burned up in the Martian atmosphere. The orbiter was lost, and the project failed, in part, because NASA scientists did not convert data from metric to non-metric units [41]. A failure to convert data to the appropriate *representation* scale is a serious DQ problem.

The *interpretability* dimension means that the information must be in languages or units that are clear. This includes clear definitions of all terms. Research has shown that employing user terms instead of computer jargon is a critical factor in helping the user make proper decisions [12].

The *ease of understanding* dimension may at first seem obvious, but if it is not planned for and measured, then it might not be realized. This dimension states that data must be clear, unambiguous, and easily comprehended [45].

The *consistency* dimension refers to the use of common formats from system to system and application to application. Consistency means the representation of the data values is the same in all cases [2-4]. Consistency also requires common definitions such as when merging two source files that contain a gender attribute. If one of the source files codes a male as a 1 and a female as a 0, and the other source file defines them the other way around, then there will be a problem after the merge. This is also a good illustration of our earlier point. The merger of two files that are 100% accurate does not always produce a third file that is 100% accurate. Consistency implies that there is no redundancy in the database, and that referential integrity is enforced. It has implications beyond just the data. This dimension has been shown by human factors professionals to be a major consideration in the design of systems [33, 34].

The *manipulability* dimension means that the data is easily modified such as joined with other data. It is easily changed, downloaded or uploaded, aggregated, reproduced, integrated and customized. These features make it easy to use data for multiple purposes [45].

The *conciseness* of representation dimension means being brief and to the point. In our efforts to be brief, we often shorten phrases and create acronyms or codes. We strive to eliminate extra words, but there is a fine line to follow. If the expression is too long, the user may be distracted and have trouble finding the essential point. However, if it is too short, the user might have trouble remembering the code or acronym, which leads to errors. The best solution is to create multiple versions and discuss them with the user. The analyst should ask pertinent questions that go beyond which one they like best. The analyst should also ask questions of several users at different times.

The accessibility category includes only two dimensions, but complete books could be written about both of them. *Accessibility* and *security* are inversely related dimensions. Access is the "extent to which data are available or easily and quickly retrievable" ([45] p 14). Security is usually made tighter by adding levels of checks, usually passwords, at multiple levels of systems and across databases. Security features make it more time consuming and difficult for a user to access their data, thereby restricting access. One of the benefits of employing the user-defined dimensions as standards for quality is that we can measure the users' perspective on how suitable the information is to them. This approach opens communication between users and system support personnel that was previously unavailable.

In an unpublished study, 34 users of a system rated accessibility as poor, while systems support people rated the same system as having good accessibility. Furthermore, for the same system, system support people rated the system as having poor security, while users rated security as good. These ratings were major eye-openers for the system support personnel. They would not have considered improving accessibility without the study, and they planned to keep adding more and more levels of security—just the opposite of what the users believed they needed.

Acxiom Corporation® uses the concept of dimensions to compare a variety of information elements and information sources. Analysts at Acxiom Corporation® determine ratings for each dimension for each data element and build matrices of them. Similarly they rate each source of information along each dimension. The results of these studies inform them as to the strengths and weaknesses of their data and information [35]. Significantly they rate the importance of the dimensions as part of their studies.

To review, note that IS and management attempt to deliver quality systems. However, there were numerous DQ problems, as we learned in chapter 1 during the discussion of the impacts of poor-quality data. We then indicated it was appropriate to provide a full definition of DQ, since measurements are needed, and people do what you inspect, not what you expect. Researchers found 179 DQ attributes. Since that was too many to work with, researchers applied advanced statistical analysis techniques, including factor analysis, to reduce the number to 15 dimensions. Those dimensions were subsequently put into four categories, giving us a hierarchy of DQ, and providing a framework for managing DQ. Later a sixteenth dimension, manipulability, was added.

INTERACTIVE RELATIONSHIPS OF DIMENSIONS

In reviewing the dimensions of DQ, you may notice that some are in relationship to others. To be in relationship, in our context, means that when one dimension varies—increases or decreases; improves or deteriorates—another dimension also varies. If they vary in the same direction, it is a *direct* relationship; if they vary in opposite directions, it is an *inverse* relationship. For example, if accessibility increases and security decreases, it is an inverse relationship. The dimensions provide a framework for organizations to review all aspects of DQ and IQ. It is important that these reviews are done with full awareness of the other dimensions; quality analysts now study the relationships of dimensions.

The identification of dimensions and the study of their relationships is thought to be a critical breakthrough toward improving the quality of information produced by IS. As mentioned in chapter 1, although there have been IS developers writing systems and improving techniques for 50 years, there is still a plethora of DQ problems. The demand for information and related services is expected to increase with data warehouses and Internet use. Strong and others state that IS project development generally treats DQ problems as intrinsic, missing many of the contributing issues and organizational effects [37]. In the past, it is likely that well-meaning

IS professionals did everything possible to improve quality along the lines of intrinsic dimensions, but without sufficient awareness of the effects on the other dimensions. Thus, the study of the 16 dimensions and their relationships is a major step toward improving IQ.

Decision makers are sometimes forced to decide between incomplete but consistent data or complete but less consistent data ([3], p. 240). There are many cases where this tradeoff surfaces. Ballou and Pazer highlighted a case in a human resources IS [3]. Many people generate information about an employee over several years. Now, suppose that employee applies for a promotion. It is possible that, over the years, the employee's evaluations were inconsistent. The decision maker has to make a tradeoff; should all the evaluations be used so the data is complete, or is consistency more important? The manager knows that by using all of the evaluations, an element of inconsistency is introduced. The manager could use a subset of the data based on some rule, such as most recent, in an attempt to introduce consistency, but then incompleteness results.

Another example involves accessibility and security. If data is not accessible, then the quality is decreased because users cannot access it in a timely manner. The quality analyst reviews the entire framework and knows that all barriers to accessibility cannot be simply removed, since that would seriously jeopardize another dimension, security. Security and accessibility have an inverse relationship. As a corollary, it can be readily seen that accessibility and completeness are directly related. Increasing accessibility should improve completeness.

Timeliness and accuracy also have an inverse relationship [4]. Much research is needed to further analyze the relationships between dimensions. One could ask a question such as, "When can relevant information that is complete and accurate not be useful?" Consider all aspects of the following case.

Let us suppose a firm learns that a competitor is going to lower prices, but does not know by how much, or when. The marketing information about the competitor is neither complete nor accurate. However, because it is timely, the organization can begin to make plans. The organization may develop what-if plans, or build a model of possible price changes and study the impacts, so that they can be prepared for any price change. But high-level managers could have missed this point by focusing on exact details that are not yet known. Also, to avoid criticism, some IS professionals may say they can't report that information yet, because it is incomplete. They may want to wait until all the data is available. But if they wait too long, the data, even if complete and accurate, will not be useful.

It is easy to speculate on the pairs, but not easy to reach conclusions without sophisticated modeling or experiments. Ballou and Pazer reached the surprising conclusion that if time is short the most important thing to focus on is accuracy [4].

There is much room for more research, analysis, and modeling of the interactions between these dimensions. The research has been restricted to just a few pairs, but a more comprehensive picture is needed. A clear understanding of the relationships is imperative to be sure that when we are fixing one problem, we are not causing another.

Data Quality Dimensions and Reasons for Developing New Systems

Many reasons for developing systems have been described in the PIECES framework described by Wetherbe and Vitalari [46]. 'PIECES' is an acronym for performance, information, economics, control, efficiency, and service and is used as a checklist for identifying problems and determining priorities for developing new information systems. The combination of the Pieces framework with the 16 data quality dimensions is a valuable area for further research.

Performance is related to timeliness in terms of the system responding to user requests to provide current, up-to-date data. Performance also extends to a consideration of the total amount of work that can be put through the system in a given time.

The *information* category of PIECES is related to several DQ dimensions. It includes lack of necessary information, irrelevant information, too much information, information that is not formatted properly, inaccurate information, information that is not timely, and information that is difficult or costly to produce. It also includes data capture, data redundancy, data inconsistency due to redundancy, and data that is not secure, not organized, not flexible, and not accessible [46, 47].

The *economics* category covers costs (unknown, untraceable, too high) and profits (find new markets, improve old markets, increase orders).

Control involves security, either too much or too little. Inadequate security can lead to fraud, embezzlement, and potential privacy violations;

excessive security can result in bureaucratic red tape that slows people, or excessive controls that cause processing delays [47].

Efficiency considers time wasting activities, especially those caused by redundancy.

Service includes many aspects of accuracy as well as ease of use.

As you can readily see, an Information Systems strategy plan examines the business as a whole. Information system standards require IS professionals to consider the organizational environment in which the system is used. These standards include technical, organizational, and economic (TOE) feasibility. For example, if the system does not meet the organizational objectives and the strategic plan, then the system is not funded. The goal of the IS professional is to develop systems that meet user requirements for information, with minimal errors, within an approved budget. Most authors of IS texts that describe requirements and processes emphasize the total environment of a system [10, 18, 22, 24] but are not aware of the 16 dimensions of information quality.

When researchers Strong, Lee, and Wang say that Information Systems projects tend to treat DQ problems as intrinsic problems rather than organizational problems, what is the issue? Are systems getting too big or too complex? Excessive focus on one dimension, without knowledge of the effects on other dimensions, could be a major negative factor. Another factor could be the size and purpose of a system; the needs of users might be lost in the shuffle. The growth of data warehouses (DW) and the Internet are contributing factors to the complexity of systems that both demand higher quality but yet yield data quality problems. Consider whether systems are being used for their original intended purposes, and whether the creation of 100% accurate source data is enough to assure that a comprehensive DW is accurate. Some researchers say the answer is no, while others say that developing 100% source data accuracy is the number one priority. We need some background prior to a full analysis of this issue.

Food for thought: *If all the source databases that are used to create a DW are 100% accurate, would the DW be accurate? Why or why not?*

NASA's Space Shuttles

Columbia

On February 1, 2003, the space shuttle *Columbia* was coming in for a landing after a productive 16-day mission, but instead of a smooth landing, the shuttle disintegrated in the earth's atmosphere. The heat resistant tiles either malfunctioned or were lost.

Our task in this text is not to understand the engineering aspects of the problem, but to discuss the important role of information and the systems that deliver it. The first and most important element is that information must be of good quality and fit for the users. Before reading this text, you may have assumed data must be accurate, but you now know to analyze an IS by looking at the 16 dimensions and asking about their fitness for each specific user or user type. The facts surrounding the space shuttle *Columbia* disaster showed deficiencies in several dimensions of DQ. The information was incomplete, inaccessible, inaccurate, not believed, and too late to do any good.

Officials missed warning signs because they didn't believe that pieces of foam falling off part of the rockets could damage the heat shield on the shuttle; this is the DQ dimension believability. Certain analysis charts omitted problems with the foam and pictures were not available for analysis; these are the DQ dimension completeness. A task force that was working on fixing a ramp problem fell behind and scheduled their report to be completed after the *Columbia* was scheduled to land. A meeting of engineers that was called to analyze the risks of the loss of heat shield tiles was concluded too quickly with the leader saying, "Let's wrap it up. We have got to go to Linda Ham's meeting at 8, and we just have got 5 or 10 minutes. Let's speed it up here" ([6] p. 128). These are examples of the DQ dimension timeliness.

Various models that were meant to illustrate where debris would hit the shuttle, if the debris fell from varying points along the rockets, were not accurate. NASA engineers asked the Department of Defense (DOD) for pictures of the shuttle in flight, but were overruled, and the protocol for engaging DOD managers was not clear. The strict protocols, and the ignorance of them, made the info inaccessible. Since the information was inaccessible, the overall information used for analysis was incomplete.

Thus, DQ dimensions of believability, accessibility, completeness, timeliness, and accuracy had serious problems and contributed to the failed landing of the *Columbia*.

Challenger

NASA launched the space shuttle *Challenger* on January 28, 1986. Moments after takeoff, solid rocket booster joint seals burst, leading to an explosion that destroyed the multi-million-dollar shuttle and killed seven people. There is no doubt that O-ring failure caused the accident [30]. The O-rings did not reseal properly after being subjected to pressure during liftoff in the cold. The cold, brittle O-rings allowed gases to leak; the gases caught fire, burnt through the sides of the fuel tanks, and caused the explosion [5]. NASA had been aware of the potential O-ring problem for several years, and had conducted special investigations six months before the accident. The results of these investigations indicated that problems remained [32].

In addition, an engineer, R. Boisjoly, wrote a letter in July 1985 stating that the O-ring problem could cause a "catastrophic failure of the highest order" [30]. The presidential commission that investigated the accident found that NASA used a flawed decision-making process to approve the launch of the shuttle. This process resulted in the launch of the *Challenger* in the face of evidence suggesting a pending disaster [30]. The elements of the flawed decision-making process included incomplete and misleading information, conflicts between engineering data and management judgments, and a management structure that allowed problems to bypass key managers [30].

The decision-making process was a carefully planned procedure containing several levels and rules [30]. The planned process included four levels of review, as well as a final review by a decision-making body called the mission management team. Regardless of the status of other levels and components, failure to meet certain standards at any level could halt the launch process. For example, Thiokol, Inc. was a level IV contractor responsible for the solid rocket booster; a failed O-ring test at this level should have stopped the entire launch process.

At 5:45 P.M. on January 27, Thiokol objected to the launch, citing the engineers' lack of confidence that the O-rings were safe in cold weather [10]. According to the launch process, this objection should have stopped the launch. However, the NASA level III manager challenged Thiokol management, and after six hours of debate, Thiokol agreed to launch.

Several theories have been offered to explain NASA's flawed decision-making process. Some researchers have highlighted the role of perceptions as a contributing factor to the poor decision making [20, 32]. Some have argued that groupthink was a key factor in the decision-making process [20]. One clear symptom of groupthink is that NASA level III managers deliberately controlled information feedback by not passing concerns to upper management as required. Additional theories include interactions of images and technology [23], information format [42], and incomplete information statistics [40]. The relationships of these factors to DQ dimensions should be readily recognizable to the reader. An exercise for the student is to discuss the relationship of the images and technology, information format, and incomplete statistics to the dimensions of DQ.

We argue that DQ problems in the database and the reporting system of the management information system (MIS) were critical. Corrections to these MIS deficiencies might have mitigated the negative effects of the factors that led NASA to make the flawed decision to launch.

Management Information System

An MIS provides information to management in a usable format. A decision support system (DSS) is a special form of an MIS that focuses on the comprehensive database, the mathematical models, and the ad hoc inquiry facilities. A comprehensive, integrated database is at the heart of a modern MIS and DSS. A key factor in the success of an MIS is the quality of the data behind the system. The database should have minimal redundancy and maximum reliability [21].

There were serious DQ problems in NASA's MIS, including database inconsistencies and errors, reporting violations, lack of modeling for trend analysis, and poor integration of components and tests.

In the following paragraphs, we will describe several key elements of the decision process that illustrate DQ incidents.

Database

There were several types of DQ problems in the NASA database. First, the O-rings were misclassified and misreported. In some cases, the O-rings were classified as redundant (C1-R), meaning other equipment backed up the O-rings. In other cases, the redundancy (C1) was not reported [30], which designated the O-rings as critical equipment vital to the success of the mission. This problem falls into both the consistency and accuracy categories of DQ problems. A data dictionary with one definition for each data element might have prevented the engineers and the safety consultants from miscoding information in the database [11], thus avoiding these issues.

A second failing of the database was that critical components were not cross-referenced with the test plans [30]. It was almost impossible for NASA to verify that all of the hundreds of critical components received the right tests, because there was no list that cross-referenced tests with components (completeness). The dictionary for an MIS contains relationships between all related data elements. These dictionaries have been available since the mid-1970s. The investigating commission stated that such cross-references would have made the critical items list a more efficient management tool [30].

A third failing of the database was that it was inaccurate. One manager had proposed that NASA close the O-ring problem as resolved, but there was no agreement to do so. Despite this lack of agreement, the O-ring issue was closed without an authorizing signature [30]. A database security feature that restricted updating might have prevented this critical error.

Reporting

The Rogers Commission stated that there were several flaws in the reporting system of the decision-making process. NASA middle-level managers did not inform NASA upper-level managers about Thiokol's objections to the launch. There were unreported waivers of launch constraints; all such waivers should have been reported to upper management ([30], p. 137). These reporting violation flaws left upper management with the data quality problem of incomplete information.

NASA middle managers did not alert system reliability and quality assurance (SR&QA) to the launch debates as required. Thus, SR&QA, the reliability and safety experts, had incomplete information. A formal MIS could have informed NASA upper management and SR&QA of the current debates and required their approval signatures as part of the pre-launch decision-making process. This technique has been used in many large computing centers for years, beginning in the late 1970s.

The comprehensive database, combined with mathematical models, allows the decision makers to examine relationships between variables. For example, if a question were raised about two variables, such as temperature and O-rings, an inquiry that triggers a statistical function could be executed. This facility could have helped articulate the relevancy of temperature to O-ring erosion incidents and do so in time to influence NASA's decisions.

In fact, the data needed to analyze the temperature effects on the O-rings was available at the time of the launch, but was not used correctly. The Thiokol engineers used incomplete data in their regression graphs [40, 42]. When complete data is used, a clear relationship between temperature and O-ring performance is visible; this information would have been much more convincing than the graphs used by the engineers. Bunn, the Marshall Space Center Director, said, "Even the most cursory examination of failure rate should have indicated that a serious and potentially disastrous situation was developing" ([30], p. 155). Instead, engineers and administrators argued opinions and used charts that were in a format familiar to engineers but not suited (fitness for use) to the decision makers [42]. While the Thiokol engineers were confident in their belief that the shuttle was not safe, they had difficulty articulating that belief in a convincing way to the NASA decision makers.

Consequences of information overload (quantity) include the difficulty of finding relevant data [25], a decrease in innovation in decision making [15], a lack of ability to verify data (accuracy), and an inability to determine data completeness.

In the *Challenger* case, staff reductions that occurred after the shuttle program was declared operational, contributed to an increase in information overload. NASA managers, administrators, auditors, and technicians became buried under an avalanche of information. The 170,000 pages of shuttle-related documentation contained complex, confusing, and contradictory information ([5], p. 51). Reporting requirements were scattered in numerous individual documents, and there was little agreement about which documents applied to specific circumstances ([30], p. 155). This is the DQ problem of relevance.

One of the solutions to information overload includes filtering information to reduce its volume. But when there is too much data, managers, administrators, and engineers may filter out data necessary for a complete picture. For example, the original objections made by the Thiokol engineers associated with the *Challenger* case clearly stated, "O-ring temp must be greater than or equal to 53 degrees F at Launch" ([30], p. 90). However, the memorandum detailing Thiokol's final management position failed to include this statement [30]. It was filtered out.

The most pertinent point related to experience levels is that the single, foremost expert on the O-rings, Roger Boisjoly, is the person who became our most famous whistleblower of the 1980s. Boisjoly wrote letters and made middle-of-the-night phone calls in an attempt to stop the launch. Administrators, with much less domain-specific experience than Boisjoly, overrode Boisjoly's objections and ordered the launch.

The O-ring deficiencies caused the *Challenger* disaster, but flaws in the decision-making process allowed the disaster to happen. Enhancements to correct the quality deficiencies in NASA's MIS and DSS could have addressed every flaw cited in the *Challenger* launch's decision-making process. The specific areas that had quality deficiencies included the database, the reporting systems, and the modeling and analysis processes.

THE USS *VINCENNES* AND IRAN FLIGHT 655

On July 3, 1988, the Navy Cruiser USS *Vincennes* fired two missiles at what it believed was a hostile aircraft in attack mode. State-of-the-art technology aboard the USS *Vincennes* apparently misidentified the civilian plane as a military aircraft, which resulted in the destruction of Iran Flight 655. DQ problems may have contributed to the decision that killed 290 people.

At least four official investigations of the USS *Vincennes* incident were conducted. Admiral Fogarty conducted the first investigation from July 13 to July 19, 1988, and the results were published on July 28, 1988. The second investigation was to determine if emotional issues and panic were factors in the decisions made or the discrepancies noted between the crews' report and the information recorded by the onboard computer system. The report was dated August 7, 1988 [28]. The U.S. Senate Committee on Armed Services conducted the third investigation in September of 1988. The final investigation was conducted by the Defense Policy Panel of the House Armed Services Committee in October of 1998.

Rogers said, "The USS *Vincennes* is one of the U.S. Navy's newest and most technically advanced ships, an anti-air warfare (AAW) cruiser equipped with the world's finest battle management system, Aegis Battle Management System. Aegis is capable of simultaneously processing and displaying several hundred surface and air radar tracks. Its great tactical advantage is the speed with which it determines course, speed and altitude" ([29], p. 2). Research showed that the Aegis system did not make errors in identification, but that certain errors manifested themselves in the socio-technical seam of the overall system. An IS includes more than just the programmed hardware and software; it includes interfaces, procedures, and people. When looked at from this perspective, DQ problems become apparent; problems that, if fixed, might have prevented the disaster.

Data Quality

DQ was a major factor in the USS *Vincennes* decision-making process. DQ problems appeared in the use of wrong target identifiers (accuracy), incomplete information, conflicting information, voice-communication problems, and information overload (quantity). The USS *Vincennes* case illustrated at least one instance of poor-quality data in five of six DQ dimensions.

When multiple ships simultaneously identify an aircraft, multiple track numbers are initially assigned to the entity (the air contact). The Aegis system resolves these duplicate numbers to a single, unique, track number, TNxxxx. However, the Aegis system recycles the numbers that were initially assigned to the contact. This reuse of identifiers was at the heart of the USS *Vincennes* disaster. An inconsistency error can occur at the socio-technical seam: the interface. Human users may note the initially assigned number and not realize the computer has replaced it with a different tracking number. There is no system alert to notify human users to the system's reuse of the original number. Once an error has been introduced, there may be a chain reaction of errors as various people use that data. In the *Vincennes* example, a target identifier, TN4474, was used twice, once to identify Flight 655, and then again later to identify a fighter plane that was 110 miles away. The identifier used to track Flight 655 changed from its initial value of TN4474 to TN4131. Seconds before firing, the *Vincennes* Captain asked for the status of TN4474 and was told it was a fighter, descending and increasing in speed. He and his crew had been discussing and tracking the radar blip of Flight 655, and confused its tracking number, TN4131, with the fighter's number, TN4474. To make matters worse, there were severe communication problems that were, coincidently, happening at the same time. When the Captain gave the order to fire, the *Vincennes* shot down TN4131 rather than TN4474. If the duplication of identifiers had been recognized, the involved parties could have exchanged information and avoided the disaster.

Incomplete information resulted from the computer-generated displays. Aegis displays aircraft as white dots on large display consoles. The dots are in half-diamonds for hostile aircraft and in half-circles for friendly aircraft. The relative length of the white lines projecting from the dots indicates course and speed. The use of relative length for speed restricts the use of relative length for size, which deprived the ship's officers of another visual check. A commercial airliner is much larger than a fighter plane; if the size of the symbol had been linked to the size of the air contact, it would have been possible for the *Vincennes*' crew to note that TN4131 was much too large to be a fighter. Improvements in the representation could have led to easier-to-understand information.

Information inconsistencies also complicated the decision-making process. Captain Rogers explained ". . . we had indications from several consoles, including the IDS operator, that the contact's IFF readout showed a mode III [civilian] squawk but more significantly to me, a mode II [military] squawk . . . previously identified with Iranian F-14s was also displayed" ([29], p. 147).

The most significant discrepancy was between the Aegis system's tapes and the reports of five crewmembers. The Aegis system's tapes and system data indicated that Flight 655 was in ascending mode; five crewmen operating five consoles reported that the aircraft was in a descending mode (Roberts, 1992). In addition, Captain Rogers stated that the aircraft was at an altitude of 7,000-9,000 feet at the time of the shooting [29]. Data captured from the Aegis system indicated that the aircraft was at an altitude of 13,500 feet [28].

Communication problems contributed to poor-quality information. Captain Rogers explained that, "It looks like the system worked the way it's supposed to . . . . However, there are fitness for use problems with the way the consoles are designed, the displays are presented, and the communication nets work" ([29], p. 152). Captain Rogers' staff discovered that the voice quality of the internal communication net deteriorated when the circuit was heavily loaded. This is a very serious problem, as voice traffic increases during real or potential crises.

Time

Captain Rogers believed that the time-constraint—less than four minutes—was a critical variable in the decision-making process [29]. In addition, Captain Rogers' commanding officer did not have enough time to validate (accuracy), as per normal procedures, the information that Rogers presented to him [9].

An aircraft launched from an Iranian military airbase in Bandar Abbas, Iran, headed directly toward the USS *Vincennes*. Captain Rogers said, "The aircraft was designated as assumed enemy per standing orders" ([29], p. 137). The target aircraft was initially traveling at about 250 knots. In a three-minute period, Petty Officer (PO) Leach observed the display screen five times and noticed the consistent pattern of increasing speed and decreasing altitude. At 11 miles, the aircraft began to descend at a rate of 1000 feet per mile. Captain Rogers reported that at the time of impact the aircraft had an altitude of only 7,000 feet and was moving at 437 knots [29].

SUMMARY

In the space shuttle *Challenger* and *Columbia* cases, there were ten incidents of poor-quality data spread over many categories of DQ. In the USS *Vincennes* case, there were eight incidents of poor-quality data spread over five dimensions of DQ. Good-quality information on all of the dimensions would have mitigated those potential problems. It is extremely important for IS developers of the future to be well-versed in the 16 dimensions of DQ. As we move further into the 21st century, with technology advancing at an astounding rate, and dependence upon information becoming critical (especially in major well integrated global applications such as Customer Relationship Management [16] and Enterprise Systems [38], researchers must do everything possible to bring the importance of DQ to the forefront. Identifying sources of DQ and the moderator variables that impact decisions is important to avoid future disasters. John Talburt and his colleagues are using commercial data integration technologies to improve the quality of entity resolution in the public sector across many dimensions at once [39].

One of the next major improvements in the system development processes should be to include full analysis of all of the dimensions of DQ with significant user interaction. User feedback about these dimensions during the development process is critical to the success of the system.

CHAPTER THREE QUESTIONS

Review Questions

1. Which dimensions of IQ have counterparts in the physical product analogy? Which do not?
2. Give an explicit example of a consumer requirement for each dimension of IQ.
3. What is meant by fitness for use?
4. Define intrinsic DQ.
5. Explain the PIECES framework.
6. List and explain the four categories of DQ.
7. Give two definitions of accuracy.
8. How do the space shuttles *Columbia* and *Challenger* illustrate the DQ problem of incompleteness? Of accuracy? Of believability?
9. Differentiate between conciseness and consistency.
10. What is the difference between interpretability and ease of understanding?

Discussion Questions

1. Discuss whether you believe that productivity should be included as a measure or component of quality. Be sure to consider both sides of the equation. Argue for and against the proposition. Include in your argument the factors or criteria that were important in helping you reach your conclusions.
2. Pick eight pairs of dimensions of DQ, identify possible relationships between them, and explain your rationale.
3. Provide example scenarios that clearly illustrate your points made in discussion Question 2.

4. Ask ten people to define data quality. Summarize your results and bring your findings to class. Prepare an informal presentation of your findings. What, if any, common themes arise?
5. Explain the DQ problems that were found in the USS *Vincennes* case.

REFERENCES

1. *The Merriam-Webster Dictionary*, ed. H.B. Woolf. 1974, New York, NY: Pocket Books. 848.
2. Ballou, D.P., *Computer Network Architectures*. 1996: Lecture Notes, Fall Semester.
3. Ballou, D.P. and H. Pazer, *Modeling Completeness vs Consistency in Information Decision Contexts*. IEEE Transactions on Knowledge and Data Engineering, 2003. 15(1).
4. Ballou, D.P. and H.L. Pazer, *Designing Information Systems to Optimize the Accuracy-Timeliness Tradeoff*. Information Systems Research, 1995. 6(1): p. 51-72.
5. Bell, T.E., and Esch, *The Fatal Flaw in Flight 51-L*. IEEE Spectrum, 1987. 24(2): p. 36-51.
6. Cabbage, M. and W. Harwood, *COMM CHECK . . . The Final Flight of Shuttle Columbia*. 2004, NY: Free Press. 320.
7. Davenport, T.H., *Information Ecology*. 1997, New York, NY: Oxford university Press. 255.
8. Deming, W.E., *Out of the Crisis*. 1986, Cambridge, MA: MIT, Center for Advanced Engineering Study.
9. Dotterway, K.A., *Systematic Analysis of Complex Dynamic Systems: The Case of the USS Vincennes*. 1992, Naval Postgraduate School: Monterey, CA. p. 254.
10. Feinstein, D.L. *Information Systems Curriculum Update*. in *Seventh International Conference on Information Quality*. 2002. Cambridge, MA.
11. Fisher, C.W., *NASA's Challenger and Decision Support Systems*. The Journal of Computing in Small Colleges, 1993. 9(2): p. 145-152.

12. Fisher, C.W. *An Empirically Based Technique for Improving Communication Skills of Systems Analysts.* in *Information Systems Educators Conference (ISECON).* 2000. Philadelphia, PA: AITP.

13. Fisher, C.W. and B.R. Kingma, *Criticality of Data Quality as Exemplified in Two Disasters.* Information & Management, 2001. 39(2): p. 109-116.

14. FMS, *FMS' Procedures for Implementation of the Information Quality Act.* http://fms.treas.gov/index.html, 2003: p. 13.

15. Herbig, P., & Kramer, Hugh, *The Effect of Information Overload on the Innovation Choice Process: Innovation Overload.* Journal of Consumer Marketing, 1994. 11(2.): p. 45-54.

16. Hess, K. and J. Talburt. *Applying Name Knowledge to Name Quality Assessment.* in *The Ninth International Conference on Information Quality.* 2004. Cambridge, MA: MIT TDQM Program.

17. Jarvenpaa, S.L., *The Effect of Task Demands and Graphical Format on Information Processing Strategies.* Management Science, 1989. 35(3): p. 285-303.

18. Kendall, K.E. and J.E. Kendall, *Systems Analysis and Design.* 5 ed. 2001, Englewood Cliffs, NJ: Prentice Hall. 914.

19. Klein, B.D. *User Detection of Errors in Data: Learning through Direct and Indirect Experience.* in *AIS98.* 1998.

20. Maier, M., *Space Shuttle Challenger Disaster.* SUNY Binghamton, 1992.

21. McLeod Jr., R. and G.P. Schell, *Management Information Systems.* 9 ed. 2004, Upper Saddle River, NJ: Pearson Prentice Hall. 420.

22. McLeod, R.J., *Management Information Systems: A Study of Computer-Based Information Systems.* 6 ed. 1995, Englewood Cliffs, NJ: Prentice Hall. 754.

23. Morgan, M., *The Challenger Decision: The Interaction of Image and Technology.* Human Systems Management, 1986. 6.

24. O'Brien, J.A., *Management Information Systems: A Managerial End User Perspective.* 2 ed. 1993, Homewood, IL: Irwin. 571.

25. Orr, K., *Data Quality and Systems Theory.* Communications of the ACM, 1998. 41(2): p. 66-71.

26. Pradhan, S. *Believability as an Information Quality Dimension.* in *Ifternational Conference on Information Quality.* 2005. Cambridge, MA: MIT TDQM.

27. Redman, T.C., *Data Quality for the Information Age*. 1996, Norwood, MA: Artech House, Inc.

28. Roberts, N.C., *Reconstructing Combat Decisions: Reflections on the Shootdown of Flight 655*, in *Administrative Sciences Department*. 1992, Naval Postgraduate School: Monterey, CA. p. 29.

29. Rogers, W., and Rogers, Sharon, *Storm Center The USS Vincennes and Iran Air Flight 655*. 1992, Annapolis, MD: Naval Institute Press. 264.

30. Rogers, W.P., *Report of the Presiential Commission on the Space Shuttle Challenger Accident*. 1986, Washington, D.C.: United States Government Printing Office.

31. Schkade, D.A., and Kleinmuntz, Don N., *Information Displays and Choice Processes: Differential Effects of Organization, Form, and Sequence*. Organizational Behavior and Human Decision Processes, 1994. 57(3): p. 319-337.

32. Schwartz, H.S., *Organizational Disaster and Organizational Decay: The Case of the National Aeronautics nd Space Administration*. Industrial Crisis Quarterly, 1990. 3: p. 319-334.

33. Shneiderman, B., *Designing Menu Selection Systems*. Journal of the American Society for Information Science, 1986. 37(2): p. 57-70.

34. Shneiderman, B., *Designing the User Interface*. 2E ed. 1992, Reading, MA: Addison-Wesley.

35. Smith-Adams, W. and J. Talburt. *Conducting an Information Product Competitor Analysis: Case Study*. in *The Eigth International Conference on Information Quality*. 2003. Cambridge, MA: MIT TDQM.

36. Stone, D.N., and Schkade, D.A., *Numeric and Linguistic Information Representation in Multiattribute Choice*. Organizational Behavior and Human Decision Processes, 1991. 49: p. 42-59.

37. Strong, D.M., Y.W. Lee, and R.Y. Wang, *Data Quality in Context*. Communications of the ACM, 1997. 40(5).

38. Strong, D.M. and O. Volkoff. *Data Quality Issues in Integrated Enterprise Systems*. in *Tenth International Conference on Information Conference*. 2005. Cambridge, MA: MIT TDQM.

39. Talburt, J., C. Morgan, T. Talley, and K. Archer. *Using Commercial Data Integration Technologies to Improve the Quality of*

Anonymous Entity Resolution in the Public Sector. in *International Conference on Information Quality*. 2005. Cambridge, MA: MIT TDQM.

40. Tappin, L., *Analyzing Data Relating to the Challenger Disaster.* The Mathematics Teacher, 1994. 87(6): 423.

41. Tayi, G. and D.P. Ballou, *Examining Data Quality.* Communications of the ACM, 1998. 41(2): p. 54-57.

42. Tufte, E., *Visual Explanations: Images and Quantities, Evidence and Narrative*. 1992, Cheshire, CT: Graphics Press.

43. Wand, Y. and R.Y. Wang, *Anchoring Data Quality Dimensions in Ontological Foundations*. Communications of the ACM, 1996. 39(11): p. 86-95.

44. Wang, R.Y., Y.W. Lee, L.L. Pipino, and D.M. Strong, *Manage Your Information as a Product*. Sloan Management Review, 1998(Summer): p. 95-105.

45. Wang, R.Y. and D. Strong, *Beyond Accuracy: What Data Quality Means to Data Consumers*. Journal of Management Information Systems, 1996. 12(4): p. 5-34.

46. Wetherbe, J. and N. Vitalari, *Systems Analysis and Design: Traditional, Best Practices*. 4 ed. 1994, St. Paul, MN: West Publishing.

47. Whitten, J.L., L.D. Bentley, and K.C. Dittman, *Systems Analysis and Design Methods*. 6 ed. 2004, Boston, MA: McGraw Hill. 780.

41. Mars Climate Orbiter Mishap Investigation Board, *Phase I Report*, November 10, 1999.

Information Products and Total Data Quality Management

*I*n the first few chapters, we learned the importance of data and information quality (IQ). It has been shown that one of the most important things a corporation can do is fix its data quality (DQ). We also learned the principles of TQM as applied to physical products in the manufacturing world, but as of 1998 there was a scarcity of theoretically grounded methodologies for application of TQM principles to the IS field.

INTRODUCTION

Most would agree that there are fewer defects in manufactured products than in databases and the information outputs from those databases. What can be done to bring IS quality to the same level as physical manufacturing? With this in mind, researchers have begun to apply TQM to *information products* in the IS world. Information systems focus on data, so we refer to the TQM concept as total *data* quality management (TDQM). "The purpose of TDQM methodology is to deliver high quality information products to consumers of that information" ([16] p 58). In addition corporations are beginning to create strategic information products that compete in the marketplace of information products. Acxiom Corporation® creates and sells many such information products. Their management realizes that there is a need for an overall information quality strategy that includes an "objective view of the Strengths, Weaknesses, Opportunities and Threats (SWOT) for each product" ([13], p. 17). To accomplish this, Acxiom Corporation® uses an approach that defines the IPs and their important dimensions for comparison, measures the products on those dimensions, and analyzes the products for improvement opportunities [13].

The information product (IP) concept requires that organizations treat data and information much like the products found in a manufacturing environment. If they are successful, they should be able to apply the same quality improvement techniques that work in manufacturing to their data and information processes. The quality disciplines used in manufacturing that have been built over the last 200 years are applicable to information products. Our main goal is to transfer manufacturing knowledge to the IS world.

INFORMATION PRODUCTS

Our first step is to define the term *Information Product* (IP). Think of it as any output that a system delivers to its environment. Presumably, the information output provides value to the receiver. The system's environment may be another system, a database, or a person. Right now, we will not place a limit on the environment. However, whatever the environment, it must be well understood by the system developers. According to Kock, data is a carrier of knowledge and information, a way through which knowledge and information can be stored and transferred [3]. In this context, data is transformed into information or knowledge only when it is interpreted by its receiver.

Generally speaking, the output of an IS is a report, a form, a response to an inquiry, or a database record (entity and related attributes). Reports are organizational documents that contain predefined data such as an invoice, shop floor activity, accounts receivable details, customer orders received, products shipped, or delinquent payment records. There is practically no limit as to the types of reports possible. Reports also come in a variety of formats, for example summary, exception, and detail in a textual format. A report may consist of graphs instead of text or in addition to text. It may be electronic instead of printed, and may include data and information that is combined, integrated, or summarized from multiple databases.

A form may provide information to, as well as collect information from, the user. Usually there is enough information on a form to make it clear what is required from the consumer. Examples include product order forms, college applications, and class registration forms. These may be printed or electronic.

IS designers must ensure that the reports and forms serve the intended purpose, that they are in the correct format, and that the people who need them get them when they need them. IS specialists spend a significant amount of time learning to design reports and forms to meet user needs [5, 8].

As mentioned earlier, we do not usually feel it is necessary to distinguish between information and data, although sometimes it can be useful. The distinction is mostly academic. Conventional wisdom defines data as the raw material for information. This implies that once data is combined with other data, it becomes information. Data, the raw material, was processed to create information. Now, what if that information is combined, through a second process, with other information to form new information? The information output of the first process is raw material of the second process. There is a cliché here: one person's information is another person's data. In other words, the distinction is relative. For readability purposes, we will sometimes switch between the two terms, but we are open to their interchangeable use in most cases. There is an analogy to physical parts, assemblies, and products.

In the physical world we can ask a similar question, when is something a raw material, and when is it a finished product? Consider the process of building assemblies from parts. Spokes, a rim, and a hub are combined to make a wheel. That wheel is a product, and it is an assembly of the raw materials that went into it. The wheel is then combined with other parts to make an even larger assembly, a bicycle. From this perspective, the wheel is just a part of the bicycle assembly, the finished product. The cliché still applies: one person's product is another person's part. To take this argument to the extreme, consider that the spokes, rim, and hub were products fabricated out of raw material—metal. One might say that the most fundamental part is the metal ore.

Clearly, there are differences between information and physical products, but that should not deter us from using the analogy when it can propagate ideas from one discipline to the other. However, it may be useful to make some differentiations between information and physical products now, so that we can distinguish between what may or may not be a concern further down the line.

A stock room becomes depleted as parts are removed from stock. If there were 100 parts at the beginning of the day, and 60 parts were used to assemble a product, then the 40 parts left would not satisfy the same need the next day. However, an information stock room never gets depleted in the same fashion. An unlimited amount of information can be given out without any concern about depletion of the data reserve.

The manager of an information database and the manager of a physical stock room share some concerns. They are both concerned about security, maintenance, obsolescence, accessibility, consistency, acquisition, and distribution. Some concerns are unique to information, and further research is needed. For example, believability, reputation, conciseness, and objectivity are key dimensions in deciding how well information products will fit the needs of consumers.

What does it mean to manage information as a product? It means to treat it as an *end-deliverable* that must satisfy customer needs. An organization typically has manufacturing disciplines, marketing disciplines, and financial disciplines to manage physical products. The goal is to be able to transfer the knowledge of those disciplines into the world of IS. Heretofore, this world has been building its own procedures and methods for developing IS. Several of the steps reference quality, but there were no overarching principles of doing business around the information product. Dr. Richard Wang, Co-Director of MIT's TDQM program, believes that the information product and TDQM approach will provide the basis for theoretically grounded methodologies for addressing IQ problems [16].

Product manufacturing includes gathering and inspecting input, performing processes on that input, and delivering output or products to consumers. In the physical product world, the input is the raw material that is analogous to the raw data input into the IS. The manufacturing process for product manufacturing is the assembly line. For an information-manufacturing environment, the IS is the process that captures the raw material and transforms it to output. In one world, the output is the tangible physical product; in the other it is the various reports, databases, forms, and graphs that are the outputs of those information systems. Table 4.1 illustrates the similarities between product manufacturing and information manufacturing. Product manufacturing can be viewed as a processing system that acts on raw materials to produce physical products such as automobiles, appliances, and furniture. Information manufacturing can be viewed as a processing system that acts on raw data to produce information products such as reports, summaries, and graphs.

Table 4.1
Comparison of Physical Product Manufacturing to
Information Manufacturing
(Source Wang et al. 1998 [19])

	Product Manufacturing	**Information Manufacturing**
Input	Raw Materials	Raw Data
Process	Assembly Line	Information System
Output	Physical Products	Information Products

The IS profession has long recognized the analogy. McLeod describes the physical system of the firm as one that transforms input resources into output resources. The input resources come from the organization's environment, then a transformation process acts on those resources to produce output resources [9]. However, recognizing the analogy and taking full advantage of it are two separate issues. Given the state of quality in manufacturing versus the state of quality of our information, it can be safely said that we still have a lot to learn from manufacturing. "Use of the term information manufacturing encourages researchers and practitioners to seek cross disciplinary analogies that can facilitate the transfer of knowledge from the field of product quality to the less well defined field of information quality" [3]. What physical product activities should be modeled by IS professionals?

Two of the major tasks in the physical product manufacturing system are:

- Design and development of products.
- Production and distribution of the products.

Product quality is a function of both activities. In addition to these, there are numerous activities in the internal and external environments that surround and influence the success of the enterprise and quality of products. For example, market research helps determine the customer requirements, while product research and development determines how to best meet those requirements. Vendor analysis helps determine which suppliers will provide the best-quality raw materials at the most reasonable price in time to meet customer requirements. Without listing all of the related processes, systems like accounts receivable, accounts payable, cost accounting, purchasing, competitive analysis, and pricing are long established processes that support the manufacturing environment. Manufacturing plants have long studied the flow of parts from the vendor to the stock room, to the shop floor, and to the assembly line, as well as the flow of the finished products to the warehouse, to the shipping docks, and to customers. The flow of information is also critical to IS.

The field of IS uses data flow diagrams (DFD) to document the flow of information. There are four basic symbols that, when used properly, provide an easy-to-read picture of how information flows. The symbols are shown in figure 4.1. Information flow is shown with arrows. Sources or inputs of information, as well as destinations or outputs, are indicated by rectangles. The processes performed on the information are represented by circles or curved rectangles, and the storage of information is illustrated by thin rectangles which denote files and databases. Analysts use DFD to document information flow throughout the organization and to determine who uses the information; when, how, and who changes the information; what information is stored; and what relationships exist to other data. Information systems students study DFD in their systems analysis and design courses so that they will be able to completely and accurately document the flow of information through an organization when developing a new system.

The external entity is the source or destination of information. Normally, these are nouns that describe a role such as customer, supplier, manager, or government. The data store is what many people think of as a file or a database, and it is where the information is saved. A process, normally a verb, is the action performed on the data. A process may be as simple as reading the data from a data store or accepting it from an external entity. A process may also be an extremely complicated series of mathematical algorithms performed on multiple databases simultaneously. Finally, one of the key symbols is the arrow, which represents a data flow. The information carried on the data flow arrow may be one field of data; several fields, records, reports, and forms; or it could be an entire database.

A simple glance at a DFD informs the viewer where the data came from, what processes acted on it, where it is stored, and who uses it. For those who would like to investigate further, we recommend Hoffer's textbook, *Modern Systems Analysis and Design*, or Kendall's book on the same subject [5, 8].

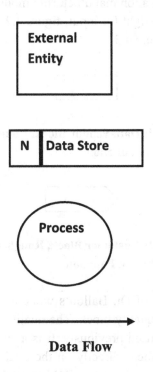

Figure 4.1 Basic DFD Symbols

Data flow diagrams lack two major concepts when compared to manufacturing systems: a clear distinction between inputs and outputs, and a clear picture of the DQ validity checks, edits, and inspections. A well known researcher in the field of IQ, Dr. Donald Ballou, has addressed this problem with his concept of information manufacturing systems [3]. Dr. Ballou created an information manufacturing system model that evaluates IS quality in light of timeliness, accuracy, value, and costs. Dr. Ballou's model is beyond the scope of this introductory textbook, but the reader should be aware that he used mathematical models to analyze the tradeoffs between those four elements. His landmark work [3] should be studied by all serious data and IQ analysts. Researchers are encouraged to build on his model by adding more DQ dimensions.

Ballou's model distinguishes between external entities that are sources of information and external entities that are receivers of information products. Whereas the DFD uses the rectangle to represent both sources and receivers, the information manufacturing model uses a rectangle with an arrow pointing to the right for input, figure 4.2, and an arrow pointing to the left for output, figure 4.3.

Figure 4.2 Dr. Ballou's Data Vendor Block, Roughly Equivalent to an Input or Collection Function

Figure 4.3 Dr. Ballou's Customer Block, Roughly Equivalent to an Output or Distribution Function

A major innovation of Dr. Ballou's work is the specification of an entirely new block, the quality block. The quality block is a triangle that is half of the rectangle used previously. It is a subset of processing, but it forces the analyst to focus directly on the quality tasks and activities. Every data flow can have one or more DQ blocks that specify exactly how the quality of that data unit is managed and controlled.

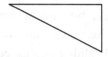

Figure 4.4 Data Quality Block

When these new blocks are combined with the symbols used in the DFD, we have a very powerful tool for documenting the information flows with emphasis on inputs, outputs, and quality. If an organization finds itself in a reaction mode because of multiple DQ problems, the analyst can study the flow of information and analyze the validity checks that take place within the DQ blocks for each and every data unit. In a proactive mode, the organization may form a quality committee of consumers, data collectors, and data custodians (virtually all stakeholders) who can brainstorm the possible validity checks that could be developed for every data unit. Although DFD are still heavily used in industry, there is movement to the unified modeling language (UML) found in the object-oriented paradigm.

"An information production map (IP-MAP) is a graphical model similar to a data flow diagram that is designed to help people comprehend, evaluate, and describe how an information product such as an invoice, customer order or prescription is assembled" [10]. The IP-MAP is aimed at creating a systematic representation for capturing the details associated with the manufacture of an IP [3, 12]. Recently, consistent with the trend toward object-oriented analysis and design, researchers are beginning to implement IP-MAPS with the UML [12]. "UML is used in multiple application domains and is increasingly becoming the *de facto* standard language for object-oriented analysis and design" [12]. As organizations move to object-oriented processing, they are advised to implement IP-MAPS with UML.

Now that we have information products and recognize the information manufacturing system, we can focus on the application of TQM principles to IS.

TOTAL DATA QUALITY MANAGEMENT

The foundation for an IQ program is the adapted version of TQM, total DQ management. The TDQM cycle follows the Deming cycle of plan-do-check-act described in chapter 2. "In applying the TDQM methodology, an organization must clearly articulate the IP in business terms; establish an IP team consisting of a senior executive champion, an IP engineer and members who are suppliers, manufacturers, consumers and IP managers; teach IQ assessment and management skills to all the IP constituencies; and institutionalize IP improvement" ([16] p. 61).

These steps are drawn as a continuous cycle, figure 4.5. The planning step includes a thorough definition of all information products. Once the definitions are agreed on, the measurements are selected or defined and applied to determine current level of quality. Once that is known, analysis can determine root causes of any area in which the organization is not satisfied with the current quality. Then improvement projects may be defined and prioritized. After the projects are completed, a fresh assessment of the organization, or subset of the organization, related to the pertinent IP follows, and the cycle begins anew.

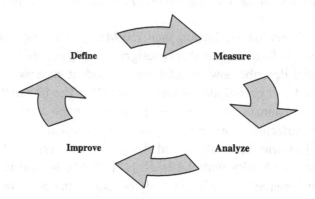

Figure 4.5 TDQM Cycle [16]

TDQM's FOUR STEPS

Define the Information Product

The definition component identifies, tailors, prioritizes, understands, and filters the relevant IQ dimensions. One must first define the characteristics for the IP and assess the IP's information quality requirements in light of the known IQ dimensions. All 16 dimensions should be reviewed and considered, but they may not all be relevant or equally important to every single task within all IS projects all the time. After this is accomplished, the project team identifies the information manufacturing system for the IP [3]. This first step is the most difficult, partly because it is new, and partly because there are many factions, players, and components that must be clearly defined. If any of the steps are taken for granted, or the dimensions ignored, then there may be DQ problems when the system is implemented and actually used by the consumers. Wang and his colleagues have shown that once these initial tasks have been accomplished, then concepts become well understood, and the process may be easily repeated for other information products [16]. Also, once the first few tasks are accomplished, the next series of steps, measurements, analysis, and improvements follow.

Measurement

Measurement is important to determine the extent of problems and the success of solutions. Unfortunately, there is a paucity of good measurements and measurement tools in the IS world. In the TDQM cycle, the measurement component produces IQ metrics. Following the theory that IQ is in the eye of the beholder, or user defined, the ultimate measure for IQ is whether the information is fit for use by consumers. Therefore, we need a measure that is based upon users' perceptions and encompasses all 16 dimensions. In addition to measurements for different uses of information by different users, there are also measurement problems based upon the source of the data. A data warehouse (DW) integrates data from a variety of sources: internal operations, confidential databases, and external databases outside the organization. Internal operations data include transaction processing systems such as order entry and accounting. Confidential data may be stored in private databases with various formats throughout the organization. External data include financial indicators, information about competitors, and market research information. Dealing with this wide range of sources, platforms, and formats, and combining them into useful data for integrated storage, is one of the most important challenges in a DW implementation.

Dr. Wang and his colleagues developed an ideal instrument for this purpose [16]. He includes this portion of the measurement in his seminal paper, "A Product Perspective on Total Data Quality Management" [16]. The Information Quality Assessment (IQA) is a survey given to all stakeholders—collectors, custodians, consumers and managers of information—for each IP, figure 4.6. The IQA is a major breakthrough in measuring how the stakeholders perceive quality across all dimensions. We have repeatedly stated the IQ should be determined by the view of the user, but until now not enough has been done to understand that view across all dimensions and as compared to the technologists. The survey asks for an evaluation on a scale from 0 to 10 for each dimension. Plots of the

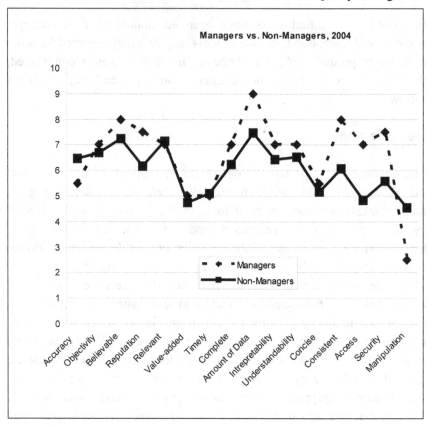

Figure 4.6 Information Quality Assessment

evaluations on a graph highlight the problems as viewed by the stakeholders. The plots provide insight into where the effort should be placed to improve quality. This topic will be covered further in chapter 7 when we discuss measurements. But before we move on it is worth mentioning that the DQ analyst is not obtaining the ratings for each dimension by a single user type. One of the major contributions is that the ratings for different groups of stakeholders may be compared to each other.

Figure 4.6 shows the ratings of managers versus non-managers. Notice that in several dimensions the perception of IQ is very similar, but in a few there is a big difference. Managers believed that there was a good amount of data; it was consistent, easy to access, and secure. However, they also believed it was quite difficult to manipulate. The non-managers believed that the data was easy to manipulate. One of the key jobs of the DQ analyst is to delve into the root causes of these differences and determine how to resolve them. Perhaps the non-managers were more familiar with the data and knew all the tricks for manipulating it. If so, then an easy way to improve the satisfaction of the managers with the data is to train the managers on those techniques, or create new and easier ways for them to manipulate the data.

As the reader will discover in chapter 7, these comparisons between groups can be an eye opener. A comparison between an information technologist's point of view and a user's point of view often leads to great followup discussions. In one case, the technologists thought a system had very little security, partly because they were trained to know all of the ways to break into a system. However, the users felt there was too much security because it hampered accessibility. The IQA brought the issue to the attention of the DQ analyst, who then worked with both groups to reach a satisfactory solution.

In addition to these perceptual measurements, Dr. Wang and others give tangible IQ measurements that can be captured in the database [1, 18]. These include specific accuracy measurements such as the percentage of incorrect client addresses, the timeliness of updating, the percentage of missing data, and a count of records that violate various business rules [16]. Traditionally, MIS also tracks quality problems to a person who may have committed the error.

However, before starting a major project, an in-depth understanding of the causes of the problems must be developed. Root cause analysis is the next stage in the TDQM methodology.

Analysis

The analysis component pinpoints causes of IQ problems and identifies their various effects on the organization. This step is directly analogous to the major systems analysis effort of a normal IS project. However, it is now done in light of the relevant dimensions included with the tangible IQ metrics. Each dimension must be considered for each IP. The IQ professional and IP manager must analyze the impacts of a change of one dimension on the other dimensions. As discussed earlier, one cannot simply improve the security dimension in a vacuum. Any changes to the security dimension have a high probability of adversely affecting the accessibility dimension. Likewise, changes to the accuracy dimension might affect timeliness, changes to completeness and amount of information might affect conciseness, and so on. The relationship and importance of these perceptions of quality by the stakeholders must be analyzed and documented.

Analysis is also performed using the tangible measurements mentioned in the last section. Here the IS custodian strives to uncover actual causes of problems. For example, IS departments keep track of which fields have the most errors in a database or on an input form. If possible, they track the errors to the actual source, not in order to punish the culprit, but to identify root causes of problems. It is important to know if a high percentage of the errors in a record involve one field from one source. In a case where errors in one or two fields account for 80% of the errors, it is relatively easy to focus all energies on the one problem area. Most likely there is a design problem that can be easily rectified. Sometimes, something as simple as an instruction change on how to fill out a form can be implemented, saving thousands of dollars and hours of error correction.

Analysis was performed on the input forms used by an agency that provided various social services to members of the community. One error kept occurring in the database because the field was improperly labeled. The collectors did not always enter the data into the right place on the form. This simple correction saved a significant amount of time in trying to recreate the value of the data, as well as improving the accuracy of the database. The impact of any error is usually more far-reaching than just the time to correct it. If it was in error and a report was based on it, then many users may have read the report and already made decisions based upon that misinformation.

There are several analysis tools and techniques. First and foremost is the information quality assessment (IQA) technique developed by the Cambridge Research Group. The IQA tool is a survey that collects stakeholders' perception of the quality and importance of each dimension for the IP of interest. The IQA focuses on intangible perceptions, and is covered in chapter 7.

The Integrity Analyzer

The Integrity Analyzer (IA) performs many tangible tests on the data itself, and is also covered in chapter 7. "An outgrowth of research from MIT's total data quality management (TDQM) research, the IA embeds a TDQM methodology that combines the principles of the TDQM cycle with the principles of integrity constraints in relational databases" ([6], p. 72). The tangible tests are the integrity constraints as defined by Codd: domain, entity, referential, column, and user-defined integrity. With the IQA establishing a clear picture of user perceptions of DQ, and the IA establishing that the integrity constraints are being met, an organization is well on its way to improved IQ. There are a few additional tools and concepts taken from the field of quality control in manufacturing. The combination of all techniques provides a powerful movement toward total DQ.

Pareto Chart Analysis

"The Pareto chart is a graphical too for ranking causes of problems from the most significant to the least significant" ([15], p. 75). In a quality control study, the data refer to defects found in manufacturing. The defects by sub-parts are plotted to show both frequency and percent of total defects. The example below itemizes five components of a final product for the frequency of defects with each component is calculated. Then, a plot of the defects is developed as in figure 4.7. The left vertical axis indicates total defects, and the right vertical axis indicates cumulative percentage of defects. The line graph depicts the effect of each component's errors on the cumulative errors for the product.

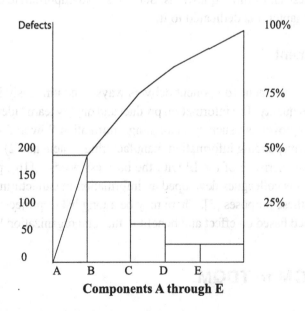

Figure 4.7 Pareto Chart

The Pareto diagram indicates which problem should be solved first. These bar graphs are extremely helpful in factory quality control. Graphs are much easier to follow than a list of numbers, especially in a manufacturing environment that may have hundreds of parts. Pareto techniques will be explored further in chapter 6. One of our important goals is to transfer knowledge from key quality techniques in manufacturing to information products.

Statistical Process Control

When quality control experts examine sample products produced from a mass production line and find that there are n defects, what meaning can be attached to this finding? Did the n defects occur by chance? Is n so large that it is an outlier and was not a result of random chance? Suppose that improvements were made to the production line; can management determine if the changes significantly helped (or hurt) the situation? Without a specific and overt change engineered by management, it is possible that machines and equipment deteriorate over time to cause a negative change in the output quality? How can we monitor the process to determine if the equipment is deteriorating? The subject of statistical process control answers these and similar questions. Statistics is so important to the quality field that chapter 5 is dedicated to it.

Improvement

The improvement component delivers ways of continuously improving information quality. The information product and quality team "identifies key areas for improvement such as 1) aligning information flow and work flow with the corresponding information manufacturing system and 2) realigning the key characteristics of the IP with the business needs" ([16], p. 65). Dr. Ballou and his colleagues developed an information manufacturing analysis matrix for these purposes [3]. There may be a long list of projects that must be prioritized based on effect and benefit to the total organization [2].

FROM TQM TO TDQM

In this section we review and reinforce the relationship of the TQM concepts in our current TDQM approach. An IQ vision must be clearly stated in business terms. This is similar in structure to the mission statement of an organization. The vision must be clearly understood by upper-level management, and it is their responsibility to heighten awareness throughout the company that IQ is a top consideration. Once this is done, central responsibility for information quality control needs to be established. It would be much easier to have everyone be responsible for his or her own part of the ship, so to speak, but this would not give the intended results.

First, the workers may be so busy with their current responsibilities that they could not give the high level of priority to IQ stated in the vision. Secondly, there would probably be different interpretations of exactly how the task should be handled. Thirdly, workers may have limited view or control over the processes used. This would create a variety of solutions or precautions that may not mesh well with each another.

Information product suppliers, manufacturers, and consumers all must be educated on how to take charge of not only IQ in general, but on how to apply it to their individual projects and tasks in particular.

Lastly, a policy for continuous IQ improvement must be institutionalized. This responsibility should fall to the CIO or top-level management. It will be up to these people to maintain the employees' interest in the program throughout the organization. Techniques to do this include feedback from their efforts, regular meetings, and informative presentations. Information improvement projects should become a regular part of the budgetary process.

Development Stages and Activities

In an effort to understand the information manufacturing system itself, we will review the three major stages and nine major activities within those stages. All nine activities are required to produce the information. All are important, just as all nine links in a chain are. If one link is broken, so is the chain. This should make the internal processing system clearer.

Table 4.2
The Three Stages of Systems Development (Source [17])

Dev. stages	Design	Implementation	Deployment
Dev. activities	Requirements analysis	DB implementation	Training
	Conceptual model	Software engineering	Maintenance
	System specification	Software quality assurance	Information quality management

There can be specific problems associated with one or more activities. To make effective use of this table, we attempt to map DQ problems into the area where there is the most chance of catching and fixing the original error. For example, if we notice that the information designed into the system is not the information required by the consumer, then we have inadequate requirements analysis under design.

Additionally, if we notice bugs occurring in the software, then there was most likely inadequate testing under implementation. There may be several reasons for poor retrieval and distribution, but we can start with consideration of inadequate training of custodians or inadequate procedures in deployment.

To illustrate the relationship and interdependencies of these activities, consider the tests for validating data that are taught in a fundamental programming course on specific program techniques. Programmers are taught to ensure that their program receives only good input data. First, there is a simple test for *missing data*, accomplished by checking for blanks where there should be data, although it is possible that *blanks* are acceptable data in certain situations. The determination of whether blanks are acceptable should be done during the requirements analysis activity. Once that is determined, then the decision must be communicated to the program and database designers by a system specification document. These designers must define allowable input so that the programmer and database implementer put in the proper tests. Then it is up to them to implement what is required. Often this step requires some creativity, since blanks must be allowed sometimes, for some fields, but not other times, for other fields. Programmers may distinguish between null fields and blank fields during the software engineering. The programs and database must be fully tested to verify that the programs meet the specifications. If the business rules change, then changes must be made to all of the programs involved. Making changes requires knowing which programs handle the input tests, and what techniques were used to implement the tests. For a medium-to-large business there could be hundreds of thousands of lines of code that a programmer has to search to find the correct program. Obviously, the program documentation is one of the most important factors in the maintenance and ongoing quality of a system. Finally, the system must be retested.

There are several conditions that require a similar process. For example, programs test for field length, composition of the attributes, range of allowable values, class of information, relationship to previously stored data, and the use of check digits or self-validating codes. These conditions must be analyzed and determined by users, explicated in specifications documents, planned for by designers, implemented by database administrators and programmers in software engineering, measured as to effectiveness by quality assurance personnel, and well documented so that changes can be made according to business needs during the maintenance activities.

Dr. Wang identified four key roles in an information manufacturing system [16]. The people who create or collect raw materials—data for the system—are *providers*. The providers are the first step in the information production process. Without raw material, data, the system would be useless.

The people who design, develop, and maintain data and computer systems are *custodians*. These are the typical roles found in the application development and maintenance, as well as system support departments of an IS organization. They are responsible for data storage, maintenance, integrity, security, recovery, and applications.

The users of the information are the people who work on the immediate output of the system, from those who process a business transaction to all levels of management who use summary reports and graphs to make far-reaching decisions. These users are considered *consumers* of the IP. It is the consumers who must want to buy the products. Consumers determine product quality.

An investment broker in a financial firm who creates accounts and executes transactions must first collect information necessary to open the accounts, and therefore is an information provider. An IS professional is a custodian of the data. A financial controller, who makes decisions based on information, is a consumer of the information.

The fourth role is the *manager* of the overall process. A manager is assigned responsibility for the production process and the IP's life cycle. Many organizations believe that it is enough to simply tell everyone in the organization to be sure that good-quality data is received (the input is good), that their own department only modifies or transforms (manufacturing process) the data in such a way that the new information is of good quality, and that only good-quality information (output or IP) leaves their department or station. The theory is that if everyone practices good DQ, then the organization will have good-quality information.

Information Product Manager

An information product manager must be appointed to manage the overall process; we cannot overemphasize the importance of this. The key responsibility of the information product manager is to coordinate and manage the three stakeholders using an integrated, cross-functional approach. The three stakeholders are:
- Supplier (provider) of raw information.
- Manufacturer (custodian) of deliverable information.
- Consumer of information (consumer).

The four main principles of managing information as a product are:
- Thoroughly understand the consumer's information needs.
- Manage the information as the product of a well-defined process.
- Manage information as a product within a life cycle.
- Appoint an information product manager.

Understand the consumer's information needs

Information system professionals are much more aware of this problem than they used to be. It has been shown that faulty requirements are the biggest factors in failed information processing systems, including over budget and late delivery, i.e., missed due dates [7, 11, 20]. It is also well known that if there are problems in an IS, it is significantly cheaper, with much less of a negative effect on users, if the problems are identified and fixed in the requirements analysis stage, as opposed to later stages such as program coding, system testing, or—worst case—after release to full production. The later an error is found, the more rework is needed in earlier stages, and the more widespread the error may have become [14].

One advantage of the IQ approach is that the scope of the requirements is made much broader and more realistic because all 16 dimensions must be considered. For example, more factors are considered in context of other factors. As was demonstrated in the section on dimensions, work on one dimension might impact another dimension. Earlier system development projects did not always take this into consideration. Then when systems were released for use by consumers, quality issues arose. Consumers may say they want high security, but become dissatisfied when they find that in order to achieve the highest security, they have to sacrifice accessibility. Consumers may insist on perfect accuracy until they realize that the report they need may be delayed for two weeks, or even a month. A well-known example of time and accuracy tradeoffs is the nation's gross national product (GNP). If you wanted a 100% accurate GNP, then you would have to wait at least six months instead of getting a much earlier approximate version.

Manage information as the product of a well-defined process

The DQ analyst must thoroughly document the systems through either DFD with the new Data Quality blocks[3] or the UML with Data Quality blocks. The process crosses department and function boundaries to deliver the required information products.

Manage information as a product within a life cycle

The stages of information from origination to obsolescence are: introduction (creation), growth, maturity, and decline [6]. These four stages follow the classical life cycle of a product [6]. A chemical company failed to update databases, and the quality of the database deteriorated over time. Regardless of the quality of a database, it will eventually become unfit for use.

Appoint an information product manager

The main responsibility of the information product manager is to coordinate and manage the three major stakeholders. These are the supplier of raw data, the manufacturer of the deliverable information, and the consumer of the information [6].

Information as a Byproduct

The IP approach requires that the information be managed instead of the hardware and software, as in the byproduct approach. The byproduct approach follows the stovepipe systems approach, in which there is a linear flow that controls individual components with emphasis on cost controls, instead of viewing the overall system. In the IP approach, an integrated cross-functional approach is used that includes suppliers, manufacturers, and consumers.

An eyeglass company lost $1 million annually because of DQ problems [6]. The company had no known bugs in its system or application software, but it had inadequate methods of communicating information from suppliers of data to consumers of data. The wrong prescriptions were sent to the lens grinders, resulting in good lenses being produced to bad specifications.

The goal of managing information as a product is to deliver quality information products to the user and to improve what the user needs—not what IS needs. Success is based upon delivering a quality IP continuously over the IP life cycle. In the byproduct approach, success was often measured by whether a system worked without any bugs. The product approach claims that bugs are the wrong criteria for measuring success. The consumers of the information must be able to perform their jobs better in order to claim success of an information manufacturing system. One company's system never had any bugs, but they didn't keep the database up-to-date. Since the database was outdated, the users had to deal with obsolete information and lost confidence in the system [6].

IP manager's responsibilities during the life cycle stages

The four stages of information from origination to obsolescence follow the classical life cycle of products as follows: introduction (creation), growth, maturity, and decline [6]. During the *introductory stage*, the emphasis is on design and development, which resembles an engineering effort. The essence of the IP manager's duties is process management and coordination. The information product manager (IPM) must ensure that the entire organization understands all of the consumer requirements and integrates them into meaningful products. Quality goals and standards have to be set for each IP. The IPM needs to use every available resource to overcome the natural resistance to a new way of approaching business processes. This does not imply, or even remotely suggest, that the IPM will use authority as a big stick to force compliance. But it does imply that the manager will be the most knowledgeable, enthusiastic, and persuasive advocate of all aspects of the TDQM program. The IPM needs to persuade executives on the importance of all steps in the TDQM process, and convince middle—and lower-level managers of the benefits of following it religiously. A natural phenomenon in organizations is that when a highly-respected knowledgeable person begins winning executives and middle managers over to a concept, others readily follow, especially when the results support the claims. Therefore, monitoring is crucial.

During the *growth stage*, the IPM works with the teams to improve and monitor the IP. Here, the organization uses emerging tools and performs periodic reassessments. In order to accurately monitor something, it is necessary to have a set of quantifiable standards. A measurement without standards is virtually useless. For example, suppose a store sold 10 dresses in a day. How useful is that data? The goal, or standard, could be a target as part of an aggressive sales promotion, or it could be a measure as to what was sold the same day last week, last month, or last year. It could also be a measure as to what the competition sold. For example, what if the goal was to sell 100 dresses? What if only a single dress was sold last week? Or 40 last month? What if the competitor sold 2? Or 90? Only when there is a target, a standard, or a goal, is a measurement useful. This is not only true in retail, but it is extremely important in quality planning and controls. One of the best ways to sell the TDQM project to upper-level managers and to lower-level workers, is to provide meaningful goals and show the measurements that indicate success of the improvement projects.

As the IP *matures*, even more emphasis is placed on continuous reassessment of all aspects of the product, the standards, and measurements. The organization must be aware of changes in the competitors' product, the consumers' needs, and the suppliers' abilities. The organization's management must be willing to initiate changes to products, even though this may entail long negotiations with many constituents. The monitoring should include consumer opinions, and the organization must be ready to revise quality goals based on evolving consumer needs. The IP monitor process measures product production and determines when product modification is necessary. Emerging information quality assessment tools, covered in later chapters, can provide the mechanisms to do this.

The area of *Obsolescence* is difficult for many organizations to face. The organization must consider terminating a successful product if the IPM is no longer providing the consumers the information they need.

ESTABLISH TDQM PROGRAM

To realize the benefits of the TDQM philosophy, an ongoing TDQM program, firmly entrenched in the corporate culture, must be established. There are five key steps to formally establishing a TDQM program.

1. Articulate IQ vision in business terms.
   - Set standards and goals for the quality of information products in business terms.
   - Upper-management should visibly endorse this vision and propagate it throughout the organization.
2. Establish central responsibility for IQ.
   - Create an IP management position such that one person has day-to-day responsibility for IQ.
   - This person must have the authority and accountability to adopt new techniques and make organizational changes.
3. Educate IP suppliers, manufacturers, and consumers.
   - Train all constituents and participants in IQ principles.
   - Learn methods of managing quality.
4. Teach new IQ skills.
   - All constituents must learn the skills required to put IQ programs into place.
5. Institutionalize continuous IQ improvement.
   - Establish regular meetings, talks, and organization changes.
   - Track the corporation's progress in meeting IQ goals.

Acxiom Corporation Introduced TDQM

"In well researched data quality systems, [information] products have specific data quality metrics that reflect the needs of their customers and the way their customers use their data product" ([4], p. 257). Extending the TDQM approach across multiple products is not easy for a corporate-wide DQ strategy. Many organizations can only provide a relative assessment of the quality of their data in general terms such as good, poor, excellent, or getting better.

Acxiom Corporation is an organization with many working components. The solutions and products organization within the corporation is likened to a data factory, manufacturing data products from raw source data into marketable products ([4], p. 258). Each product has its own metrics. Differing quality measurements and systems make it difficult to discuss corporation DQ, and organizations can easily lose statistical process control over the data quality across the entire factory. Acxiom has shown that DQ can become a sustainable competitive advantage for the organization that is able to gain statistical process control.

Acxiom was able to achieve this goal through the implementation of TDQM. Acxiom's first step was to form "an overarching 'Data Quality Scorecard Review Team' to communicate and achieve their goals" ([4], p. 259). This team developed the scorecard system to provide a unified system for measuring DQ. All IP teams were required to submit their metrics quarterly, enabling a review of DQ every three months. This alone was a major accomplishment, as people tend to do "what you inspect not merely what you expect." The corporation is now fully aware of DQ metrics and measuring them quarterly. The review team looked for improvement plans at one quarter and for improvement results at subsequent quarters, putting the TDQM cycle into the forefront. A system was established whereby multiple project teams could describe, monitor, and publish their DQ metrics internally throughout the organization, leading to the data quality scorecard approach. While individual products followed the TDQM approach, they still had difficulty with consistency across the organization. The scorecard approach sought to define, measure, analyze, and improve DQ for the entire organization.

Acxiom selected four of the DQ dimensions and added a new one to use for their universal scorecard approach. Individual products could still use all 16 dimensions, but for cross-organization evaluation and comparisons the five selected dimensions were accuracy, completeness, consistency, access timeliness, and grouping accuracy. The scorecard team consults with each IP team to establish specific metrics and methods for collecting measurements.

Every IP team took the following actions:
- Establish quantifiable goals for each of the five dimensions.
- Establish a methodology for measuring each dimension.
- Convince the scorecard team that the measurements chosen are, in fact, appropriate.
- Explain how the IP team is using the results to improve its DQ.
- Make all results available to all people involved with the IP processes.

Resistance was encountered from many IP teams, especially in the area of developing metrics for each of five dimensions. They complained that some dimensions were not relevant to their IP. They also pointed fingers at who else was responsible outside their control, such as vendors. This resistance is typical with the start of a new program and only serves to emphasize the importance of putting the IPM in place and securing upper-level management support very early in the process. Continuous education and training on the importance of all aspects of following the TDQM (TQM!) process were also instrumental in the success of Acxiom's new quality program.

SUMMARY

Researchers and practitioners have recently begun to apply the techniques of total quality management that have been effective on physical products to data and information products. This application of TQM to data and information is referred to as total data quality management. TDQM follows the same four basic steps found in TQM: define the product, measure the product quality, analyze problems to identify causes, and improve the products. The important distinction is that there are 16 dimensions to IQ, and all of them must be considered when developing an IQ improvement program. An IP manager is necessary to oversee this process. There are five steps to achieving a TDQM program. The Acxiom Corporation has successfully implemented a TDQM program by fully integrating the IP concepts with the principles and steps of TDQM.

CHAPTER FOUR QUESTIONS

Review Questions

1. Define the four steps of the TDQM process.
2. What are the four principles of treating information as a product?
3. Describe the key difference(s) of treating information as a product verse treating it as a byproduct.
4. What does information manufacturing have in common with physical product manufacturing?
5. Distinguish between information providers, custodians, and consumers of information. What tasks are associated with each?
6. List the principles of TDQM that Acxiom followed.
7. Explain the differences between data flow diagrams and Dr. Ballou's blocks for information manufacturing systems.
8. Explain the concept of IQA.
9. Explain the four principles of managing information as a product.
10. Define a Pareto diagram and state its main purpose.

Discussion Questions

1. Inventory management is a critical part of physical production processes. A company cannot afford to run out of inventory, because the company would not be able to meet product build and delivery commitments. However, carrying too much inventory is very costly. How does data inventory differ from material product inventory?
2. As shown earlier, data differs from a material product because the use of data does not deplete the supply of data. Do the multiple uses of data deplete the value of data?
3. In the IP model, we introduced four roles: information suppliers, manufacturers, consumers, and managers. What are the implications of one person holding multiple roles?
4. For each of the three business types listed below identify a possible IP and describe who might fill the 4 IP roles in each organization.
   a. Mom and pop insurance agency.

      b.   National fast food chain.

      c.   A small college.

5.   In a physical manufacturing system, someone quite familiar with the content and value of the material product usually designs a product.

      a.   In what ways is an IS designer familiar with the content of the IS product?

      b.   In what ways is an IS designer not familiar with the content of the IS product?

6.   Considering that much work has been previously done on defining customer and user requirements, what is the new main advantage of following the IQ approach to understand consumer's information needs?.

7.   Why manage information as a product and not as a byproduct?

8.   In what ways is it important for an IS designer to be familiar with the content of the IS product? Why? What are the risks or costs involved?

REFERENCES

1.   Ballou, D.P. and H.L. Pazer, *Modeling Data and Process Quality in Multi-Input, Multi-Output Information Systems.* Management Science, 1985. 31(2): p. 150-162.

2.   Ballou, D.P. and G.K. Tayi, *Enhancing Data Quality in Data Warehouse Environments.* Communications of the ACM, 1999. 42(1): p. 73-78.

3.   Ballou, D.P., R. Wang, H. Pazer, and G.K. Tayi, *Modeling Information Manufacturing Systems to Determine Information Product Quality.* Management Science, 1998. 44(4): p. 462-484.

4.   Campbell, T. and Z. Wilhoit. *"How's your Data Quality?" A Case Study in Corporate Data Quality Strategy".* in *Eigth International Conference on Information Quality.* 2003. Cambridge, MA: MIT Total Data Quality Management Program.

5.   Hoffer, J., J. George, and Valacich, *Modern Systems Analysis and Design.* 4 ed. 2004, Upper Saddle River, NJ: Prentice Hall. 683.

6.   Huang, K.-T., Y.W. Lee, and R.Y. Wang, *Quality Information and Knowledge.* 1999, Englewood Cliffs, NJ: Prentice Hall. 209.

7. Kendall, K.E. and J.E. Kendall, *Systems Analysis and Design*. 5 ed. 2001, Englewood Cliffs, NJ: Prentice Hall. 914.

8. Kendall, K.E. and J.E. Kendall, *Systems Analysis and Design*. 5 ed. 2004, Englewood Cliffs, NJ: Prentice Hall. 914.

9. McLeod Jr., R. and G.P. Schell, *Management Information Systems*. 9 ed. 2004, Upper Saddle River, NJ: Pearson Prentice Hall. 420.

10. Pierce, E. *Extending IP-MAPS: Incorporating the Event-Driven Process Chain Methodology*. in *Seventh International Conference on Information Quality*. 2002. Cambridge, MA: MIT TDQM Program.

11. Ray, H.N. and J.E. Oliver, *Teaching Interpersonal Skills in Systems Analysis and Design*. Interface: The Computer Education Quarterly, 1989.

12. Scannapieco, M., B. Pernici, and E.M. Pierce, *IP-UML: A Methodology for Quality Improvement Based on Information Product Maps and Unified Modeling Language*, in *Information Quality*, R.Y. Wang, et al., Editors. 2005, M. E. Sharpe: Armonk, NY. p. 265.

13. Smith-Adams, W. and J. Talburt. *Conducting an Information Product Competitor Analysis: Case Study*. in *The Eigth International Conference on Information Quality*. 2003. Cambridge, MA: MIT TDQM.

14. Stair, R.M. and G.W. Reynolds, *Principles of Information Systems*. 6 ed. 2003, Boston, MA: Course Technology. 692.

15. Summers, D.C.S., *Quality*. 2006, Upper Saddle River, NJ: Pearson/ Prentice Hall. 819.

16. Wang, R.Y., *A Product Perspective on Total Data Quality Management*. Communications of the ACM, 1998. 41(2): p. 58-65.

17. Wang, R.Y. and H.B. Kon, *Toward Total Data Quality Management (TDQM)*, in *Information Technology in Action: Trends and Perspectives*, R.Y. Wang, Editor. 1993: Englewood Cliffs, NJ.

18. Wang, R.Y. and Y.W. Lee, *Integrity Analyzer: A Software Tool for Total Data Quality Management*. 1998, MIT: Cambridge, MA.

19. Wang, R.Y., Y.W. Lee, L.L. Pipino, and D.M. Strong, *Manage Your Information as a Product*. Sloan Management Review, 1998(Summer): p. 95-105.

20. Whitten, J.L., L.D. Bentley, and K.C. Dittman, *Systems Analysis and Design Methods*. 6 ed. 2004, Boston, MA: McGraw Hill. 780.

Statistics

*T*his chapter is intended to provide an introduction to statistical analysis. The reader should develop an appreciation of statistics that will help foster an adequate understanding of the strengths and limitations of statistical data analysis and its application in data quality (DQ), at least from the perspective of a consumer of statistics.

Introduction

The term statistics is used to describe the body of techniques used to collect, organize, and analyze data, as well as interpret it and draw valid conclusions on the basis of such analysis. The field of statistics provides a set of standard procedures for describing and making inferences on data. Statistics is used in the domain of DQ to help make better decisions by uncovering hidden relationships and unknown patterns, as well as interpreting the sources of variation in the data.

Probability and statistics are closely related disciplines which are often confused. As described by Brownlee, in probability theory, the structure of the problem is defined, a mathematical model is built, and the values of the parameters of the model are specified [2]. Then, given a specified model, inferences are made about specific cases of the problem at issue, for example, in terms of the distribution of occurrence of each possible outcome. In statistics we argue in the reverse direction. The structure of the problem is given and a model is assumed, but not specified (the model's parameters are unknown). Then data is collected and summarized, and the observations are used to infer the values of the parameters of the model.

These attempted definitions can be further clarified with a simple example in DQ. Consider a case in which an accounting firm audits financial statements searching for potential errors or misstatements. Suppose that a random sample of size n is taken from a lot of N financial statements with a known proportion of π erroneous statements. What is the distribution of occurrence of erroneous statements (X) in repeated random samples? If we assume for the sake of this analysis that $N = 1000$, $n = 50$, and $\pi = 0.1$ (10%), then we can expect that the number of erroneous statements X will often be 10% of the 50 statements in the sample (5 statements); but it will *not* always be 5. In fact, 5 will be the most common outcome, but we can expect other results as well (3, 2, 7, 1, . . .). Probability will help us understand what proportion of the time in repeated random samples the number of erroneous financial statements X will take a given value x.

On the other hand, if a random sample of n financial statements is taken from the population of N available cases, and X erroneous statements are detected, what can be said about the proportion parameter π? What summary measures can be calculated to help describe the data sample? How can π be estimated from the sample? These are the kind of questions answered by statistics.

Descriptive statistics deals with summarizing the collected data; and *inferential statistics* deals with analyzing the data and drawing conclusions from that assessment.

Common to all aspects of the definition of statistics is *data*. Data, plainly stated, is the set of facts collected, recorded, and organized, from which conclusions are drawn.

The set of all possible cases that could be considered within the context of the problem under analysis is commonly known as the *population*. Examples of populations are all U.S. citizens, all the customer records in a database collected this month, and the heights of all female students in a given university. In our example of the previous section, the set of N cases represented the population of financial statements audited by the accounting firm in a given period.

When gathering data to try to characterize a population, it is usually impossible to collect data about the entire population, especially if it is very large. Instead, we usually resort to examining a part of the population referred to as a *sample*. The sample is more manageable than the population with respect to the statistical operations to be performed on it. In the financial statements audit example described before, the auditor considered samples of size *n*.

In describing the population to analyze, the nature of the data should be identified: grades of students, gender of customers, or income of credit applicants. Data can be either quantitative (numerical) or qualitative (categorical). Quantitative data is usually divided in two groups, continuous and discrete. Continuous variables can take on any real value within its range of definition (heights cannot be negative, for example). Discrete variables are limited to a discrete number of attainable numerical values (when counting events, it would be meaningless to have any fractional values, for instance).

Any value or measure that describes some characteristic of the population is called a parameter of the population (such as the average income of U.S. citizens). If we wanted to estimate the value of a particular parameter, we would most likely obtain a sample of the population and use it to compute the estimate. For example, to estimate the average income of U.S. citizens, we would obtain a sample of the population of U.S. citizens and compute the average income for those citizens belonging to the sample. The measured characteristic of the sample that has been observed or obtained from the sample is known as a statistic. Whereas the measured characteristics of a statistical population are known as *population parameters*, the measured characteristics of a sample are known as *sample statistics*.

DATA COLLECTION

Data can be collected by direct observation or reported by individuals. Systematically collecting data to measure and analyze the variation of one or more processes forms the foundation of statistical process control [5]. The process under analysis may be time dependent, with several potential factors acting as the source of variation of the quality of the output over time. There is more on this in chapter 6.

Another form of direct observation is by means of an experiment. A statistical experiment is a planned activity in which the factors that have the potential of affecting the response variables under analysis are under the control of the researcher. According to Bernard, a statistical experiment has five distinct stages [1].

1. Formulate the hypothesis.

2. Assign members to the intervention group or to the control group at random.

3. Measure the response variables in one or both groups.

4. Introduce the intervention.

5. Measure the response variables again.

Testing a new quality improvement process can be seen as a simple example of a statistical experiment. The existence of the quality improvement process might be seen as the independent variable (the factor to be controlled), and the potential improvement on quality of the response variable. At least two groups are considered, the intervention group on which the improvement process (the intervention) is tested, and the control group on which the intervention is spared. Each group is tested before applying the improvement process on the intervention group. Then the intervention is applied. As a final step, the test is performed again to measure the effect of the intervention. In a statistical experiment, members are randomly assigned to each of the groups to ensure that any differences between the groups are due to chance and not to a systematic bias. On average, the intervention and control groups will be equal in terms of their associated attributes (such as gender, experience on the job, age). If we observe that the group that receives the intervention has better results, we can conclude that it is caused by the intervention, rather than by some extraneous cause. More details on random sampling are covered in the next section.

Sometimes it is not possible to gather data directly, which requires that data be collected from individuals. A survey is the process of gathering data by asking participants to provide data. There are several methods for collecting survey data: face-to-face interviews, self-administered questionnaires, and telephone interviews. Surveys are the most widely used data-gathering technique in social science, but despite their popularity, it is easy to conduct surveys that yield worthless or misleading results [6]. Recall that knowing how to collect data is a critical task of a systems analyst who is in the process of determining the requirements for a new system. Failure to use proper techniques to prepare surveys may contribute to poor requirement definitions.

RANDOM SAMPLING

Random sampling, also called probability sampling, is the type of sampling in which every item of the population of interest has a well-defined—often equal—chance of being chosen for inclusion in the sample. The primary goal is to get a representative sample of the population, such that it can be used to produce valid generalizations about the population under analysis. Random sampling ensures that the data samples are chosen in an unbiased manner and, therefore, are most likely to render samples that are truly representative of the population. In addition, by allowing the possibility of calculating the relationship between the sample and the population, known as the sampling error, random sampling provides the statistical basis for determining the confidence that can be associated with the inferences on the population obtained from the samples. There are four principle random sampling methods.

- Simple random sampling: Items are chosen at random from the entire population, generally using a list of random numbers to decide on the numbers to be selected. Random numbers can be obtained using a random-number table or by means of a random-number generator.

- Systematic sampling: Instead of using a list of random numbers, samples are selected from the population at regular intervals (such as every fifth financial statement of the population of audits).

- Stratified sampling: The population is divided into mutually exclusive groups, known as strata, based on one or more relevant population features. Then samples are drawn randomly from each stratum. The proportionate representation of each stratum within the sample is guaranteed by controlling the relative size of the strata.

- Cluster sampling: Used in the case of a dispersed population, for which it is excessively expensive to reach each sample element. The total population is divided into clusters, each of which should be a small-scale version of the total population. Random sampling is then used on the set of clusters to choose which clusters to include in the study.

The importance of obtaining a representative sample should be stressed. Many people fail in this critical data collection task because they use what is known as sampling by convenience. They happen to know addresses or phone numbers of a particular segment of the population or had a list of companies in the Midwest. These types of mistakes are common and contribute to DQ problems. Wonnacott and Wonnacott provide a good example of DQ issues in random sampling.[9]. In 1936, the editors of the *Literary Digest* tried to predict the U.S. presidential election, and for that purpose they used a sample of voters chosen from telephone books and club memberships, a sample which was heavily Republican oriented. Even worse, the list of respondents (approximately 25% of the original survey) tended to be proportionately even more Republican than the non-respondents. All in all, the sample was so biased and non-representative of the U.S. voting population that it resulted in a prediction of a Republican victory. Instead, Roosevelt ended up winning the election by a large margin.

DESCRIPTIVE STATISTICS

Descriptive statistics deal with organizing and summarizing collected data. In order to make sense out of a set of observations, we must arrange them in an understandable form. Grouped data usually loses much of the original detail, but in exchange, a clear overall picture can be obtained of the underlying relationships embedded in raw data. An almost intuitive approach organizes data in terms of categories or classes, and determines the amounts of individuals corresponding to each category, known as the class frequency. A data table, together with the corresponding frequencies for each class, is called a frequency distribution. The cumulative sum of all frequencies for all categories must be equal to the total number of observations. Consider, for example, the case of a random sample of salaries of IT consultants taken from an industry survey. Let X be the salaries in thousands of dollars.

For the 40 employees surveyed, X turns out to be:
X = 62, 54, 75, 66, 65, 55, 65, 89, 67, 52, 57, 70, 63, 78, 85, 92, 52, 55, 67, 69, 88, 82, 58, 90, 95, 79, 85, 82, 75, 70, 67, 56, 70, 67, 75, 69, 67, 75, 79, 90

A frequency table can be constructed, table 5.1, organizing the data into categories. If data is numerical, categories become class intervals, with the extreme values of each class interval referred to as class limits. For example, we can organize salary data into 5 class intervals: 50-59, 60-69, 70-79, 80-89, 90-99.

Table 5.1
Frequency Table for Salary Survey

Class Interval	Frequency	Cumulative Frequency	Relative Frequency	Cumulative Relative Frequency
50-59	8	8	0.20	0.20
60-69	12	20	0.30	0.50
70-79	10	30	0.25	0.75
80-89	6	36	0.15	0.90
90-99	4	40	0.10	1.00

If salaries are recorded to the nearest $1,000, the class interval 50-59 includes all values within those two limits. Note that a relative frequency column has been added to the table. The relative frequency distribution is obtained by dividing the frequency distribution by the total number of observations. Therefore the cumulative relative frequency is 1.

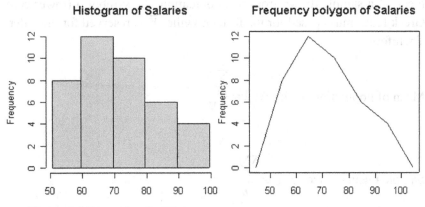

Figure 5.1 Example of a Histogram

A good way of graphically representing a frequency distribution is by way of a histogram, figure 5.1. A histogram is a bar chart of a frequency distribution, with bar widths equal to the class interval sizes and numbers of observations listed along the vertical axis. Another useful graphical representation is the frequency polygon, a line graph of the frequency distribution, where the midpoint of each class interval is displayed along the abscissa.

Shape, Location, and Spread

As we see in figure 5.1, a histogram presents a graphical display of the data in which three properties of the data are identifiable: the shape of the distribution of the data, the central tendency (location), and the spread (variability) of the data.

Measures of central tendency are measures of the location of the middle or the center of a distribution. The definition of middle or center is purposely left vague so that the term central tendency can refer to a wide variety of measures. We will describe three of them, arithmetic mean, median, and mode.

Generally, we wish the measure to be representative of all values in the group, and therefore we seek some kind of average. The most common measure of central tendency is the *arithmetic mean* (average) usually defined as $\sum_{i=1}^{M} X_i \big/ M$, where X_i are the M data values assumed by variable X. When it is necessary to distinguish the mean of a population from the mean of a sample drawn from this population, the symbol μ (lower case Greek letter mu) is used for the former, while $\bar{X}$ is reserved for the latter. Therefore,

Mean of population of size N: $\mu = \dfrac{\sum\limits_{i=1}^{N} X_i}{N}$;

Sample mean of size n: $\bar{X} = \dfrac{\sum\limits_{i=1}^{n} X_i}{n}$

If we denote by f_x the frequency in the data sample which variable X takes value x, then the sample mean can also be expressed as $\sum\limits_{x} f_x \cdot x / n$.

The *median* of a group of values arranged in order of magnitude is the value of the middle item, or the average of the two middle items, if the number of values is even. Geometrically, it is the value in the abscissa's axis that divides the histogram into two equal parts. For example, if we arrange in order the data set of salaries described in previous paragraphs, X would be (52, 52, 54, 55, 55, 56, 57, 58, 62, 63, 65, 65, 66, 67, 67, 67, 67, 67, 69, 69, 70, 70, 70, 75, 75, 75, 75, 78, 79, 79, 82, 82, 85, 85, 88, 89, 90, 90, 92, 95) and the median would be 69.5.

The *mode* is the value that occurs most frequently in the data set. It corresponds to the peak of the histogram if each value is taken as a class interval. Distributions for which there is only one mode are referred to as *unimodal*. In the previous example, the mode of the data set is 67, as it appears five times, more than any other value in the data set.

Both the mean and the median represent the general level of data values (location) but from different perspectives. Mathematically, the mean minimizes the sum of the squared deviations with respect to the individual members of the data set. The median, on the other hand, minimizes the sum of the absolute values of the differences with each member of the data set.

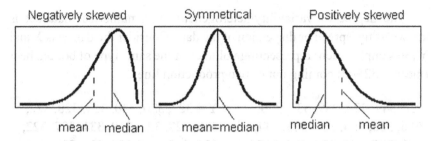

Figure 5.2 Shape of Distributions

Figure 5.2 shows the shape of three different cases of data distributions. When the distribution is symmetrical, the mean, median, and mode coincide. For a negatively skewed distribution (nonsymmetrical with a tail to the left), the mean is typically smaller than the median. Conversely, in the case of positively skewed distributions (nonsymmetrical with a tail to the right), the mean is typically greater than the median.

Although the arithmetic mean is by far the most popular measure of central tendency, the median is a more robust measure, since it is not affected by extreme values (outliers), which can drastically distort the mean, dragging it to one side. Also, for very skewed data sets, the median is likely to be a more sensible measure of center than the mean. This is typically the case of income data distributions, for which the median is generally quoted rather than the mean. This is because the median, being the midpoint, is better at reflecting the center than the mean. The latter can be badly inflated by the presence of just a couple of millionaires![6]

As mentioned before, the median is the center value of an ordered set of data that divides the set into two equal parts. This concept can be extended to consider those values that divide the set into four equal parts. These values are known as quartiles and are usually denoted as Q_1, Q_2, Q_3 and Q_4 (note that the median coincides with Q_2). Similarly, the values that divide the sorted data into 100 equal parts are known as percentiles. The 25th, 50[th,] and 75th percentiles correspond respectively to Q_1, Q_2, Q_3.

---

[6]   The following (true) story illustrate this point: Rik Smits graduated from Marist College in 1988 with a BS degree in Business. He signed a multi-million dollar contract with the NBA's Indiana Pacers. The dean of the School of Business told parents (jokingly) that the average salary of the graduates that year was around $180,000.

The degree of variability/heterogeneity of a numerical data set is known as the spread or dispersion of the data. Consider the data sets X and Y (30 samples each) representing volumes of the same type of bottled beer (mean = 325ml) coming out of two production lines.

X = 349, 324, 289, 339, 330, 306, 306, 354, 302, 303, 334, 343, 337, 349, 335, 282, 307, 351, 328, 298, 375, 294, 296, 325, 353, 368, 265, 336, 337, 395

Y = 322, 320, 330, 323, 320, 322, 330, 327, 327, 319, 331, 327, 322, 326, 330, 332, 326, 325, 317, 320, 329, 321, 322, 323, 323, 327, 337, 332, 325, 322

The histograms depicted in figure 5.3 show a much larger spread in data set X than in data set Y.

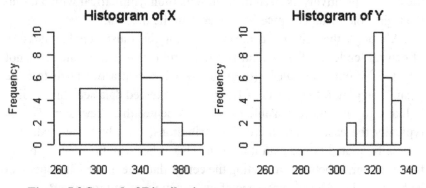

Figure 5.3 Spread of Distributions

Spread measures are based on calculations of distances between points in a distribution. The *range* is the distance between the highest and the lowest measurements in a distribution. It is calculated by subtracting the smallest value from the largest measurement. The *interquartile range* is the distance between the first quartile ($Q_1 \equiv 25^{th}$ percentile) and the third quartile ($Q_3 \equiv 75^{th}$ percentile).

The *standard deviation* of a set of data is a measure of the distance of the individual data elements with respect to their mean value. If the data set is tightly grouped, the standard deviation will be small; if the data is widely dispersed, the standard deviation will be quite large. The measure is calculated as the square root of the mean squared difference between each individual point and the mean value. The standard deviation of the entire population is denoted by σ (lower case Greek letter sigma) and has

the following expression: $\sigma = \sqrt{\sum_{i=1}^{N}(X_i - \mu)^2 \Big/ N}$. The squared differences between each point and the mean value are computed to avoid the canceling effect of positive and negative deviations when added. When computing the standard deviation of a sample of the population (the data will almost always be a sample) we use the sample mean $\bar{X}$. The standard deviation

of the sample of size n (s), is given by $s = \sqrt{\sum_{i=1}^{n}(X_i - \bar{X})^2 \Big/ (n-1)}$.

Note that sum of squared differences is divided by $(n-1)$ instead of n. Think of this as a corrective factor that helps more accurately represent true variability in the population. For large samples ($n>30$) the difference is almost imperceptible.

Let us apply the standard deviation formula to the X and Y samples of bottled beer presented in the previous example. We get $\bar{X} = 327$ and $s_X = 29.4$ for data set X, and $\bar{Y} = 325.2$ and $s_Y = 4.7$ for data set Y. The much smaller value of s_Y indicates that the spread is much smaller in Y.

The *variance* of a set of data (denoted σ^2 for a population and s^2 for a sample) is the square of the standard deviation. Unlike the variance, the standard deviation describes variability in the original units of measurement.

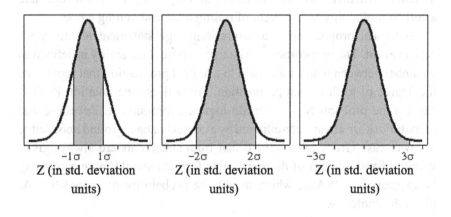

(a) shaded area $\cong$ 68%   (b) shaded area $\cong$ 95%   (c) shaded area $\cong$ 99%

Figure 5.4 Normal Distribution

Each point value in the data set can be represented in terms of its deviation with respect to the mean, measured in standard deviation units. This dimensionless score, Z, is independent of the units used, and is equal to (deviation/standard deviation). For example, the Z score for each X value in a population with mean μ and standard deviation σ is $Z = \frac{X - \mu}{\sigma}$. For normal distributions, figure 5.4, 68.27% of all cases will be found within one standard deviation unit of the mean, 95.45% of all cases are included within two standard deviations of the mean, and nearly all the data, 99.73%, is included between three standard deviations on either side of the mean. For moderately skewed distributions, these values may hold approximately.

PROBABILITY THEORY

The starting point for probability theory is the concept of a state of nature, which is a description of everything that happens in the universe. The set of all possible states of nature is called the outcome space, which we will represent as Ω (upper case Greek letter omega). The notion of probability is associated with the possible outcomes of a certain event. An event is a subset of the outcome space with the property that one can, in principle, determine whether the event occurs or not. For example, one can associate a certain probability to the event of rolling a die and getting a one.

A logical proposition is a natural language statement identifying a certain event. The proposition can be true or false. Probability is defined as a number between 0 and 1 attached to a logical proposition that represents the degree of truth in that proposition. We will use the notation P(A) to express the probability of a certain logical expression A. Recalling that probabilities are always conditioned by a context or background knowledge ξ (lower case Greek letter xi), so that truth statements are always given within a fixed domain of discourse, this formula should more rigorously be expressed as P(A|ξ), which means the probability of proposition A, given the context ξ.[7]

---

[7]   In order to keep the notation as understandable as possible, we will exclude the reference to the context I_0 in the subsequent expressions. Also, we will represent a conjunction of events $A_1 \cap .. \cap A_n$ by means of a comma-separated list $A_1, A_2, ..A_n$.

Basic axioms of probability:

1. $0 \le P(A) \le 1$
2. $P(A) = 1$ if and only if A is certain (A coincides with outcome space Ω)
3. Sum rule: Given two logical statements A and B,
   a. $P(A \cup B) = P(A) + P(B) - P(A \cap B)$
   b. $P(A \cup B) = P(A) + P(B)$ if and only if A and B are mutually exclusive
4. Total Probability: If outcome space Ω is partitioned in m events $\{E_1, E_1, ..., E_m\}$, then $P(E_1) + P(E_2) + ... + P(E_m) = 1$
5. Product rule:
   a. Given two logical sta tements A and B, $P(A,B) = P(A|B) \cdot P(B)$
   b. For n
      $A_1, A_2, ..A_n$,
      $P(A_1, A_2 ..., A_n) = P(A_1) \cdot P(A_2|A_1) \cdot ... \cdot P(A_n | A_{n-1} .. A_1)$

These properties are either part of the definition of probability measure or can be derived mathematically. We will take them as valid without further demonstration.

Conditional Probability and Independence

Note that the product rule gives way to the notion of conditional probability. The probability of occurrence of event A may be influenced by another event B, and this is expressed in terms of a conditional probability. It follows from the axioms of probability that $P(A|B) = P(A, B)/P(B)$. If event A is independent from event B, then $P(A|B) = P(A)$. This means that if A and B are independent from each other, $P(A, B) = P(A) \cdot P(B)$.

Example 1: If three critical system components are down 10% of the time, what is the availability of the system?

Answer: Assuming that the availability of each component C_i , (i=1...3) is independent from each other, $P(system) = P(C_1) \cdot P(C_2) \cdot P(C_3) = 0.9^3 = 73\%$.

Example 2: In a sample of 100 records from a medical insurance claim database which is being audited in search of errors, 40 records are erroneously coded in the diagnosis code (ICD9CM) field, and 30 have errors in the gender field. However, 20 records exhibit errors in both the

ICD9CM and gender fields, and so are included in both counts. What is the probability that a randomly chosen record had errors in the diagnosis code, in gender, or both?

Answer: To solve this exercise, let us assume that D represents those records with diagnosis errors, and G represents records with error in gender. In such case, $P(D) = 40/100$, $P(G) = 30/100$, and $P(D,G) = 20/100$. If we apply the sum rule (Axiom 3) we have $P(D \cup G) = P(D) + P(G) - P(D,G) = 0.5$. We have 50% chance of finding records with errors in the ICD9CM code, in gender, or both.

Example 3: (adapted from O'Donnell and Meredith [7]) At 10:00 P.M. you get an email from your office requesting you to attend an urgent meeting at the Chicago headquarters the next afternoon. To find a seat on a flight early next morning, you call all three airlines that fly into Chicago. They each have one flight which would get you to Chicago in time, but they are all fully booked. You ask each airline what the likelihood is of you getting a seat because of a cancellation or no-show. You are told that your chances of getting a seat are 25%, 30%, and 35% respectively for the three airlines. When you email headquarters, what likelihood do you report that you will be able to make the meeting?

Answer: How likely is it that you will catch a flight? Well, most people would say, not very likely. In this kind of situation, humans tend to underestimate. Actually, you have a good chance of catching a flight. Let us consider the following:

F_1: boarding flight in airline 1; $P(F_1) = 0.25$ (25%)
F_2: boarding flight in airline 2; $P(F_2) = 0.30$ (30%)
F_3: boarding flight in airline 3; $P(F_3) = 0.35$ (35%)

The probability of not boarding a flight on airline 1 (we'll call this event F_1) is:

$P(X_1) = 1 - P(F_1) = 0.8$ (axiom 4)

The same criteria apply to the rest of the airlines. Therefore, $P(X_1) = 0.75$; $P(X_2) = 0.70$; $P(X_3) = 0.65$;

Consider the probability of not getting a flight at all, rather than getting a flight, since the calculation is easier. This is the probability of the conjunction of events X_1, X_2 and X_3, also known as the joint probability of X_1, X_2 and X_3 and denoted by $P(X_1, X_2, X_3)$. According to the product rule, axiom 5, and given the fact that each flight booking event is independent from each other (we assume independence among airlines), the joint probability $P(X_1, X_2, X_3)$ is equal to the product of the probabilities of each event:

$$P(X1, X2, X3) = P(X1) \cdot P\ X2) \cdot P(X3)$$
$$= 0.75 * 0.70 * 0.65 = 0.341 \quad (34.1\%)$$

Once again applying the law of total probability, axiom 4, the probability of boarding a flight is 1-0.341 = 0.659 (65.9%)—actually pretty good. This shows that humans are not very intuitive when dealing with uncertainty conditions.

Bayes Theorem

The classical approach to probability estimates probability as the frequency of a repeated experiment. Since frequencies can be measured, this could be considered as an objective estimate of the underlying probability of the event under study. For example, if we were to estimate the probability of getting tails when we toss a coin, we could repeat the experiment a number of times and use the frequency of tails as a probability measure.

There are certain situations in which this frequentist approach is invalid, such as if repeated experiments are not possible. For example, if we tried to predict who is going to be the next president of the U.S., there would be no possible way of counting frequencies of occurrence of this event, because the event has a single occurrence. It would be far fetched to think of probability in terms of repetitions of an experiment when there are none. As Sivia states, "we are at the liberty to think about a problem in any way that facilitates a solution, or our understanding of it, but having to seek a frequentist interpretation for every data analysis problem seems rather perverse" [[8], pp 8].

The Bayesian approach provides an elegant alternative to deal with this kind of probability problem. Bayesian thinking postulates that the probability of a certain event represents the degree of belief that such event will happen. Moreover, such degree of belief is associated with a probability measure (prior probability) that can be updated by additional observed data. New observations are added in order to update the prior probability and therefore obtain a posterior probability distribution. But how should this belief update be performed?

A theorem published posthumously in 1763 by Reverend Thomas Bayes, Presbyterian minister and amateur mathematician, solved this problem. The paper, a mathematical piece on probability, provided a way of updating prior beliefs (based on a probability distribution) by means of observational data. *Bayes theorem* derives from a simple reordering of terms in the product rule of probability, axiom 5:

$$P(H|D) = \frac{P(D|H) \times P(H)}{P(D)}$$

with $P(D) = P(D|H) \times P(H) + P(D|{\sim}H) \times P({\sim}H)$ (${\sim}H$ means H negated)

The above expression is known as Bayes Theorem. Actually, its present form is a reformulation by Laplace, the famous French mathematician who took interest in Bayes rule and used it in different domains of application.

If we assume that H is a hypothesis under consideration and D the evidence, or set of observational data, the factors in Bayes formula can be characterized as:

- $P(H|D)$, the probability of a certain hypothesis based on a set of observational data given a certain context (posterior probability of hypothesis H).

- $P(D|H)$, the likelihood of the data given a certain hypothesis in a given context.

- $P(H)$, the intrinsic probability of hypothesis H, before considering the evidence D (prior probability).

- $P(D)$, the probability of the observations, independent of the hypothesis, that can be interpreted as a normalizing constant rendering $P(H|D)$ to a value interval of [0,1]. As shown before, $P(D)$ can be factorized by application of a combination of the product rule, axiom 5, and the law of total probability, axiom 4.

Bayes Theorem can also be rewritten as: the (prior) probability of a certain hypothesis is updated by the likelihood of the observed data. Or in other words, posterior is proportional to the prior times the likelihood of the data that was observed.

$$\text{Posterior} \propto \text{Prior} \times \text{Likelihood}$$

The result of the update process is the posterior probability distribution of the hypothesis that represents a revision of the prior distribution in the light of the evidence provided by the data.

Example 4: In a data staging process of a DW implementation, data is integrated from two sources: 80% of the data received from source A is of exceptional quality, while only 50% of the data received from source B is of exceptional quality. Given the amount of data coming from each source, it is estimated that 60% of the data comes from source A, and 40% from source B. If a sample is taken and inspected and found to be of exceptional quality, what is the probability that it came form source A?

Answer: Using A to identify data coming from source A, B to identify data coming from source B, and Q for data of exceptional quality, $P(A) = 60\%$; $P(B) = 40\%$; $P(Q|A) = 80\%$; $P(Q|B) = 50\%$ (note that $B \equiv \sim A$). Applying Bayes' theorem:

$$P(A|Q) = \frac{P(Q|A) \times P(A)}{P(Q|A) \times P(A) + P(Q|B) \times P(B)} = 70.6\%$$

The probability that data of exceptional quality came from source A is 70.6%.

Example 5: Korb & Nicholson present a nice discussion. of *People vs. Collins*, one of the first cases of misapplication of probabilistic reasoning in the legal system [4]. In 1964, in the town of San Pedro, California, two thieves snatched an old woman's handbag in the street. Witnesses to the crime testified that they had seen a blonde woman with a ponytail and a black man wearing a beard and mustache fleeing in a yellow car. Probabilities were estimated for the occurrence of each of these events in the LA area:

1. A man with a mustache   1/4
2. Who was black and bearded   1/10

3. A woman with a ponytail   1/10
4. Who was blonde   1/3
5. An interracial couple   1/1000
6. Driving a yellow car   1/10

Answer: Janet and Malcolm Collins were charged with the crime. Nobody could actually identify them, but they matched the guilty couple on all these characteristics: The couple drove a yellow car. Janet was blonde and had a ponytail, and Malcolm was a black man with a beard and a mustache at the time of the crime. The prosecution's case rested on the fact that it was hardly conceivable that the two suspects could match up with all of these pieces of evidence just by chance. The mathematician acting as expert on behalf of the prosecution testified that the product rule applied, and that the features described above were independent from each other, which meant that the joint probability was equal to the product of the probabilities of the individual pieces of evidence: 1/12,000,000. The prosecution went on to assert the chance the couple were innocent was 1/12,000,000.

An outrageous fact in this case is that the product rule does *not* apply! The individual pieces of evidence are not independent. If we know that the man has a mustache, does the probability of him having a beard remain unchanged? If we know that one of the occupants of the car is blonde and the other is black, what is the probability that the occupants are an interracial couple?

But there is a more fundamental error in the prosecution reasoning. If we label the probability of guilt given the evidence as $P(H|D)$ and the likelihood of the evidence assuming innocence as $P(D|{\sim}H)$, $P(H|D)$ is *not* equal to $1-P(D|{\sim}H)$. Instead we should apply Bayes theorem:

$$P(H|D) = \frac{P(D|H){\times}P(H)}{P(D|H){\times}P(H) + P(D|{\sim}H){\times}P({\sim}H)}$$

With a few reasonable assumptions, most of which even favor the prosecution and which detail goes beyond the scope of this example, Korb & Nicholson come to demonstrate that the probability of guilt given the evidence $P(H|D)$ becomes 0.002, which means a 99.8% chance of innocence and a very nasty error in judgment [4].

RANDOM VARIABLES

A random variable X is a function that maps the outcome space $\dot{U}$ to the set of the real numbers. It can be viewed as the name of an event with a probabilistic outcome. For example, consider the event of tossing two coins. The outcome space is:

Ω = ([tail, tail], [tail, head], [head, tail], [head, head]), where each element in the set represents each possible outcome. If X is a random variable representing the number of heads obtained after tossing both coins, X can take the following values:

X([tail, tail]) = 0; X([tail, head]) = X([head, tail]) = 1; X ([head, head]) = 2

Probability Distributions

A probability distribution for a random variable X determines the probability $p(x)$ that the random variable X will take the value x for every possible value x. It is denoted as $p(x) = P(X = x)$. If the random variable is discrete, from the axioms of probability it follows that $\sum_x P(X = x) = 1$.

When random variables are continuous, $P(X = x) = 0$ for every real value. We must therefore calculate probabilities within a certain interval of values of X. Probabilities are then expressed in terms of probability density functions where the density function f(x) is such that:

$$P(a < x < b) = \int_a^b f(x)dx$$
$$f(x) \geq 0, \forall\ x \in \Re$$

The total area under the density function curve is equal to 1, and the area between $\underline{a}$ and $\underline{b}$ is equal to $P(a < x < b)$.

For both continuous and discrete values, the expression $F(x) = P(X \leq x)$ is known as the distribution function. Its value for a certain value x is the probability that the random variable X will be less than or equal to x.

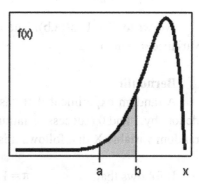

Figure 5.5 Continuous Distribution

Expected value and variance

The expected value of a random variable X that takes values $(x_1, x_2, ..., x_N)$ with probabilities $(p_1, p_2, ..., p_N)$ is defined as $E(X) = \sum_x x \cdot p(x)$.
Remembering that the arithmetic mean can be expressed in terms of the frequency of the data values as $\sum_x f_x \cdot x / N$, we can conclude that as the data size N grows larger, the relative frequencies (f_x / N) approach the probabilities p_x, which means that $E(X)$ represents the mean of the population (μ) from where the sample is drawn. A similar analysis can be done on continuous variables.

As mentioned before, the variance of a random variable is a measure of the spread around the mean. It is calculated as the expected value of the square of the difference between the observations and the mean of the observations and denoted by σ^2.

Examples of common probability distributions

Uniform
A uniform distribution describes variables that can assume any value in a particular range with equal probability. Given the endpoints a, b of the interval as parameters, the probability density function for a uniform random variable is defined as:

$$f(x) = \begin{cases} \dfrac{1}{b\text{-}a} & a < x < b \\ 0 & \text{otherwise} \end{cases}$$

We write $X \sim \text{Unif(a,b)}$. The expected value is $E(X) = \dfrac{a+b}{2}$ and the variance $\sigma^2 = (b\text{-}a)^2/12$.

Bernoulli
A random experiment that has only 2 possible outcomes, which we denote by 1 and 0 (success or failure), is called a Bernoulli experiment. A random variable X that follows this distribution is such that:

It follows that: $\pi = P(X = 1)$ and $1\text{-}\pi = P(X = 0)$

$$E(X) = \pi \ ; \ \sigma^2 = p(1\text{-}\pi)$$

Binomial

The number of successes in n identical repeated Bernoulli trials follow a Binomial distribution with probability of success π, denoted as $X \sim \text{Bin}(\pi, n)$. The probability distribution function is

$$P(X = x \mid \pi, n) = \frac{n!}{x! \cdot (n - x)!} \pi^x (1 - \pi)^{n-x}$$

. The expected value is $E(X) = n \cdot p$ and the variance $\sigma^2 = n \cdot \pi \cdot (1 - \pi)$.

Example 6: A company reports that 20% of its accounts receivable are overdue. If an auditor takes a random sample of 10 accounts, what is the probability that none of the chosen accounts will be overdue?

Answer: If X is the number of overdue accounts, we need to compute the probability that $X = 0$, with $\pi = 0.2$ and $n = 10$:

$$P(X = 0 \mid\mid \pi = 0.2, n = 10) = \frac{10!}{0! \cdot (10 - 0)!} 0.2^0 (1 - 0.2)^{(10-0)} = 0.107$$

There are 10.7% chances that none of the accounts will be overdue.

Poisson

Poisson is the limiting case of a binomial distribution, where the probability of success (π) is very small, and the sample size (n) is very large. The discrete probability distribution function is $P(X = x \mid \lambda) = \frac{\lambda^x \cdot e^{-\lambda}}{x!}$ as is denoted as $X \sim \text{Poisson}(\lambda)$. Both the expected value $E(X)$ and the variance σ^2 are equal to λ. The Poisson distribution is suitable as an approximation of the binomial distribution with parameters (n, π), when n is large and π or $(1-\pi)$ is small (a rule of thumb is $n > 30$ and $n \cdot \pi < 5$). The expected value is in this case $\lambda = n \cdot \pi$.

Normal

The normal (or Gaussian) distribution is one of the most important continuous distributions. It is unimodal, bell shaped, and symmetric about its mean. Given $E(X) = \mu$ and variance σ^2 as parameters, the probability density function for a normal random variable $X \sim N(\mu, \sigma^2)$ is defined by

$$f(x \mid \mu, \sigma^2) = \frac{1}{\sqrt{2\pi} \cdot \sigma^2} e^{-(x-\mu)/2\sigma^2}.$$

When the variable X is expressed in terms of Z scores $(Z = \frac{X - \mu}{\sigma})$, the density function takes the form $f(z) = \frac{1}{\sqrt{2\pi}} e^{-\frac{1}{2}z^2}$. Z is said to normally distributed with $\mu = 0$ and $\sigma^2 = 1$. The probability distribution of Z is known as the standard normal distribution.

Example 7: The time required for routine quality check process is normally distributed with mean $\mu = 10$ min and standard deviation $\sigma = 2$ min. What is the probability that a given quality check process would take more than 15 minutes to complete?

Answer: If X is the time required for each quality check, we need to calculate $P(X \le 15)$. Transforming X into a Z-score with $\mu = 10$, $\sigma = 2$ and $X = 15$, Z is therefore equal to $\frac{15 - 10}{2} = 2.5 \, min$.

This means that $P(X \le 15) = P(Z \le 2.5)$, the grayed area below the curve in figure 5.6. Looking up in a table of standard normal probabilities (Z-scores) for $Z = 2.5$, we find that the probability is equal to 99.38%. Therefore $P(X>15) = (100-99.38)$ % $= 0.62\%$.

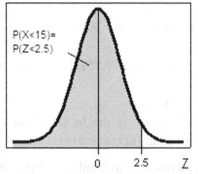

Figure 5.6 Grayed Area is $P(Z \le 2.5)$

Note: Standard normal probability tables usually report the area under the curve between 0 and the value Z that serves as input value to the table. In our example, this means that we look up $Z = 2.5$ and we obtain 0.4938. As the area under the other half of the bell curve is equal to 0.5 (total area under the curve is equal to 1), $0.5 + 0.4938 = 0.9938$ (99.38%).

The normal distribution can be used as a good approximation to the binomial distribution for large samples. As a rule of thumb, given a binomial distribution $Bin(n, \pi)$, when $(n \cdot \pi)$ and $n \cdot (1-\pi)$ both exceed 5, the normal distribution with mean $\mu = n\pi$ and $\sigma^2 = n \cdot \pi \cdot (1 - \pi)$ is a good estimate.

Example 8: A retail store has discovered that 12% of its receipts contain errors. Management wants to know the probability of less than 100 errors out of the next 1000 sales.

Answer: Considering that $X = 100$ is the number of errors out of $n = 1000$ sales, and $\pi = 0.12$ is the proportion of errors in the population, $\mu = 1000 \cdot 0.12 = 120$ and $\sigma^2 = 1000 \cdot 0.12 \cdot 0.88 = 105.6$. We calculate the Z-score as $\dfrac{100 - 120}{\sqrt{105.6}} = -1.946$ errors. Therefore $P(X<100) = P(Z<-1.946)$ = $P(Z>1.946)$ = $1-P(Z<1.946)$. Looking up 1.946 in the standard normal probability table, $P(Z<1.946) = 0.9741$. The probability of having less than 100 errors is $1-0.9741 = 2.59\%$.

INFERENTIAL STATISTICS

This term encompasses the set of methods used to make a generalization, estimate, prediction, or decision on a population based on collected samples. Statistical inference is the relationship between a population and samples drawn from the population. We sample the population in a manner to ensure that the sample correctly represents the population. We then take measurements on our sample and infer (or generalize) back to the population. We try to make inferences or judgments about a larger population based on the data collected from a small sample drawn from the population, together with indications of the accuracy of such inferences based on probability theory.

Sampling Theory and Point Estimates

In general, a point estimate is a single number determined from a sample and used to estimate the population value. When the sample is perfectly representative of the population, the sample mean equals the population mean (μ), and the standard deviation of the sample equals the standard deviation of the population (σ). In reality, however, it is unlikely that the mean of a sample taken from a population will be identical to μ and that the standard deviation of the sample will be σ. The difference between the sample statistic and the population parameter is known as the *bias* or *sampling error*.

Consider all possible samples of size n that can be drawn from a population. For each sample, we can compute a statistic (such as the mean or the standard deviation) that will vary from sample to sample. The sampling distribution of a sample statistic is the probability distribution consisting of all possible values of the sample statistic paired with the probability values associated with each sample statistic value. This concept applies to different types of sample statistics, including means, standard deviations, variances, proportions, and medians.

The *central limit theorem* claims that the sampling distribution of the sample mean $\bar{X}$ exhibits three properties.

Fact 1: The expected value of the sample mean is equal to the population mean μ.

Fact 2: The standard deviation of the sample mean is always less than the standard deviation of the population from which the samples were taken. This deviation of the sample mean $\bar{X}$ from μ represents the sampling error, and so it is commonly known as the *standard error* (SE). For samples of size n drawn from a population with standard deviation σ, $SE = \sigma/\sqrt{n}$.

Fact 3: In random samples of size n, and with increasing values of n, the sampling distribution of $\bar{X}$ tends to be normally distributed with mean equal to π and standard deviation equal to $SE = \sigma/\sqrt{n}$.

Example 9: Suppose that a large population of measurements has mean value $\mu = 80$ and standard deviation $\sigma = 10$. The sample distribution of the sample means for a sample size $n = 40$ is given by the statistics E($\bar{X}$) $= \mu = 80$, and SE $= 10/\sqrt{40} = 1.58$. Note that SE (the standard deviation of the sample mean) is substantially smaller than σ.

Sampling distribution of proportions

Answer: Given an infinite population, the proportion parameter π is the probability of occurrence (or success) of a given event. As we see, this concept is strictly related to the binomial distribution where on n trials, the probability of success is given by π.[8] Consider all possible samples of size n, and for each sample determine the proportion p of successes. We thus obtain a sampling distribution of proportions p with mean equal to π and standard deviation (SE) equal to $\sqrt{\pi \cdot (1-\pi)/n}$.

Example 10: If the proportion of defects of a given population is $\pi = 0.1$, in random samples of size $n = 50$, the sample proportion fluctuates around 0.1 with a standard error $SE = \sqrt{0.1 \cdot (1-0.1)/50} = 0.04$.

---

[8]   Note that a proportion can be seen as a special case of the mean of a population that can only take values 0 or 1.

Sampling distribution of differences

Answer: Consider two populations with parameters θ_1 and θ_2 respectively (θ is lower case Greek letter theta). If we extract samples of size n_1 from the first population and samples of size n_2 from the second population, we can calculate a sample statistic w_1 for population 1 and a sample statistic w_2 for population 2. The sampling distribution of w_1 will have a mean value that fluctuates around θ_1 with standard error SE_1. Similarly, w_2 will fluctuate around θ_2, with standard error SE_2. From all possible combinations of the samples coming from populations 1 and 2, the sampling distribution of ($w_1 - w_2$) can be obtained. The expected value of the mean of this distribution is equal to ($\theta_1 - \theta_2$) and the standard error is $SE_{w_1-w_2} = \sqrt{SE^2_{w_1} + SE^2_{w_2}}$. Table 5.2 below shows the sampling distribution of differences of proportions and means.

Table 5.2

Sampling Distribution of Differences of Proportions and Means

Population Parameter	Point Estimate	Standard Error
Mean (μ)	$\bar{X}$	$\sigma/\sqrt{n}$
Proportion (π)	p	$\sqrt{\pi \cdot (1-\pi)/n}$
Difference between means of two populations ($\mu_1 - \mu_2$)	$\bar{X}_1 - \bar{X}_2$	$\sqrt{\dfrac{\sigma_1^2}{n_1} + \dfrac{\sigma_2^2}{n_2}}$
Difference between proportions of two populations ($\pi_1 - \pi_2$)	$p_1 - p_2$	$\sqrt{\dfrac{\pi_1 \cdot (1-\pi_1)}{n_1} + \dfrac{\pi_2 \cdot (1-\pi_2)}{n_2}}$

Note: We have assumed in this section that as the size of the sample is large enough ($n>30$), the sampling distributions are approximately normal. We have also made the assumption that if the population parameters are not known, they can be estimated closely using the corresponding sampling statistics ($\mu \cong \bar{X}; \pi \cong p; \sigma \cong s$). Later on we will deal with those cases in which some (or all) of the population parameters are not known and/or the sample size is small.

Unbiased, Efficient, and Consistent Estimators

For any population parameter θ, an estimator $\underline{w}$ is said to be *unbiased* if, on average, w is equal to θ. This is the same as saying that $E(w)-\theta = 0$ (bias is equal to 0). In figure 5.7(a), w_1 is an unbiased estimator of θ; instead, w_2 is a biased estimator $-E(w_2)-\theta \neq 0$. For example, we have mentioned that the expected value of the sample mean $\bar{X}$ is equal to the population mean μ. This implies that $\bar{X}$ is an unbiased estimator of μ.

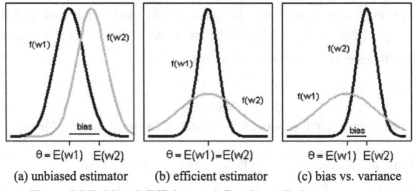

| (a) unbiased estimator | (b) efficient estimator | (c) bias vs. variance |

Figure 5.7 Unbiased, Efficient and Consistent Estimators

As well as having an estimator with a small bias, we want the statistic to have a distribution with a small spread, that is, a small variance. If the sample distributions of two statistics have the same expected value, the one with the smaller variance is known as an *efficient estimator*. In figure 5.7(b), both estimators have the same mean θ, but w_1 has a smaller variance, for which w_1 is an efficient estimator, and w_2 is called an inefficient estimator of θ.

The question arises when comparing estimators of different biases and variances, how can we define the best overall estimator that takes into account the smallest combination of bias and variance? Statistical theory shows that we should choose the estimator that minimizes the mean squared error (MSE), the expected value of the squared bias. It can be proved that the MSE is indeed a combination of bias and variance:

MSE = (bias of estimator)² + (variance of estimator)

A *consistent estimator* is that for which both bias and variance tend to zero for large sample sizes. The sample mean $\bar{X}$ is a good example of a consistent estimator: $E(\bar{X}) = \mu$ (i.e. bias = 0), and the SE $= \sigma/\sqrt{n}$ gets smaller and smaller as n increases.

Confidence Interval Estimates

The interval estimate is an estimate of a population parameter given by two numbers

   (lower and upper bound) between which a population parameter probably lies. The confidence interval for the population parameter is the interval that has a high probability of containing the population parameter. For example, a 95% confidence interval implies that about 95% of similarly constructed intervals will contain the parameter being estimated. The general format for the confidence interval is:

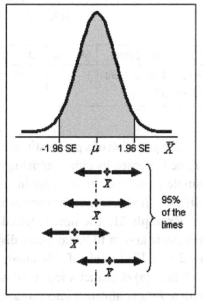

Figure 5.8 Confidence Interval

Parameter = Point estimate $\pm$
   (interval coefficient) $\times$ SE

The interval coefficient is the number of standard errors on either side of the population parameter necessary to include a percentage of the point estimate equal to the confidence level.

For example, a 95% confidence interval for the mean of a sample of size n ($n \geq 30$) implies that 95% of the times the sample mean $\bar{X}$ will lie within 1.96 standard errors of the hypothesized population mean μ, figure 5.8. In other words:

$P(\bar{X} - 1.96 \cdot SE \leq \mu \leq \bar{X} + 1.96 \cdot SE) = 95\%$

When the sample size is large ($n \geq 30$) and the population standard deviation is known, the sampling distribution of the statistic is approximately normal, and the interval coefficient is a Z-score. For example, the confidence interval for the mean $\bar{X}$ may be written as $\mu = \bar{X} \pm Z \cdot SE$, and we can expect to find $\bar{X}$ lying in the interval $(\mu \pm SE)$ 68.27% of the times, in the interval $(\mu \pm 2 \cdot SE)$ 95.45% of the times, and in the interval $(\mu \pm 3 \cdot SE)$ 99.73% of the times. Table 5.3 shows some characteristic Z-scores and their corresponding confidence levels.

Table 5.3
Confidence Levels and Z-scores

Confidence Level	68.27%	90.00%	95.00%	95.45%	99.00%	99.73%
Interval coefficient (Z-score)	1	1.645	1.96	2	2.58	3

The precision of a point estimate, that is, the confidence interval width, can be increased by either reducing the confidence level or increasing the sample size. Since an increase in sample size will reduce standard error (SE), it will also reduce the confidence interval width.

Example 11: The time required to complete a routine quality check process is known to be normally distributed with a standard deviation of $\sigma = 2$ min. If a sample of 100 quality check records yields a mean of $\bar{X} = 10.5$ min, (a) construct a 95% confidence interval, (b) show the difference with a 90% confidence interval, and (c) what happens if the sample size is $n = 50$?

Answer: (a) $\mu = \bar{X} \pm Z \sigma / \sqrt{n}$. Replacing the values in the formula, and acknowledging that for a confidence level 95%, $Z = 1.96$ (table 5.3), we obtain $\mu = 10.5 \pm 1.96 \cdot 2 / \sqrt{100}$. The 95% confidence interval for $\bar{X}$ is (10.108, 10.892). (b) For a 90% confidence interval, $\mu = \bar{X} \pm 1.645 \cdot 2 / \sqrt{100}$. Therefore $\bar{X}$ lies between 10.171 and 10.829. The 90% confidence interval width is smaller than the one corresponding to the 95% confidence interval (the precision of the estimate is higher). (c) With a smaller sample size ($n = 50$), the precision of the point estimate is reduced for a given confidence level: with probability 95%, the confidence interval for $\bar{X}$ is $\mu = 10.5 \pm 1.96 \cdot 2 / \sqrt{50} = (9.945, 11.054)$.

Small Sampling and the Student's *t* Distribution

In previous sections we assumed that the standard deviation of the population (σ) was known, or that it can be replaced by the standard deviation of the sample $\left(s = \sqrt{\sum_{i=1}^{n}(X_i - \bar{X})^2 \big/ (n-1)} \right)$. If the sample size n were large enough, replacing s by s would still render an approximately normal sampling distribution of the sample statistic.

But with a small sample size ($n<30$), the additional variability introduced by s in the conversion formula of the Z-score $\left((\bar{X}-\mu)/s\right)$ affects the shape of the sampling distribution, which is no longer normal. To maintain the same level of confidence (95%, for example) the interval width must be increased. This is done by replacing the Z-score taken from the standard normal with a *t*-score taken from a Student's *t* distribution.

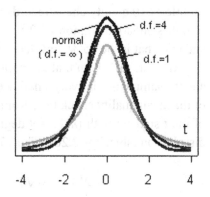

Figure 5.9 Student's *t* distribution

The *t* statistic, similar to the Z-score is formulated as $t = \dfrac{(\bar{X} - \mu)}{s/\sqrt{n}}$, where μ is the population mean, $\bar{X}$ is the sample mean, and s is the sample standard deviation. The Student's *t* distribution is the sampling distribution of the *t* statistic, the best we can do when σ is unknown and has to be replaced by s. The Student's *t* distribution is a family of distributions indexed by the number of *degrees of freedom*.

The number of degrees of freedom (d.f.) of a statistic is the sample size n minus the number of population parameters (k) which must be estimated from the sample to compute the statistic. The expression of the number of degrees of freedom is therefore d.f. = $(n-k)$. In the case of the *t* statistic, with the sample of n observations we can calculate both $\bar{X}$ and σ, but we still need to estimate μ. Therefore $k = 1$, and d.f. = $n - 1$.

As the sample size increases, the degrees of freedom get larger, and the *t* distribution gets closer to the standard normal distribution. A normal distribution is a *t* distribution with infinite degrees of freedom. We can see in figure 9 that the t distribution is very similar to the standard normal, except that it has slightly heavier tails.

We can now express the confidence interval for estimating the population mean in terms of the t statistic as $\mu = \bar{X} \pm t_{d.f.} \cdot s/\sqrt{n}$.

Note that ($s/\sqrt{n}$) is the estimated standard error.

Example 12: Consider a variation on the previous exercise in which the time required to complete a routine quality check process is assumed to be normally distributed, but the standard deviation is unknown. If a sample of 10 quality check records yields a mean of $\bar{X} = 10.5$ min, and a sample standard deviation $s = 2.5$, (a) construct a 95% confidence interval, and (b) what is the 95% confidence interval with a sample size of $n = 50$?

Answer: (a) Given that the population standard deviation is unknown and the sample is relatively small, we estimate the 95% confidence interval of the mean quality check time from which this sample was taken in terms of the t statistic with $(n-1) = 9$ degrees of freedom. From the Student's t distribution table, $t_9 = 2.262$. The 95% confidence interval is:

$$\bar{X} \pm t_{d.f.} \cdot s/\sqrt{n}$$
$$10.5 \pm 2.262 \cdot 2.5/\sqrt{10} = (8.71, 12.29)$$

(b) With a larger sample ($n = 50$) we can probably assume that the sampling distribution is normally distributed. We can check this by calculating the 95% confidence interval using both Z and t scores, and comparing them. The 95% confidence interval, in terms of t, with d.f. = 50-1 = 49, is:

$$\bar{X} \pm t_{d.f.} \cdot s/\sqrt{n}$$
$$10.5 \pm 2.00 \cdot 2.5/\sqrt{50} = (9.79, 11.21)$$

Assuming a normal distribution replacing σ with s, the 95% confidence interval is:

$$\bar{X} \pm Z \cdot s/\sqrt{n}$$
$$10.5 \pm 1.96 \cdot 2.5/\sqrt{50} = (9.81, 11.19)$$

As we can see, the confidence intervals calculated with both approaches are quite similar.

HYPOTHESIS TESTING

A hypothesis is a claim about some aspect of a situation. In some cases, we are interested in testing that some specific hypothesis is true, rather than determining the confidence interval of a population parameter. This essential aspect of inferential statistics is known as hypothesis testing: hypothesizing about the parameters of the population under consideration and setting up a test procedure in which a sample statistic is tested to verify the claim. We may be interested in testing whether an expected outcome is likely to be true, or whether there is any difference between two procedures if they belong to different populations, or if the difference is due to variations in the samples drawn from the same population.

In order to perform hypothesis testing, the competing hypotheses need to be identified. There are usually two alternatives, the null hypothesis (H_0) and the alternative hypothesis (H_a). The null hypothesis is the hypothesis or claim being tested; the alternative to this claim is the alternative hypothesis. Any value not contained in the null hypothesis is contained in the alternative hypothesis.

The goal of a hypothesis test is to use a data sample to decide whether to accept or reject the null hypothesis about a population parameter. It is achieved by comparing the sample statistic with a predetermined decision rule. That is, before collecting sample data, a critical value of the statistic (w_c) is determined. The sample result (w) is then compared to the critical value w_c, and the corresponding decision is made. The region containing the values for which we reject the hypothesis is called the rejection region or critical region. The region containing the values for which we do not reject the hypothesis is called the acceptance region.

Let θ be an unknown population parameter. If the critical value is w_c, we may want to test the null hypothesis H_0: $\theta = \theta_0$. There are three alternatives to consider: (a) $\theta > \theta_0$; (b) $\theta < \theta_0$; (c) $\theta \neq \theta_0$, figure 5.10. Alternatives (a) and (b) give way to a *one-tailed test* (testing for a possible deviation in only one direction). In case (a), the rejection region goes from the critical value w_c to ∞; in case (b), H_0 is rejected for values between $-\infty$ and w_c. Alternative (c) implies a *two-tailed test*, that is, testing for a possible deviation in either direction). Two critical values (w_{c_1} and w_{c_2}) may be considered; any value located between $-\infty$ and w_{c_1}, or between w_{c_2} and ∞, entails that H_0 is rejected.

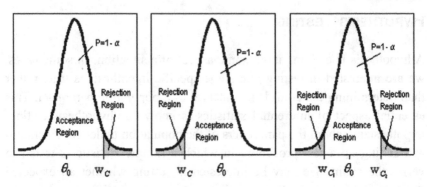

Figure 5.10 One-Tailed and Two-Tailed Tests

There are four possible outcomes of a hypothesis testing procedure:
1. The null hypothesis H_0 is true, and it is accepted.
2. The null hypothesis H_0 is true, but it is rejected.
3. The null hypothesis H_0 is false, but it is accepted.
4. The null hypothesis H_0 is false, and it is rejected.

The outcomes of the decision are shown in table 5.4. If number 2 or 3 occur, then to accept or reject the null hypothesis is wrong—an error has been made. Type I error (α) is the error of rejecting a true null hypothesis. Type II error (β) is the error of accepting a false null hypothesis. The probability of correctly rejecting a false null hypothesis is known as the *power of the test*.

Table 5.4
Decision Making Scenarios

	Accept H_0	Reject H_0
H_0 true	No error (probability = $1-\alpha$)	Type I error (probability = α)
H_0 false	Type II error (probability = β)	No error: power of the test (probability = $1-\beta$)

Once the critical value of the statistic (w_c) is determined, the probability of making a Type I error can be computed from a probability distribution (a normal distribution). It is the area under the curve beyond the critical value of the probability density function that corresponds to the rejection region. The area under the curve denotes the probability of rejecting a true null hypothesis. The chance of committing a Type I error is typically reduced if the critical value, w_c, is moved farther from the mean, consequently reducing the rejection region.

An alternative way of approaching the problem is to set the probability of Type I error (α), and then compute the corresponding critical value w_c. The value α is known as the significance level of the test; it is the maximum probability with which we would be willing to risk a Type I error. A typical value for α is 5%. Table 5.5 lists the typical steps in a hypothesis testing procedure:

Table 5.5
Steps in Hypothesis Testing

1. Define the null hypothesis (H_0) and the alternative hypothesis (H_a)
2. Define the statistic to be used to test H_0
3. Specify the significance level α
4. Derive the critical value of the statistic w_c for the given α
5. Determine the actual value of the test statistic
6. Compare the value of the test statistic with the critical value and make a decision

Example 13: Consider the situation adapted from Kazmier, in which an auditor wishes to test the claim that the accounts receivable in a given firm have a mean value of $300 [3]. We assume, in this case, that the standard deviation of the accounts receivable population is known to be σ = $40. For this purpose, the auditor sets the significance level at α = 5%, takes a sample of size n = 36, and computes the sample mean $\bar{X}$ = $290. The auditor will reject the hypothesized value of $300 if it is contradicted by $\bar{X}$.

Answer:

1. Following the roadmap in table 5.5, we start by defining the null and the alternative hypotheses: The null hypothesis H_0 is μ = 300 and the alternative hypothesis H_1 is $\mu \neq 300$ (as we see, the " $\neq$ " comparison suggests a two-tailed test).

2. The test statistic is $\bar{X}$ based on a sample of size $n = 36$ and known $\sigma = 40$. Having a rather large sample size and known σ, we can assume normality for the sampling distribution of $\bar{X}$, denoting that a Z-score can be used to formulate the comparison.

3. The significance level is specified at $\alpha = 5\%$.

4. The Z-score for a two-tailed normal hypothesis test with $\alpha = 5\%$ (the critical Z-score) is $Z_C = 1.96$. (Note: since is double-tailed, the Z-score corresponds to a confidence interval level of 95%.) The critical values $\bar{X}_{C_1}$ and is $\bar{X}_{C_2}$ are calculated as:

$$\bar{X}_C = \mu \pm Z_C \, \sigma \, / \sqrt{n} = 300 \pm 1.96 \cdot 40 / \sqrt{36}$$
$$= 300 \pm 13.07 \Rightarrow (\bar{X}_{C_1} = 286.93, \bar{X}_{C_2} = 313.07)$$

5. The actual value of the test statistic is computed. In this case $\bar{X} = \$290$.

6. The test statistic $\bar{X} = \$290$ is compared with the critical values. In order to accept the null hypothesis H_0: $\mu = 300$, $\bar{X}$ must be greater than $\bar{X}_{C_1} = 286.93$ and less than $\bar{X}_{C_2} = 313.07$. As in this case, $\bar{X}_{C_1} < \bar{X} < \bar{X}_{C_2}$, the auditor accepts the null hypothesis that $\mu = 300$.

Example 14: A one-sided test would have been appropriate if the auditor were verifying whether the mean value of the accounts receivable is less than \$300. In this case, the alternative hypothesis H_a would be $\mu < 300$ (the null hypothesis, H_0, remains the same). The critical value $\bar{X}_C$ would be:

$$\bar{X}_C = \mu \pm Z_C \, \sigma \, / \sqrt{n} = 300 - 1.645 \cdot 40 / \sqrt{36}$$
$$= 300 - 10.97 = 289.03$$

Answer: Remembering that $\bar{X} = 290$, we verify that $\bar{X}_C < \bar{X}$, and consequently the null hypothesis is accepted. Note that Z_C takes the value 1.645 in this case, because the given proportion of the area (5% probability) corresponding to the significance level α is in one tail of the distribution.

Example 15: If σ is not known (is estimated through s), and the sample size is small, the test is performed replacing the Z-score with a t score. Suppose that in our previous example σ is unknown, and is replaced with $s = 38$. Also assume that the auditor obtains a sample of size $n = 9$ and, as before, wants to verify if the mean value of the accounts receivable is less than $300.

Answer: The null hypothesis H_0 is $\mu = 300$, and the alternative hypothesis H_a is $\mu < 300$. The critical value is calculated using a t statistic with d.f. $= n-1=8$, and $t_{8(C)}$ is obtained from the Student's t table for $\alpha = 5\%$ (one tail). Its value is $t_{8(C)} = 1.860$. The critical value $\bar{X}_C$ is therefore calculated as:

$$\bar{X}_C = \mu \pm t_{8(C)} \cdot s/\sqrt{n} = 300 - 1.860 \cdot 38/\sqrt{9}$$
$$= 300\text{-}23.56 = 276.44$$

$\bar{X}_C < \bar{X}$, and therefore we accept the null hypothesis: the mean value of the accounts receivable is equal to $300.

Example 16: A firm has shifted to a new software virus protection platform in order to reduce the number of incidents. The senior security officer wishes to test the hypothesis that the fraction of infected personal computers is currently 3% ($\pi = 0.03$). The significance level is set at 5%. In a random sample of 50 personal computers, 4 are found to be infected with virus.

Answer:
  H_0: $\pi = 0.03$; H_a: $\pi > 0.03$ (one-tailed test)
  $p = 4/50 = 0.08$ (the sample proportion)
  $\alpha = 0.05$ (significance level of 5%)
  $n = 50$ (since the sample size is large, we can assume normality)

The Z-score for a one-tailed test, 5% test is $Z_C = 1.645$.

Since we are testing proportions in this case, the expression for the critical value becomes:

$$p_C = \pi + Z_C \cdot SE_p = \pi + Z_C \cdot \sqrt{\pi \cdot (1-\pi)/n}$$
$$= 0.03 + 1.645 \cdot \sqrt{0.03 \cdot (1-0.03)/50} = 0.07$$

With $p = 0.08$, we verify that $p_C < p$, and on that account the null hypothesis is rejected. We accept, at a 5% significance level, that the proportion of infected computers is greater than 3%.

If the rejection region is small, there is less chance that the sample statistic will fall there, and the chance of rejecting a true H_0 is small. This logic provides the rationale for setting a very low value for the significance level α. However, this approach completely overlooks β, the possibility of accepting a false H_0 (a Type II error). If the acceptance region is large, the probability of making a Type II error is also large. It can be seen in figure 5.11 that decreasing the value of α (displacing w_c to the right, farther away from θ_0) will have the effect of increasing the value of β, and obviously, we want the power of the test to be as large as possible. It is therefore evident that setting the critical value is a tradeoff between the Type I and Type II errors (see figure 5.11). In practice, one error is usually more critical than the other one, so some kind of settlement should be reached to favor the most crucial error. The only way to reduce both errors simultaneously is to increase the size of the sample, which may not be always possible.

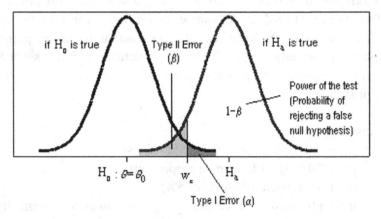

Figure 5.11 Type I and Type II Errors

Tests Involving Two Samples

We may sometimes be interested in comparing the statistics of two samples to make inferences about the populations from which the samples are drawn. For example, let us suppose that we want to compare a feature in two target groups to determine if both groups were drawn from the same population. Is the first target group different from the second target group when comparing such a feature? The conclusion should be that either there is a difference or there isn't. The null hypothesis would state that there is no difference, while the alternative hypotheses would claim that there is indeed a difference between both target groups.

To test the difference in feature between two samples, we use the difference of the sample statistics. We typically test for differences between proportions and means, table 5.2. The testing procedure looks for a zero value, with the assertion of the null hypotheses being the difference between the statistics of the two samples equals zero.

Example 17: Two routine quality check procedures are tested to identify any differences in the time they take to complete. A sample of 50 quality check records is taken from procedure 1, yielding a mean time of completion ($\bar{X}_1$) of 5 min, and a sample standard deviation $s_1 = 1$ min. For procedure 2, a sample of 40 quality check records is taken, yielding a mean time of completion ($\bar{X}_2$) of 3 min, and a sample standard deviation $s_2 = 1$ min. A significant level of 5% is considered for the test.

Answer: The test statistic is the difference of the means, $\delta = \bar{X}_1 - \bar{X}_2$. We define the null hypothesis $H_o{:}\delta = 0$, and the alternative hypothesis H_a: $\delta \neq 0$ (two-tailed test).

With large sample sizes we can assume normality, replacing σ_1 with s_1, and σ_2 with s_2. The standard error of the difference of means (SE_δ) is calculated as:

$$SE_\delta = \sqrt{\frac{s_1^2}{n_1} + \frac{s_2^2}{n_2}} = \sqrt{\frac{1}{50} + \frac{1}{40}} = 0.105$$

The Z-score for a two-tailed normal hypothesis test with $\alpha = 5\%$ is $Z_C = 1.96$. The critical values d_{C_1} and is d_{C_2} are calculated as:

$$\delta_C = 0 \pm Z_C \cdot SE_\delta = 0.105 = 0 \pm 1.96 \cdot \sqrt{\frac{1}{50} + \frac{1}{40}}$$
$$= 0 \pm 0.206 \Rightarrow (\delta_{C_1} = -0.206, \delta_{C_2} = 0.206)$$

The actual value of the test statistic ($\delta = \bar{X}_1 - \bar{X}_2 = 2$) is compared with the critical values. In order to accept the null hypothesis H_0: $\delta = 0$, δ must be greater than $\delta_{C_1} = -0.206$ and less than $\delta_{C_2} = 0.206$. As it turns out, δ is not within the range. Hence, we reject the null hypothesis, accepting that there is a significant difference in the mean time of the two procedures. Note that the lower bound δ_{C_1} is negative, and consequently makes no sense in terms of a measure of time.

The Chi-Square Distribution

The χ^2 statistic is defined as the ratio $(n-1) \cdot s^2 / \sigma^2$, where n is the sample size, s^2 is the sample variance, and σ^2 is the variance of the population from where the sample was drawn. Its sampling distribution (χ^2 distribution) is associated with the sampling distribution of the sample variance (s^2), and the sample standard deviation (s), neither of which is normally distributed. (Note: χ is the lower case Greek letter chi; χ^2 stands for chi-squared.)

The χ^2 distribution is a family of nonnegative and positively skewed probability distributions indexed by the number of degrees of freedom, figure 5.12. In the case of the χ^2 statistic, we use the sample of n observations to calculate s^2, but we still need to estimate σ^2 from the sample. The number of degrees of freedom is therefore n-1.

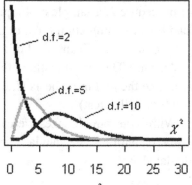

Figure 5.12 χ^2 Distribution

As in the case of the normal and the Student's t sampling distributions for means and proportions, a χ^2 distribution table can be used to construct ($1-\sigma$)% confidence intervals for the standard deviation (σ) or the variance (σ^2). In this way, σ (or σ^2) can be estimated in terms of s (or s^2) within specified confidence limits. χ^2 distributions are skewed, which means that two χ^2 values are required to determine the confidence limits (the $\pm$ interval rule used for Z-scores and t statistics does not apply).

For example, to construct the $(1-\alpha)$% confidence interval for the

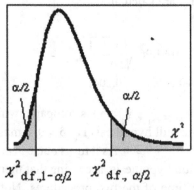

Figure 5.13 χ^2 Confidence Intervals

variance σ^2, we use the formula of the χ^2 statistic to express the variance in terms of χ^2, n and σ^2:

$$\sigma^2 = (n-1) \cdot s^2 / \chi^2$$

For a given confidence level (1-α) we obtain the two critical χ^2 values from the χ^2 distribution table, identified respectively as $\chi^2_{d.f.,1-\alpha/2}$ and $\chi^2_{d.f.,\alpha/2}$, figure 5.13.

With (1-α) = 95% and a sample size of n = 10, $\chi^2_{9,\,0.975}$ = 2.700 and $\chi^2_{9,\,0.025}$ = 19.023. The confidence interval for s ^{2} is given by:

$$\frac{(n-1) \cdot s^2}{\chi^2_{d.f.,\alpha/2}} \leq \sigma^2 \leq \frac{(n-1) \cdot s^2}{\chi^2_{d.f.,1-\alpha/2}}$$

In consequence, a sample of 10 independent observations yields a 95% confidence interval of σ^2 given by:

$$\frac{9 \cdot s^2}{19.023} \leq \sigma^2 \leq \frac{9 \cdot s^2}{2.700}$$
$$0.473 \cdot s^2 \leq \sigma^2 \leq 3.333 \cdot s^2$$

The Chi-Square Test

The χ^2 distribution has numerous applications, in addition to being used to determine the sampling distribution of the population variance and standard deviation. There are a number of other statistical quantities that follow a χ^2 distribution and for which hypothesis testing procedures have been defined. These procedures can be used to test the discrepancy between a set of observations and the expected values of these observations to measure whether the difference is statistically significant or due to random chance. The test is known as the chi-square test and has a wide number of applications, including tests of independence between two variables, tests regarding the differences between two or more population proportions, and tests of goodness of fit (how well a theoretical distribution fits an empirical distribution obtained from gathered data).

In the case of goodness of fit tests, a hypothesis about the distribution of counts is first made, and then the observations are compared, based on this hypothesis. Assuming that we have a set of k categories of observations with frequencies $(O_1, O_2, ..., O_n)$, and expected values of frequencies $(E_1, E_2, ..., E_n)$ for each category based on the null hypothesis, the expression

$$\frac{(O_1 - E_1)^2}{E_1} + \frac{(O_2 - E_2)^2}{E_2} + ... + \frac{(O_n - E_k)^2}{E_k} = \sum_{i=1}^{k} \frac{(O_i - E_i)^2}{E_i}$$

follows a χ^2 distribution, indexed by the number of degrees of freedom (d.f.). Note that d.f. = $(k-r-1)$, where r is the number of parameter estimators based on the sample. The (-1) accounts for the fact that the kth category of observations can be deduced from the rest. For example, if we want to test if the distribution of counts is normal (μ, σ), and we use the sample to estimate the mean μ and the standard deviation σ, then $r = 2$.

The following exercise makes use of the χ^2 statistic to test goodness of fit.

Example 18: In the data staging process of a DW implementation, data is integrated from 4 sources. The quality of the data sources is being compared based on the number of errors reported. The database administrator expects that the results will show that the errors are uniformly distributed across sources. The database administrator sets a significance level of 5% ($\alpha = 5\%$) and takes a random sample of 100 reported errors, finding that the distribution of errors is as listed in table 5.6. Note that the expected amount of errors per data source is included in the last row, based on the database administrator's assumption that errors are uniformly distributed.

Table 5.6
Distribution of Reported Data Errors

	Data Sources				Total
	1	2	3	4	
Observed Errors (O_i)	22	30	35	13	100
Expected Errors (E_i)	25	25	25	25	100

H_0: The number of errors is uniformly distributed across data sources

H_a: The number of errors is not uniformly distributed across data sources

Significance level: $\alpha = 5\%$

Answer: With 4 data sources and no parameters to estimate, the number of degrees of freedom is d.f. = 4-0-1 = 3.

The critical c^2 value for a = 5% and d.f. = 3 is : $c^2_{3,\,0.05} = 7.81$

Given the data, the chi-square measure is computed as:

$$\chi^2 = \frac{(22-25)^2}{25} + \frac{(30-25)^2}{25} + \frac{(35-25)^2}{25} + \frac{(13-25)^2}{25} = 11.12$$

As the actual χ^2 is greater than the critical value $\chi^2_{3,\,0.05}$, we reject the hypothesis at a significance level of 5% that the errors are equally distributed across data sources.

SUMMARY

In this chapter we provided a short introduction to statistics, an essential tool to anyone who intends to approach the topic of quality in general, and data and information quality in particular with a certain level of rigor. We discussed both descriptive and inferential statistics. We studied probability theory and its connection to inferential statistics. We have covered the most common probability distributions, as well as sampling theory and estimation, confidence intervals and hypothesis testing. For each of these topics we have supplied examples related to data and information quality. We recognize that we are just scratching the surface, given the depth and breadth of the statistical domain. We encourage students to pursue further studies on statistics. Most real world problems deal with elements of risk, uncertainty and limited information. A sound command of statistics will help professionals make more informed judgments and lead them to better decision making.

CHAPTER FIVE QUESTIONS

Review Questions

1. What is a population parameter? Explain the difference with a sample statistic.
2. What are the basic axioms of probability?
3. Describe four types of random sampling.
4. What are measures of location and spread?
5. Explain Bayes' rule.
6. What is a random variable?
7. What are the parameters of a normal distribution?
8. Define the confidence interval of a sample statistic.
9. What are Type I and Type II errors in hypothesis testing?
10. Define the chi-square statistic and give an example of its application.

Discussion Questions and Exercises

1. Given the following data set describing the time, in minutes, taken by each of 30 workers to complete a given task, organize the data in intervals, and prepare a histogram and a frequency polygon chart.

   Data: 10, 15, 12, 17, 22, 14, 13, 12, 15, 12, 16, 14, 19, 16, 12
   11, 9, 16, 15, 18, 12, 17, 16, 14, 19, 13, 12, 15, 13, 20

2. Using the data from Exercise 1, calculate the measures of location and spread of the sample.
3. The net weight of a box of Kellogg's Frosted Flakes is normally distributed with a mean of 709 grams and a standard deviation of 50 grams. What percentage of boxes has a net weight between 609 grams and 809 grams? What are the chances that a box weighs more than 909 grams?
4. Modern networking devices, including firewalls and proxy servers, make use of data mining technology to detect potential network intrusion. Assume that the intrusion detection process is 98% accurate, that is, hacker attacks will test positive 98% of the time, and normal connections will test negative 98% of the time. Assume that 0.5% of all connections are hacker attacks. How

likely is it that a connection that tested positive, signaled by the intrusion detector as abnormal, will actually be a hacker attack? Express it as a percentage. (Hint: apply Bayes' rule.)

5. A marketing firm has implemented a survey which is launched twice a year, targeting a population of 1,000 prospects. The survey's response rate is 5%. What is the probability that only one customer will respond?

6. Returning to Exercise 3, assume that as part of a quality check process, a sample of 100 boxes of Frosted Flakes is obtained from the production line. What is the probability that the sample mean will exceed 759 grams? If the sample mean is 720 grams, determine the 90% confidence interval.

7. In Exercise 3, assume that the standard deviation of the net weight of a box of Frosted Flakes is unknown, $\mu = 709$, and $\sigma = ?$. Also assume that a small sample of 10 quality check boxes is collected from the production line, yielding a mean of $\bar{X} = 715$ grams and a sample standard deviation $s = 30$, construct a 95% confidence interval.

8. As a follow up to Exercise 7, assume that as part of the quality control process, a test is performed to verify whether the mean of the population's net weight is equal to 709 grams. As before, σ is unknown and the sample size is 10, yielding a mean of $\bar{X} = 715$ grams and a sample standard deviation $s = 30$. What is the outcome of the test?

9. In Exercise 4, consider two data samples A and B used to train an intrusion detection device. Each data sample was prepared by a domain expert. The domain experts reviewed each record in the samples (a record represents a network connection), labeling them as belonging to either a normal connection or an abnormal connection. We want to verify whether there is any difference in the quality (accuracy) of data labeling provided by the two domain experts. Sample A has 1,500 records, and sample B has 1,700 records. Sample A labels are verified, yielding an accuracy of 92% (the domain expert A was right 92% of the time). Sample B labels are subsequently verified, yielding an accuracy of 96% (the domain expert B was right 96% of the time). We assume a significance level of the test of 5%. What is the outcome of the test?

REFERENCES

1. Bernard, R., *Social Research Methods, Qualitative and Quantitative Methods*. 2000: Sage.
2. Brownlee, K., *Statistical Theory and Methodology*. 1984: John Wiley & Sons, inc.
3. Kazmier, L., *Schaum's Outline of Theory and Problems of Business Statistics*. 3 ed. 1996: McGraw-Hill.
4. Korb, K. and A. Nicholson, *Bayesian Artificial intelligence*. 2003: Chapman & Hall/CRC.
5. Montgomery, D., *Introduction to Statistical Quality Control*. 4 ed. 2000: John Wiley & Sons, Inc.
6. Neuman, L., *Social Research Methods, Qualitative and Quantitative Approaches*. 4 ed. 2000: Allyn & Bacon.
7. O'Donnell, P. and R. Meredith, *Lecture Notes, Decision Support Systems*. 2003, Faculty of Information Technology, Monash University: Melbourne, Australia.
8. Sivia, D., *Data analysis: A Bayesian Tutorial*. 1996, Oxford: Oxford University Press.
9. Wonnacott, T. and R. Wonnacott, *Introductory Statistics*. 5 ed. 1990: John Wiley & Sons, Inc.

Controlling Information Product Quality

Peter Drucker, the famous management consultant, said, "You cannot manage what you cannot measure." Chapter 2 dealt with total quality management (TQM) and provided a managerial overview of the topic. In order to apply the TQM principles to data quality (DQ), we first need to establish methods for measuring quality. This chapter will begin by introducing some tools that have been traditionally used to measure quality, and then we will illustrate the use of these tools and techniques by applying them to the information quality (IQ) arena.

INTRODUCTION

Recall that raw data can be considered the input into an information system (IS). The IS processes this data to produce the output, the information product (IP). Since we established in chapter 4 that information can be treated as a product, we can apply some of the traditional tools that are used to control the quality of the output in a manufacturing process.

The management of quality begins by establishing quality standards. Managers need to determine which quality standards are relevant and how they can be met. The International Standards Organization (ISO) is an international body that sets standards for businesses and governments.

153

These standards are developed by consensus and are adopted voluntarily by organizations. The ISO 9000 standards deal with quality management by providing generic management system standards for services as well as products. ISO 9000:2000 defines *quality assurance* (QA) as ensuring that quality requirements will be fulfilled, whereas *quality control* focuses on actually fulfilling them. In the context of Information Quality, QA requires the creation of a management plan to guarantee the quality of the IP, whereas Quality Control (QC) uses tools to assess the quality of the IP. For instance, if the data is processed over multiple stages before creating the IP, these stages need to be carefully planned and structured to allow for analysis of the data at critical junctures in the production process. By implementing such systematic activities in the system it increases the likelihood that quality requirements will be fulfilled. Thus QA focuses on the quality of the processes used to create the IP and QC assesses the quality of the IP itself. QA is pro-active and is focused on error prevention, whereas QC is reactive with an emphasis on error detection.

Quality assurance starts with prevention, through design and planning of products, training of users, regular maintenance of equipment, and qualifying of suppliers and sources of incoming material. As applied to IQ, this would mean designing the IP so that it is as concise as can be, has minimum redundancy, and, as far as possible, is based on objective and reputable sources. As part of the planning process, decisions that need to be made include determining who should have access to the IP and how often it should, or could, be updated. Users need to be trained in the appropriate software that is used to generate the IP, and the software itself needs to be kept updated.

In addition, the suppliers and sources of the raw data need to be appraised and regular audits of the system need to be scheduled to confirm that the product conforms to specifications. This is where QC comes in and this could be achieved through various means ranging from spot checks to continuous inspection in order to ensure that the final IP is satisfactory. QC involves monitoring specific project results to determine if they comply with relevant quality standards and identifying ways to eliminate causes of unsatisfactory performance. One of the techniques used for inspecting lots of incoming raw material is acceptance sampling. This is a technique that has direct application to monitoring IQ, and so we will discuss this technique in more detail.

ACCEPTANCE SAMPLING

Acceptance sampling plans are used to determine whether to accept or reject a lot based on pre-specified thresholds. The lot being inspected may be taken from incoming raw material, an intermediate stage, or the final product of the manufacturing process. If an organization has a policy of requiring that the reports it produces need to be 95% accurate, then they would build an interval around 95% (analogous to a statistical confidence interval), so that as long as a sample of reports fell within the interval, the entire set would be deemed acceptable. The width of the interval would be determined by factors such as the amount of resources the organization was willing to invest, and the inherent variation in the accuracy of the reports.

Questions that arise during this phase are: what, where, and how much to inspect. Key quality characteristics for each IP need to be identified in consultation with the primary users or consumers of the IP. It could be the case that the same IP is used in different contexts or for different purposes by different users, and so multiple quality characteristics may emerge as critical. Of special concern are those quality defects that could significantly impair product performance. Where to inspect can be answered by examining the flow of data through the system. The raw data may have undergone several processes as it flows through the system; hopefully, all of them value-added. By identifying the junctures at which it is subject to high cost processes, areas of fruitful inspection can be identified. Organizations also need to make a decision about how much to inspect, including all or nothing. Note that routine inspections may not be feasible if the IP contains data that is highly confidential. Likewise if the IP is very time sensitive, 100% inspections may not be advantageous either.

When choosing between 0 or 100% inspection, a simple economic model can serve to illustrate the tradeoffs involved in this decision. (This is also known as Deming's kp rule.)

Suppose p is the true fraction of defective items in a population.
Let k_1 be the cost of inspecting an item
Let k_2 be the cost of repair due to using a defective item in the final product.
A break-even analysis gives $p = k_1/k_2$ as the break-even point

Note that if $p < k_1/k_2$, this corresponds to a scenario where the proportion of defectives is low but the cost of inspection is high relative to the cost of allowing a defective item into the final product. In such a situation, the best policy would be to perform no inspection at all.

If $p > k_1/k_2$, this implies that it would be relatively expensive to allow a defective item into the final product, suggesting that 100% inspection is best.

As an example, consider a simple spreadsheet that is the single input into a report. If the average error rate (p) in the spreadsheet is 1% and the cost of inspecting each cell (k_1) in the spreadsheet is $0.05, with the cost of fixing the final report when it is erroneous (k_2) being $50, then p = 0.01 > 0.05/50 = 0.001 and it would be advisable to perform 100% inspection of the spreadsheet cells first. However if the cost of inspection increased to $0.10 per cell and the cost of fixing an erroneous report decreased to $10, then p = 0.1/10 = 0.01 and we are at the break-even point and can choose not to do any initial inspection of the spreadsheet at all.

Clearly this simple model focuses on the extremes and should be extended to encompass other contingencies, but it provides a quick sense of where to apply resources and under what circumstances. For more complicated situations, software (e.g. Inspection Plan Management IPM/ IBS America) that create inspection plans are available in the market.

The sampling procedures themselves could vary greatly and run the gamut from using a single sample of fixed size, to item-by-item sequential sampling plans, where any number of samples could be taken, depending on the results of the sampling process. In between these two extremes are double sampling plans, where the decision to accept or reject the lot (the set of reports, in our case) is made on the basis of two consecutive samples. The first sample is of fixed size (smaller than the size of a comparable single sampling plan), and if the sample results fall between two pre-determined thresholds for acceptance and rejection, then a second sample is taken. The combined sample results are then compared to the rejection threshold. In addition to being more efficient than single sampling plans, the double sampling plans have "the psychological advantage of giving a lot a second chance" [2].

The process of sampling could also vary considerably. Conceptually, the simplest technique is that of random sampling. For example, management may be interested in knowing the accuracy of the records in a database. If there exists a master list of all the records in the database, that list can be mapped onto a random number generator. Then a given sequence of random numbers would dictate the records that belong in the simple random sample. The difficult part is the creation of the master list. A more manageable process may be that of sequential sampling where every nth record (depending on the desired size of the resulting sample) is chosen.

A different approach would be required if the tables in the database are of very different sizes. In such a situation, a stratified sample would be appropriate. Each table is considered a stratum and sampled according to its size. A variation on this is a case when it may be more important for certain tables to be accurate as opposed to others. A proportional sample that takes this into account can be designed. Sampling texts such as Lohr can be consulted for more details [2].

As may be expected, there are advantages as well as disadvantages to acceptance sampling. Its advantages are that it is relatively inexpensive, since it requires less time, and it also reduces inspector fatigue compared to 100% inspection. But the primary case against acceptance sampling is that it does not prevent poor quality, it only detects it, and in that sense it is a non-value-added activity.

There are other activities that could actually lead to improved quality [4], including:

- Design of experiments.
- Pareto diagrams.
- Control charts.
- Capability analysis.
- Six sigma.

The statistical sophistication required to use these techniques varies greatly. In addition, some of these tools, such as control charts, are used online while the production is ongoing, whereas others may be used offline, for example, design of experiments. In the following sections we explore some of these tools in more detail. We will begin with tools that can be applied during the conceptualization or design phase of the IP, and work our way down the list.

DESIGN OF EXPERIMENTS

In traditional manufacturing applications, experiments are performed while the product is still in the design or prototype phase to determine the sensitivity of the key characteristics of the product to changes in the raw materials or other parameters of the production process. As an example, consider the manufacture of catalytic converters. These are pollution control devices which work by absorbing emissions from exhaust gases in cars and trucks. They are typically ceramic-based and use a honeycomb construction to maximize the surface area. Key metrics in measuring the quality of this product include the physical dimensions of the converter and performance characteristics such as absorptive capacity. Variations in the mix or quality of raw materials, or fluctuations in the temperature at which the converters are baked, may result in changes to the walls of the honeycomb. Walls that are of uneven thickness or are too thin may collapse easily, and walls that are too thick may lead to sub-optimal absorption capacity. Therefore, controlled experiments that systematically vary the input parameters, such as raw material composition and oven temperature, are performed before the production process begins. The results of these experiments establish the optimal conditions for production. A simple example follows.

In order to isolate the impact of a single factor, such as temperature, on the absorptive capacity of the catalytic converter, the simplest design to run would be a completely randomized experiment. A few levels of temperature would be chosen as a starting point, and small batches of converters would be produced using these temperature levels. It is called a completely randomized design because the converters are assigned to the different levels of temperatures at random. The data would be analyzed using a statistical technique called analysis of variance (ANOVA), and the results would determine which temperature was best. This could then be further investigated by considering increments above or below the chosen temperature until an acceptable range was determined for the process.

It is usually the case that several factors would affect absorption capacity. As a simple extension, consider the case where both temperature and humidity may affect the final product metrics. The next step would be to investigate these two factors using a block design. If both factors were investigated using two levels, low and high, it would involve four combinations of temperature and humidity settings. One could also have mixed level designs where some factors have two levels, and others have three levels.

Factorial designs are useful in screening out the critical factors when a large number of factors are being considered. A factorial design could also establish the existence of any interactions between these two factors. However, when the number of factors to be investigated becomes very large, over five for example, factorial designs are not very efficient, and more sophisticated experiments employ fractional factorial designs where multiple factors and their interactions can be investigated using only a subset of runs. Some of these designs are referred to as Taguchi designs, after the Japanese engineer who popularized these economic experiments.

If, in addition to the factors and their interactions, we were also interested in curvature or quadratic effects, response surface models would be appropriate. Such models have the added advantage of being able to identify optimal conditions while the process is still running. Although these topics are beyond the scope of this chapter, there are several texts on experimental designs that discuss the details, such as Neter, Wasserman, and Kunter [6], as well as Myers and Montgomery [5].

Similarly, when creating IP, such as reports, experiments can be designed to probe the sensitivity of the reports to fluctuations in the quality of the raw data. Early work by Dr. Ballou and colleagues created a framework that could be systematically used to study the effects of data errors on spreadsheet results [6]. Not surprisingly, aggregating data led to reduced errors in the output, but, in general, trying to predict the impact of a certain amount of error in the input to the amount of error in the resulting output was difficult. They concluded that ". . . the seriousness of errors is highly dependent upon the manipulations that the data undergo" with computations involving ratios being more sensitive to input errors. Although the investigation on error propagation is not as conducive to easy analysis, further work on errors in spreadsheets has been done by Panko [8].

We now move to a popular tool for visually identifying problem areas with quality, Pareto diagrams. This simple technique requires almost no knowledge of statistics.

PARETO CHARTS

We briefly discussed Pareto charts in chapter 4. Recall that a Pareto chart is a vertical bar graph that displays the data according to the frequency of occurrence for each category, from highest to lowest. The Pareto chart is a widely used management tool that allows the user to focus on the "vital few out of the trivial many." In the quality arena, the Pareto rule states that 80% of the problems stem from 20% of the causes. A Pareto analysis allows users to easily assign priorities for their efforts.

The Pareto chart has two Y-axes; the left Y-axis tracks raw frequencies, and the right Y-axis tracks the cumulative percentages for the same categories. One of the unique properties of a Pareto chart is that it superimposes a cumulative percentage curve over the raw frequency bars by using two separate Y-axes. This allows users to make inferences about the impact of tackling the most egregious problems. Typically, a handful of categories will stand above the rest. If these are not immediately obvious, the cumulative percentages can be used, and the categories under the steepest part of the curve can be identified as the ones to focus on.

Example: Table 6.1 displays the DQ problems reported by users of a medical records database. Use a Pareto diagram to quantify the relative extent of the problems and prioritize the efforts of the IP manager.

Table 6.1
Sample Data Quality Problems

Dimension	# Instances
Accuracy	37
Completeness	86
Timeliness	64
Consistency	48
Objectivity	11
Relevance	59
Accessibility	22

Answer: The first step is to order the data from the category with the greatest frequency to the smallest. Next, create cumulative frequencies and convert to percentages. The result should look like table 6.2.

Table 6.2
Data Organized for Pareto Chart

Dimension	# Instances	Cumulative percent
Completeness	86	0.26
Timeliness	64	0.46
Relevance	59	0.64
Consistency	48	0.79
Accuracy	37	0.90
Accessibility	22	0.97
Objectivity	11	1.00

In Excel, use Chart Wizard, select the custom type tab, and click on Line—Column on 2 Axes. This should produce the graph shown in figure 6.1.

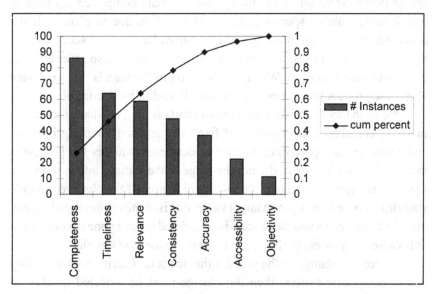

Figure 6.1 Pareto Chart for Sample Data Quality Problems

In the previous example, the completeness of the records seems to be the most pressing problem. In addition, by addressing the four dimensions with the most problems, completeness, timeliness, relevance, and consistency, the IP manager will have addressed 80% of the users' concerns about the information in the database.

The Pareto chart is a popular management tool, but its limitations should be recognized. For instance, many of the dimensions of IQ are interrelated, and we will have to make tradeoffs between some of them. In our example, it could be that by focusing on timeliness, accuracy may suffer. In order to ensure the accuracy of our data, we may need to ease up on timeliness. So, we recommend that management address the problem of poor IQ holistically rather than trying to improve each dimension of IQ in isolation.

CONTROL CHARTS

The output of any repetitive process can be studied by using a control chart. The purpose of a control chart is threefold: quantify the goal or standard the process should attain, help the process achieve that goal, and check whether that goal has been attained [9]. The theory of control charts breaks down the variation in quality into two main components: variation due to assignable or special causes, and variation due to chance. If the observed variance cannot be traced to a particular cause or set of causes, then the variation is assumed to be a chance variation, also referred to as common-cause variation. When the variation in the data is due to chance alone, the process that generated this data is said to be in control.

One of the most widely used control charts is the Shewhart, introduced in 1931. The chart takes samples of fixed size at fixed sampling intervals and computes the appropriate statistic to determine whether the process is in control or not. The chart divides the range of the statistic into two distinct regions, the signal region and the in-control region. If the observed sample statistic is too far from a preset target value, that is, it falls in the signal region, then the chart signals and the process is considered to have gone out of control. Otherwise, the process is allowed to continue to the next sample.

If there is a change in the process that leads to deterioration in quality due to assignable causes, then the change must be detected quickly so that corrective action can be taken. There is a long history of variations on the traditional Shewhart charts in order to make the control chart more sensitive to detecting changes. One of the earliest are run rules proposed by Shewhart [10] that produce a signal if a given number of consecutive sample means fall above, or below, the median. Later, Page [7] incorporated warning lines within the control limits in Shewhart control charts at one and two standard deviations above and below the target to increase the sensitivity of the control charts. He showed that this made the chart more efficient in detecting shifts, since it used information from the last few samples instead of just the last sample.

There are other methods for detecting out-of-control processes. For instance, if the chart displays a trend that has not yet gone out of control but is in the process of doing so, then the process may be stopped before any data point actually falls outside the control limits. Ideally, the chart should display points that are randomly scattered about the central target value without clustering either above or below the mean. Some of these guidelines have been codified into rules of thumb, as follows:

1. If there are 8 consecutive points either above or below the mean.
2. If there are 8 consecutive points that are increasing or decreasing.
3. 2 of 3 consecutive points above 2σ limit or 2 of 3 below-2σ limit.
4. 4 of 5 consecutive points above the 1σ limit or 4 of 5 below the-1σ limit.

---

1. If the mean is 121 and the next 8 measurements are 122, 123, 121, 124 122, 125, 129 and 126 then there are not 8 consecutive numbers above the mean so there is no problem. The third number in, 121, would have to be above 121 for there to be a problem.

2. Regardless of the mean, if the next 8 numbers are 129, 128, 127, 125, 124 123, 121, 119 then there is a problem since there were 8 consecutive decreasing numbers.

3. If a standard deviation = 10.5 and we find 2 consecutive measures = 21.6 or more then we know that there is a problem.

4. If a standard deviation = 10.5 and we find 4 consecutive measures 11, 13 12, 11.5 then we know that there is a problem.

Figure 6.2 examples of the rules of thumb.

A Shewhart control chart for monitoring a single parameter is equivalent to applying a sequence of hypothesis tests (chapter 5). At each sample, the null hypothesis that the parameter is equal to its target value is tested. If the null hypothesis is accepted, the chart continues onto the next sample, but if the null hypothesis is rejected, the chart signals. Similar to the Type I and Type II errors in hypothesis testing, there are two kinds of errors that can be made here, as shown in table 6.3. If the chart signals erroneously, then it is considered a false alarm. Overzealous use of some of the rules of thumb mentioned above may lead to an increase in the false alarm rate. Recall that by setting the control limits to three standard deviations, the rate of false alarms has been set at about 1% for a normally distributed statistic. Thus, in order to decrease the false alarm rate, one would have to move the control limits out further. Doing so, however, would decrease the sensitivity of the chart, that is, its ability to detect a shift in the process. This tension between the false alarm rate and the sensitivity of the chart to detect process changes has led users to keep the control limits at the traditional three standard deviations.

Table 6.3
Control Chart Decisions

Chart	If Common Cause	If Special Cause
Out of control	False alarm	Correct decision
In Control	Correct decision	Failure to detect

Control charts fall into one of two categories, depending on whether they are used to monitor qualitative or quantitative characteristics. If the characteristic under consideration can be counted, then an attributes chart would be appropriate, whereas if the characteristic is being measured, then a variables chart is appropriate. Variables charts are appropriate when the value under study is continuous, whereas attributes charts are used when the value under study is discrete. Often, control charts based on variables are more economical than control charts based on attributes. Also, assignable causes are more easily found using control charts based on variables.

The first question that needs to be answered when conducting QC studies, is what are the key characteristics that need to be monitored. For instance, there may be certain properties of the product that may lead to customer injury, making them critical characteristics to monitor, or there may be other characteristics that could seriously impair product performance, making them significant characteristics to monitor. Thus, key characteristics of a product are often related to cost or customer requirements.

Once the characteristic to be monitored has been selected, the next step is to determine the data collection method. Typically, the data that is plotted on a control chart is collected using rational subgroups. A rational subgroup is made from a cohesive sample, which consists of items that are created in essentially the same way, so that there is very little variation within the sample or subgroup. Therefore, it may not combine data points across different sources or workers. Different subgroups, however, may represent different sources or workers. The minimum size of a subgroup is four units, and the minimum number of subgroups required is 20. Small, frequent samples are recommended.

In many cases, a change in the process can be represented by a change in the parameter or parameters of the distribution of the quality variable. For example, if the distribution of a variable of interest is approximately normal, then a process change may result in a change in the mean, the variance, or both. In this situation, both parameters will usually have to be monitored. Typical variables charts monitor the mean and the variance. Table 6.4 summarizes some of the common variables charts.

Table 6.4
Variables Charts

Chart	Data
X-bar	sample means are plotted
R	sample ranges are plotted
S^2 or s	sample variances or standard deviations are plotted
X	individual values are plotted
MR	moving ranges are plotted

When the parameter of interest is the process mean μ, the Shewhart X-bar chart is used to monitor the mean. It is easy to implement and good at detecting large shifts from the target value. In order to apply the X-bar chart to monitor the process average, first the process dispersion has to be under control. Typically, the range or the variance of the process is brought under control, and then the X-bar chart is applied to the data. It is quite possible that the process has very little dispersion, but it is not producing items that conform to the target values. In general, it is easier to shift the mean of the process than it is to reduce the variation in the process.

When the parameter in question is the process range or variance, R charts or s^2 charts can be used. R charts use the sample range as the control statistic and are relatively simple to explain and use. S^2 charts use the sample variance as the control statistic and are more efficient. A range chart is used when the subgroup size is less than 10, whereas the s or s^2 chart is used for subgroups of 10 or more. Both charts are usually designed under the assumption that the process quality characteristic has a normal distribution.

The X chart for individual values is used if sampling is destructive or prohibitively expensive. It also assumes normality and uses the moving range as a measure of dispersion. As before, the moving range must be in control before the X chart can be used.

Five types of charts have been listed for the category, "Variables Charts." To help the student visualize which chart to use when we include the following 'flowchart.' Note that when a stop sign is reached then the data quality analyst must undertake corrective actions.

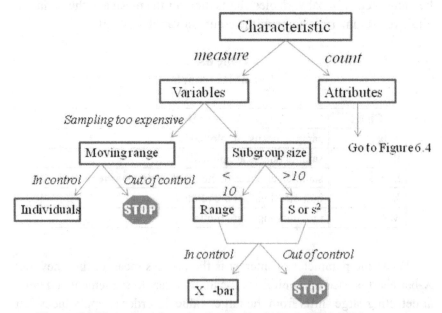

Figure 6.3 Flow chart for selecting control chart (Variables)

Often when considering IQ dimensions, proportions may be the more appropriate statistic rather than the mean. In that case an attributes chart, such as a p chart, would be used. Recall that attributes charts are used to monitor qualitative characteristics. For instance, if each report is classified as complete versus incomplete, rather than being measured on a scale of completeness, an attribute chart would be appropriate. Table 6.5 lists some commonly used attributes charts.

Table 6.5
Attributes Charts

Chart	Data	Comments
np	number of defectives	follows a binomial distribution
p	proportion of defectives	can be used with varying sample sizes
c	number of defectives per unit	follows a Poisson distribution
u	rate of defectives per unit	can be used with varying sample sizes

There are 4 control charts for attributes. The determination of which chart used can be found by following the flowchart given in Figure 6.4. Detail calculations and use of the charts follow the flowchart.

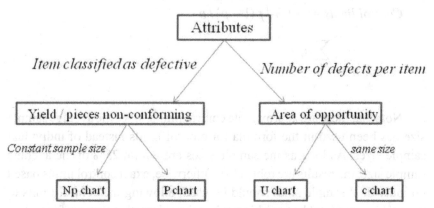

Figure 6.4 Flow chart for selecting control chart (attributes)

Number nonconforming charts (np chart):

Let X_i be the ith nonconforming item.
Average proportion of nonconforming items =
Total number of nonconforming items
Total number of items

$$Center\ line = n\bar{p} = \frac{\sum_i X_i}{k}$$

Where k is the number of subgroups and n is the common subgroup size

$$Control\ limits = n\bar{p} \pm 3\sqrt{n\bar{p}(1 - \bar{p})}$$

Fraction nonconforming charts (p chart):

$$Center\ line = \bar{p} = \frac{\sum_i X_i}{\sum_i n_i}$$

Where n_i is the size of the ith subgroup

$$Control\ limits = \bar{p} \pm 3\sqrt{\bar{p}(1 - \bar{p})/n}$$

$$Where\ \bar{n} = \frac{\sum_i n_i}{k}$$

Note that these are approximate control limits, since the average sample size has been used in the formula for control limits instead of individual sample sizes. As long as the sample sizes are within 25% of the average sample size, the results are robust [3]. Otherwise, exact control limits based on individual sample sizes should be used, allowing the control limits to vary. This would not be a problem when the calculations are performed on a computer.

P and np charts count the number of nonconforming units in a sample and are less sensitive and require larger subgroup sizes than the c or u charts, which are counts of nonconformities. C and u charts are also referred to as *area of opportunity* charts, and they measure the variation in the number of defects per unit. This count is assumed to follow a Poisson distribution, so depending on whether the unit of measurement is the same or not, the c or the u chart is used respectively. The formulae for their center lines and control limits are given below.

Areas of opportunity charts (same size):

Let c_i be the number of nonconformities associated with unit i

Average number of nonconformities =

Total number of nonconformities
Number of areas of opportunity

$$\text{Center line} = \bar{c} = \frac{\sum_i c_i}{k}$$

Where k is the number of areas of opportunity

$$\text{Control limits} = \bar{c} \pm 3\sqrt{\bar{c}}$$

Area of opportunity charts (variable size):

$$\text{Center line} = \bar{u} = \frac{\sum_i c_i}{\sum_i n_i}$$

Where n_i is the size of the ith area of opportunity

$$\text{Control limits} = \bar{u} \pm 3\sqrt{\frac{\bar{u}}{n_i}}$$

Note that the control limits will vary depending on the size of each sample.

Example: A major bank in Chicago had problems reconciling data across its branches. Samples of 10 reports from each of 7 branches were selected and each report was characterized as having discrepancies or not. This yielded the following data:

	Jones	Smith	Baker	Brown	Patel	Rao	Mishra
Officer:		7					
Number:	4	3	3	2	0	3	8

Answer: Here we are interested in recording the number of nonconforming units or defectives in a fixed sample of 10. This follows a binomial distribution, assuming that each report could either be classified as having discrepancies or not. Thus the p or np chart would be appropriate. $n = 10$ and $k = 7$

First we will attempt the np chart.

Center line = $\Sigma X_i / k$ = (4+3+3+2+0+3+8)/7 = 23/7 = 3.2857

Control limits = $3.2857 \pm 3\sqrt{3.2857(1 - 0.3286)} = 3 \pm 3\sqrt{2.2061}$

$= 3.2857 \pm 3(1.4853) = 3.2857 \pm 4.4559$

The lower control limit is calculated to be a negative number and so is set to zero, since a proportion or count cannot be negative. The upper control limit is 7.7416.

It similarly follows that the center line for the p chart is 0.3286 and its control limits are (0, 0.7742).

Based on the control limits of (0, 0.7742) for the p chart shown in figure 6.5, we see that Mishra's reports fall above the upper control limit, signaling a problem. Although technically Patel is within the control limits, it is advisable to investigate causes of better-than-expected performance, as this may either expose problems with measurement or produce guidelines that others can follow to replicate the success.

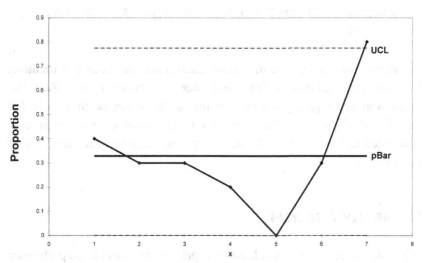

Figure 6.5 P Chart for Bank Officers' Reports

This brings us to a counterintuitive guideline. One needs to identify causes for both bad as well as seemingly too-good data points. As an example, for years, researchers have been intrigued by the reportedly low rate of deaths due to heart failure in Japan and were busy investigating diet or lifestyle implications. For instance, higher incidences of strokes were attributed to increased salt intake in the Japanese diet. Now, many public health researchers believe that the reported low rate of fatal heart attacks in Japan has little to do with disease [1]. Rather, heart attack is a low-status cause of death in Japan, connoting "a life of physical labor and physical breakdown". Other, more acceptable causes of death, such as stroke, are often reported instead, leading to underreporting of deaths due to heart attacks.

Example: Monthly sales reports from 14 sales representatives were inspected for DQ problems, and 117 problems were flagged. Determine the control limits for the control chart.

Answer: Here the number of nonconformities or defectives per report is recorded. It follows a Poisson process, and we can assume that the areas of opportunity are the same, that is, in this context the reports are of similar size allowing us to apply the c chart.

The center line is 117/14 = 8.36.
The control limits are $8.36 \pm 3 \sqrt{8.36} = 8.36 \pm 3 (2.89) = 8.36 \pm 8.67$
= (0, 17).

Regardless of the type of control chart used, the process is iterative. We start with trial control limits and after identifying any out-of-control points and investigating and eliminating the cause for the process to fall out of control, the control limits need to be recalculated. Once the process is deemed to be in control, the next step is to determine the capability of the process.

CAPABILITY ANALYSIS

When the process is in control, then a capability analysis can be performed to see if it can meet process specifications. As mentioned in an earlier example, there may be a push for IQ to meet certain standards. Once the information production process is stable, we can use process capability indices to see if the process is capable of meeting these thresholds. The capability index that is most commonly used is C_p. It is calculated as the ratio of the specification range to the natural variation in the process.

Let USL be the upper specification limit and LSL be the lower specification limit. Then if σ^2 is the natural variation in the process, the formula for C_p is given by:

$$C_p = (USL\text{-}LSL) / 6\sigma$$

If the variation in the process has been brought under control to the extent that it is smaller than the desired specification spread, then the process is capable of meeting those specifications. Thus for a capable process the C_p statistic will exceed one.

Under certain circumstances, only one specification limit will be given. Thus, the requirement may be that the completeness of a report be at least 90%, providing a lower specification limit LSL = 0.9. In that case the C_p statistic will be altered to:

$$C_{pl} = (X\text{-}LSL) / 3\sigma$$

Likewise, if only the upper specification limit is provided, then the appropriate capability index would be:

$$C_{pu} = (USL\text{-}X) / 3\sigma$$

It is possible for a process to have very little variation but fail to be capable of meeting specifications, because it is not centered on target. However, the C_p does incorporate any information about the center of the distribution. Thus, a more comprehensive index is required. If both specification limits are provided, an alternate index called the C_{pk} can be computed from the C_{pl} and C_{pu} as follows:

$$C_{pk} = \min (C_{pl}, C_{pu})$$

This is a better index than the C_p because it takes centering into account [3].

Exercise: The sales summaries at large retail store are closely monitored using a proprietary system. Management requires that the report of the number of units sold daily for a certain item be within 2 units of the actual number sold. If the standard deviation for such a report is 0.5, is the process capable?

Answer:
   Specification range is $2(2) = 4$
   $C_p = 4/6(0.5) = 4/3 = 1.33$
   As long as the process is centered, it appears that it is capable of meeting specifications.

In the continuous quest for improvement, the next step is to strive for six sigma quality. Although this term is often used loosely to convey a management philosophy, there is some statistical theory underlying it.

SIX SIGMA

A six sigma process requires that the variation in the process be reduced to such an extent that there are six standard deviations between the target mean and the closest specification limit. It should be obvious that such a reduction in variance requires heroic efforts on the part of everyone involved. In order to illustrate this, consider the following analogy. If a book is an IP, and the quality of the book is measured by the number of misspellings in it, table 6.6 shows the transition from 1 sigma to 6 sigma. Note that 4 sigma is currently the industry average. As an exercise, the reader may want to try to find a spelling error in this book to see where it falls!

Table 6.6
Six Sigma as Applied to Misspellings

SIGMA	PPM (best case)	PPM (worst case)	Misspellings
1 sigma	317,400	697,700	170 words per page
2 sigma	45,600	308,733	25 words per page
3 sigma	2,700	66,803	1.5 words per page
4 sigma	64	6,200	1 word per 30 pages (1 per chapter)
5 sigma	0.6	233	1 word in a set of encyclopedias
6 sigma	0.002	3.4	1 in all of the books in a small library

The measurements provided in table 6.6 are in parts per million (PPM), and the best case is if the process is centered at the target. Typically, a shift of more than 1.5 standard deviations is quickly detected by an X-bar chart. So the worst case is if a shift of 1.5 standard deviations occurred, and it is not detected immediately.

Often the term six sigma is used in the sense of a management tool. But following a six sigma methodology is not the same as achieving six sigma or having a defect rate of 3.4 per million. There are several texts such as *Implementing Six Sigma: Smarter Solutions Using Statistical Methods* by Breygogle that provide more detail [13].

SUMMARY

In this chapter we have introduced some basic techniques of QC and applied them to improving the quality of data. Although some of these tools required knowledge of statistics, there are others, the Pareto chart for example, that can be used with virtually no statistical expertise. We found that control chart theory could be easily applied to monitoring DQ. We saw how identifying and removing causes of problems could help us along the path to zero-defects through capability analysis and an understanding of six sigma.

CHAPTER SIX QUESTIONS

Review Questions

1. What are the ISO 9000 standards?
2. How does QA differ from QC?
3. Name some advantages and disadvantages to acceptance sampling.
4. How does a completely randomized design differ from a randomized block design?
5. List some rules of thumb for signaling that a process is out control.
6. What are the tradeoffs one should consider when setting limits for a control chart?
7. Describe a rational subgroup.
8. Compare and contrast R charts and s charts.
9. Distinguish between the use of a c and a u chart.
10. Why is C_{pk} preferred over C_p?

Exercises

1. A database in a dental office is being audited. Describe two alternative sampling techniques that could be used to generate a random sample of records.
2. Follow the above exercise with a description of an acceptance sampling based process that could be used to estimate the accuracy of the fields in the database.
3. A customer service hotline is being audited. A sample of 200 phone calls revealed the following: 15 of the complaints were prank calls, 22 did not contain sufficient information about the customer, 13 were repeat complaints, 12 did not have the correct information about the product, 16 took over the specified time to

resolve, and 23 calls were routed to the wrong department. Create a Pareto chart and state your conclusions.

4. The number of mismatches in the address fields of a billing system is being monitored as part of a quality audit. Six regional databases feed into this billing system. A random sample of 100 records was checked from each of these databases. There were 4, 19, 5, 11, 13, and 7 mismatches respectively, in each database. Use the appropriate control chart to see if the process is in control.

5. If the number of mismatches allowed in the above exercise is no more than 5, calculate the standard deviation to assess the capability of the process.

REFERENCES

1. Bowker, G. and S.L. Star. *Situations vs. Standards in Long-Term, Wide-Scale Decision-Making*. in *Twenty fourth Annual Hawaii International Conference on System Sciences*. 1991. Hawaii.

2. Duncan, A.J., *Quality Control and Industrial Statistics*. 5 ed. 1986, Homewood, Ill: Irwin.

3. Evans, J.R. and W.M. Lindsay, *The Management and Control of Quality*. 5 ed. 2005, Cincinnati, OH: South-Western/Thompson Learning.

4. Montgomery, D., *Introduction to Statistical Quality Control*. 4 ed. 2000: John Wiley & Sons, Inc.

5. Myers, R.H. and D.C. Montgomery, *Response Surface Methodology: Process and Product Optimization Using Designed Experiments*. 2 ed. 2002: Wiley-Interscience. 824.

6. Neter, J., W. Wasserman, and M.H. Kunter, *Applied Linear Statistical Models*. 3 ed. 1990, Homewood, IL: Irwin.

7. Page, E.S., *A Modified Control Chart with Warning Lines*. Biometrika, 1962. **49**: p. 171-176.

8. Panko, R.R., *What we know about spreadsheet errors*. Journal of End-User Computing, 1998. **10**(2): p. 15-21.

9. Shewhart, W.A., *Economic Control of Quality of Manufactured Product*. 1931, NY: Van Nostrand.

10. Shewhart, W.A., *Contributions of Statistics to the Science of Engineering*, in *Fluid Mechanics and Statistical Methods in Engineering*. 1941, University of Pennsylvania Press: Philadelphia, PA. p. 97-124

Measuring and Tools for Assessing Data and Information Quality

*I*n this chapter we will consider both subjective and objective measures of information quality (IQ).

INTRODUCTION TO THE NEED FOR MEASUREMENTS

An example that demonstrates the importance of understanding user needs is the salesman that arranged delivery of equipment to a customer. He made an extraordinary effort to get it delivered a week earlier than promised, believing that early delivery would give his customer a welcome surprise and earn him praise from his boss. After the equipment arrived, the salesman bragged to his boss about the early delivery. He expected praise but was severely rebuked! What insights do you think the boss had that the salesman did not?

The answer is in the failure of the salesman to define quality the way the user viewed the service, product, and situation. The unexpected early arrival of the equipment caused a number of problems. The old equipment was still in place, so the room to house the new equipment was not ready. Since the firm knew the equipment was not due for a week, they planned to remove the old equipment over the weekend. They had contracted carpenters and electricians to remodel and rewire the room to accommodate the new equipment and its greater power demands. As a result they had to obtain carpenters and electricians to come in sooner, at a higher rate. Furthermore, on the day the new equipment was delivered, the manager was on vacation, since he had planned to work the weekend to renovate the room. Executives from a client company were visiting that morning, and couldn't get past the equipment stashed in the hall—since there was no room for it anywhere else. The manager's boss, who was to meet with the customers, was embarrassed because of the mess and confusion.

The question about the boss's insight should be easy to answer now. The salesman's boss knew the meaning of the phrase *fit for use by the consumer*. Quality cannot be assessed independently of the consumers who use the products [12]. The most important factor in interpreting *fitness for use* is to investigate and completely understand the total situation from the user's viewpoint. The salesman believed that early meant better. He learned the hard way that it is important to let the user tell him if early is actually better, because, in fact, it may not be. Several authors have applied Deming's theory to IQ [2, 14, 17, 19, 22, 25]. They stress that good-quality information meets or exceeds user expectations; it is information that is *fit for use* from the user's viewpoint. The catch is that the analyst must thoroughly know those expectations.

As the salesman's miscue shows, the DQ analyst must develop a broad knowledge base about the users, the systems, the processes, the stakeholders, and the managers. However, literature does not provide an exhaustive set of metrics that organizations can apply in cookbook fashion [6]. Skills that significantly help in this regard are taken from the field of systems analysis and design, TQM, reengineering, statistics, joint application development, and prototyping, among others. However, the analyst must become proficient in a number of new skills and techniques not usually discussed in traditional IS or IT college programs. Two general areas are DQ measurement tools and database corrective or cleansing tools. Use of these tools is not presented as a magic wand with which a firm's DQ can be made perfect; quite the contrary. The use of the tools must be embedded in a full and comprehensive DQ improvement program that follows the themes given earlier in regard to IP, TQM, and TDQM. These tools are necessary, albeit not sufficient, to improve the overall IQ of an organization's information.

Since there is now significant recognition of the need to address data and IQ from users' perspectives, the following discussion will begin with an approach to measurement to ascertain fitness for use from the user's point of view. Our focus is on how to develop an assessment of an organization's perception of usability of information.

Benchmarks

Two of the primary purposes of measurements or benchmarks are:
- Help diagnose problems in systems, processes, and products.
- Assess impacts of the changes to systems, processes, and products.

Sometimes just the simple act of defining everything that must go into a benchmark test, and then running the test, will uncover bottlenecks and problems. This gives direction to the analyst on how to proceed. Exception reports are useful in finding problems. If certain processes take a little longer than normal on one day, then there might be a problem. It could be that on Wednesdays some other system is running in parallel with our process, causing a bottleneck and severely slowing the process. Without measurements, this problem would not be diagnosed.

Alternatively, if over a few weeks the processes have been running longer and longer, than perhaps a problem is beginning to surface. Maybe a machine is wearing out, and workers must redo some steps to get the product right, thereby slowing the entire process. In summary, measurements are critical for diagnoses.

The second primary purpose of benchmarks is to establish a baseline of performance, costs, productivity, steps, satisfaction, perceptions, and the like. Our recommendation is to add all aspects of quality to the list of measurements in the baseline. A normal part of project management is to reflect on the success, failures, and outcomes of a project. Suppose a new accounts-payable system was developed, installed, and implemented. How would a manager know if the new system was better than the old system? One new accounts-payable system allowed a company to layoff about a third of its clerks and was initially considered a success. However, the important measurements in the executive's eyes included customer satisfaction and reputation for integrity. The error rate shot up so high that the clerks who were laid off were rehired. One of our key perspectives is to consider all aspects of information that are important to the user.

If a new system, or a change to a system, is better, then how does an analyst know how much better it is? If it is not better, then in what areas are there still deficiencies? In a multi-plan, multi-laboratory, or multi-division corporation, many new systems may be developed, so which new systems are the best? To answer these and similar questions, benchmarks are conducted before and after changes.

A baseline and post-installation benchmark are generated as follows. After the new system is installed, the tests comprising the benchmarks are rerun and compared against the baseline benchmark. Care is taken to ensure that the measurements of the baseline benchmark and the post-installation benchmark are taken under the same conditions. This is to avoid spurious effects on the measurements. That is, if the baseline benchmark was originally taken when there was absolutely no contention, and only one or two users were executing functions at random, then the final benchmark must be taken with the same users doing the same functions with no other systems running in contention. There have been benchmark comparisons where the second benchmark was taken during the busy hours of prime shift, while the first baseline was taken off shift with very few jobs running. There cannot be an accurate assessment of benchmark results if they were taken under different conditions. The variance in the environment can make the new system look exceptionally good or exceptionally bad.

Although this chapter is not on research methods, there is significant advantage to learning and applying basics of research methods to IQ problems. Hopefully, many students will take at least one course on research methods. Several points were reviewed in the statistics and process control chapters that introduced the need for, and fundamentals of, good samples. When researchers compare two or more elements and reach a conclusion about their comparison, they must ensure that they are comparing like elements to like elements, or colloquially, apples to apples. Chapter 5 emphasized the criticality of selecting a proper set of samples for comparison. If the samples are biased in any way, then it makes little difference how perfect the rest of the test comparisons are. The invalid samples invalidate the entire test comparison. In this case, the environmental conditions of the benchmark are just as crucial as the statistical sampling.

The organization's goal is to improve data and IQ. TQM literature purports that an important aspect of improving something is being able to measure it. A related question is, "When should it be measured?" It is important to measure before and after an action to see if the action had any effect on improving it. It is also important for an organization to measure changes in case multiple actions took place at different laboratories, plants, branch offices, or retail stores. In the case of multiple actions, the organization should determine which action had the most positive effect, the least amount of cost, or both.

How should an organization measure its IQ to determine *fitness for use*? This previously unasked simple question is one of the missing links to successful IQ management programs. Researchers have agreed with Deming that quality cannot be assessed independently of the consumers who use the products but, until recently, did little about measuring quality from the users' perspectives. Subjective measures that directly ask the users for their opinion are best. This leads into the work on *Information Quality Assessment* (IQA) pioneered by Dr. Richard Wang and his colleagues [19, 23, 25].

INFORMATION QUALITY ASSESSMENT

The subjective view of information quality assessment (IQA) is a departure from past practices. They usually followed strictly objective measurements of quality and were conducted by systems technicians. These included studies that could prove if a piece of data was accurate, or whether all of the attributes were included in a response to an inquiry of a database. However, very little work actually focused on measuring fitness-for-use from the perspective of the user. In the introduction to this chapter, it was shown that an early accomplishment of some task does not always imply improved quality. In an earlier chapter on IQ dimensions it was shown that if improving the accuracy of data means that the data might be late, then that might not be considered an improvement in quality by the user.

A firm may know its competitor is planning to lower its prices, but does not know by how much or when. If they wait until they know these details, then it most likely will be too late to react. If a technologist is too focused on producing perfectly accurate and complete information, the technologist might not meet the user's needs. An executive might desire to build a proactive pricing plan based on sketchy information rather than wait until all the details are known. It is clear that to assess IQ the analyst must obtain the user's perspective. In addition, it is not enough to ask about quality in general or to specify one or two aspects of quality. If the analyst specifies just one or two aspects of quality, then the analyst is presupposing what the user's opinion is. It is best to investigate all 16 dimensions from the users' viewpoint.

Finally, the complete stakeholder perspective as discussed in the chapter on TDQM and IP must be considered. Anyone experienced in running a data center, computer center, an IS department, or IT organization knows that the users, the custodians, and the collectors all have different perspectives. We will now move from collecting the users' perspectives, to collecting and analyzing all the stakeholders' perspectives. One of the key tasks of an IP manager is to bring the groups together to develop a common understanding in order to achieve total quality improvement.

Much of the following discussion will be based on work done by the Cambridge Research Group sponsored by the MIT Total Data Quality Management Program [9, 23]. So how does an organization determine the perceptions of its custodians, consumers, and collectors of information?

Fortunately, a questionnaire has been developed based upon cumulated research conducted at MIT's TDQM Program [9, 17]. An IQA is conducted by IS analysts or DQ analysts to evaluate users' perceptions of the 16 IQ dimensions on a Likert scale [17]. The survey asks users to characterize the quality of their organization's information along each dimension of quality for a particular database within the organization. There are multiple questions per dimension so the results will be more reliable.

A drawback of questionnaires is that people accidentally—or deliberately—give inconsistent answers. Reliability refers to the consistency of the answers. Suppose you had a scale that varied every time that you stood on it. It might indicate 180 pounds in the morning and 210 pounds in the afternoon. It is very unlikely that you could gain 30 pounds in less than a day, so that variance shows the unreliability of your scale. It is time to get a new one. Increasing the number of questions and asking the same thing in different ways often improves the reliability of a questionnaire [1].

Reliability is absolutely critical if we are trying to prove a particular point. Sometimes a questionnaire may be used to set the stage for discussion purposes, and the same level of reliability is not as critical. For example, Wang's IQA questionnaire has 69 questions to assess the dimensions (four questions for each dimension), but users often get weary of answering that many questions. So some organizations use a subset of the 69 questions as a springboard for discussion. The reader should understand the purpose in using the questionnaire.

The questionnaire is divided into three equally important sections ([17], p. 67). The sections are:

- Characteristics of the information
- IQ assessment
- IQ context assessment

In addition, it is usually helpful to ask the participants to rate each dimension on a scale of 1 to 10, where 1 is the least important and 10 is the most important.

IQA Section 1, Characteristics of the Information

The first question of section 1, figure 7.1, is to identify what databases and systems the collectors, consumers, and custodians of the data are referring to as they answer the questions, since organizations often have many databases and systems. If 80 people complete the questionnaire, but they are all referring to different databases, there will be little chance of understanding their concerns about specific IP. As stated before, an important measurement concept is to know that apples are being compared to apples, so to speak.

Normally, the questionnaire is not sprung upon the stakeholders without warning. The IP manager usually arranges for the DQ analyst to work with the stakeholders and has narrowed the scope and begun focusing on a specific set of IP and their supporting databases. It is possible that the DQ analyst will change section 1 slightly in order to specifically identify the database that the stakeholder should refer to when completing the questionnaire. By focusing on a common database, the possibility of achieving usable and meaningful results is maximized.

The second question in this section asks the participants to rate their activities on a complexity scale. This information can be used toward evaluating (remember the statistics chapter) the relationships between jobs, departments, and all 16 dimensions on the basis of complexity. One use of these results is to note that if pockets of groups of people complain that there are problems with particular dimensions, and there is high correlation with high complexity, there is a very good chance that something could be designed to address these. For example, new and improved SQL statements could be written to simplify the presentation of the information or make it easier to access. Another possibility is to provide more training to users who rated the complexity high. The third and fourth questions help identify problems by area. It is useful to correlate complexity with groups of people in departments and various job titles. The fifth question identifies which of the three Cs, collector, consumer, or custodian, are reporting, as well as identifying managers. This section, coupled with the actual assessment question in section 2, provides very useful and interesting information. Later in the chapter, after all sections of the questionnaire are mentioned, reference to some actual uses of IQA will be given.

Section 1: Characteristics of the Information

1. *The primary type of information is:*
   For the purpose of this study you are reporting on:
   Accounting XYZ Database _____
   Marketing ABC Database _____
   Other (please specify) _____

2. *Complexity:*
   Rate the complexity of your activities for collecting, storing, & using the information.

Very Simple								Very Complex	
1	2	3	4	5	6	7	8	9	10

3. *Your Department is:*
   Department Name: _____

4. *Your Job Title is:*
   Job Title: _____

5. *Your main role relative to the above mentioned information:*
   (IF more than one category apply then provide numbers:
   1 is primary responsibility
   2 is secondary responsibility
   3 is tertiary etc…)

   ____ Collect this information
   ____ Manager of those who collect the information
   ____ Use this information in tasks
   ____ Manager of those who use this information
   ____ Work as systems support
   ____ Manager of system support personnel
   ____ Other _____

Figure 7.1 Section 1 of the IQA [17]

Discovering the perceptions of the various participants in the building of an IP is very educational. There have been cases where custodians have rated security low (poor) and accessibility high (good). In the same case, a whole department of consumers rated the security high and the accessibility low. Learning of this difference in perspective is one of the most valuable reasons to perform an IQA. Also, it is easy to see how important it is to ensure that apples are compared to apples; without that assurance the study would be useless. Consumers reported in followup meetings that before taking this questionnaire they were too intimidated to state their concerns. The technologists had no plans to improve accessibility, since it seemed easy to them. In another example "A major U. S. bank found that custodians viewed the data as highly timely but consumers of the same data disagreed" ([18], p. 211). Similarly, there have been huge differences in managements' perspective versus various groups of employees. In one study, managers reported that they did not have complete information, and it was not timely, while the employees said just the opposite. We cannot stress enough the value of not just getting the parties together, but getting them together with something concrete to discuss. The subjective measures collected through the IQA provide that platform.

As an organization begins to tailor section 1 of the IQA, it should pay special attention to managers whose duties are staff-like compared to those who manage employees. The organization should decide what groups are appropriate to put into common categories. The effort to determine the proper categories at the start of the study can yield more useful data from the study. For example, an organization may not want to put staff managers in the same group with line managers. We conducted the IQA at one government agency where a large percentage of people were considered managers. People were considered project managers, account managers, client managers, and other types of managers without having any of the people-managerial roles generally associated with organization hierarchy. Managers who assure that clients get the services promised do not function the same as managers responsible for directing employees on the job.

IQA Section 2, Information Quality Assessment[9]

This section has 69 questions to reliably and accurately determine the assessment of the perceptions of the 16 dimensions of DQ [17]. Although we are asking for perceptions and not for facts, we expect the participants will give honest, unbiased answers. A questionnaire is a self-report document and can be inaccurate or unreliable for a variety of reasons. Sometimes the person answering the questionnaire gets tired or careless and does not read the questions thoroughly. A person may really like an organization or deeply despise it or its management, causing the person to check off answers that appear good or bad. Reliability measures look for ways to double check the answers. Often the questions will be asked multiple times in a variety of ways. One variation is reversing the rating scheme so that sometimes 1 is good and 10 is bad; the next time the question is asked, 1 is bad and 10 is good. Different words are used to ask the same question. Statistical programs are run to examine a person's questionnaire for contradictions and inconsistencies. If a completed questionnaire has too many inconsistencies, based on a pre-established threshold, that questionnaire will be thrown out. Any comprehensive and high-quality research paper published that uses a questionnaire should also publish the reliability rating of the questionnaire.

One group to whom we gave the questionnaire told us they got tired of being asked the same question four times in different ways. They felt they had to answer 69 questions when 16-20 would have sufficed. In subsequent studies, we relaxed the reliability demands. Why? Because the first group of people stated that the survey was so much longer than necessary that they just started checking things off in order to complete it as quickly as possible. We can also ask how much reliability is needed. If the study is not for publication, and is not for *proving* one point over another, but simply to promote discussion among participants who have a common goal, the criticality of perfect research methods may be relaxed. By asking people to respond to 16 questions that inform us how they rate data and IQ along the dimensions, we achieved excellent cooperation, communication, and commitment down the road. Since the purpose was not for major proof, but to gain perceptions and then have discussions to improve the overall

---

9   For the purposes of this introductory text, we have used a modified version of the survey.

quality, the demands could be relaxed. In our future uses we asked only 16 questions, figure 7.2. The participants could finish in six minutes. The users knew it was in their best interests to make their answers as accurate as possible.

There are pros and cons to all approaches. In addition to losing reliability from a publishable research point of view, a general comparison to other locations is also lost.

We were most interested in establishing communication between the various custodians, consumers, and collectors, including both managers and non-managers of particular databases and applications. Achieving this goal contributes to the first two steps in the TDQM process of defining and measuring the problem. However, the MIT TDQM Program realizes that many organizations may want to compare their organization to others.

The MIT TDQM implementation of IQA provides for controlled data collection that is collected through a workstation system and transmitted to TDQM systems at MIT.

TDQM personnel run analysis, statistics, graphing programs, and summaries to completely analyze the organization's data. Also, since many companies use this service, MIT TDQM personnel can provide an index of the perception of the overall quality at the organization compared to other organizations. The more organizations that use this service, the more valuable it will become. MIT's TDQM creates a general benchmark that organizations use in a way similar to the Dow Jones Industrial Average. They can provide a single useable aggregate IQ measure that may be compared against many corporations' averages [17]. Suppose an organization performed an IQA one year, built a new database the next, and then performed another IQA. Ideally, the second IQA would be more positive than the first.

Section 2: Dimensions Perceptions

CIRCLE the number that most closely approximates the truth of the statement.

1. This information is accurate: Inaccurate Accurate
                                          1 2 3 4 5 6 7 8 9 10

2. This information is impartial: Very Partial Very Impartial
                                          1 2 3 4 5 6 7 8 9 10

3. This information is believable: Disagree   Agree
                                          1 2 3 4 5 6 7 8 9 10

4. The reputation of this information is: Very Bad   Very Good
                                          1 2 3 4 5 6 7 8 9 10

5. For our work this information: NOT Very Relevant Very Relevant
                                          1 2 3 4 5 6 7 8 9 10

6. The value of this information is: Very low   Very high
                                          1 2 3 4 5 6 7 8 9 10

7. This information is sufficiently timely: Disagree   Agree
                                          1 2 3 4 5 6 7 8 9 10

8. This information is complete: Disagree   Agree
                                          1 2 3 4 5 6 7 8 9 10

9. The volume of information is: Insufficient Sufficient
                                          1 2 3 4 5 6 7 8 9 10

10. It's easy to interpret this information: Disagree   Agree
                                          1 2 3 4 5 6 7 8 9 10

11. This information is easy to understand: Disagree   Agree
                                          1 2 3 4 5 6 7 8 9 10

12. This information is concise: Not Concise Very Concise
                                          1 2 3 4 5 6 7 8 9 10

13. The format of this information: Inconsistent Consistent
                                          1 2 3 4 5 6 7 8 9 10

14. This information is easily retrievable: Disagree   Agree
                                          1 2 3 4 5 6 7 8 9 10

15. The security of this information: Very Low   Very High
                                          1 2 3 4 5 6 7 8 9 10

16. This information is easy to manipulate: Disagree   Agree
                                          1 2 3 4 5 6 7 8 9 10

Figure 7.2 Perceptions of Quality by Dimensions

Several examples of the practical application have been found in the literature and as exercises for a DQ course at Marist College in Poughkeepsie, New York.

Huang described a few uses [17]. "This questionnaire has been used effectively in both public and private sectors. For example, IS managers in one investment firm thought they had perfect IQ (in terms of accuracy) in their organizational databases. However, following their completion of the questionnaire they found deficiencies such as,

- Additional information about information sources was needed so that information consumers could assess the reputation and believability of the information;

- Information downloaded to servers from the mainframe was not sufficiently timely for some information consumers' tasks;

- The currencies (e.g., dollars, pounds, yen) and units (thousands or millions) of financial information from different servers were implicit so information consumers could not always interpret and understand this information correctly" ([17], p. 61).

The DQ class at Marist College performed IQA studies at a large manufacturing corporation, a government agency, a volunteer organization, and an educational institution. A common reaction from all four organizations was that they were very impressed with the insights that college students gained about their processes and activities by simply conducting this survey. Rarely had their own IS departments gained that much understanding of the multiple aspects of data and processes.

IQA Section 3, Information Quality Context Assessment

The IQ context assessment is the third section of the IQA package, figure 7.3. A critical component of TQM, and hence TDQM, is that organizations continually improve and monitor the improvement of the quality of their products. To do so, the organization may create quality circles, conduct projects, or designate certain employees as focal points for IP improvements. The IQ context assessment determines if the people within the organization are aware of such programs. It is sometimes very surprising to an otherwise effective manager to discover that the people within an organization cannot identify the quality goals, programs, and activities of the organization. Section 3 of IQA queries the people about their degree of awareness of such programs and activities. Correlations may be drawn between the evaluations of the assessments and the knowledge of the improvement programs. It is predicted that those with lower IQ context awareness will score lower on the IQA dimension assessment index. It is also possible that the degree of awareness of the quality improvement programs will vary by job and department.

Since section 1 collects information about users, managers, custodians, and various departments, the context assessment may point to areas, either jobs or departments, that lack information about DQ activities. Management may determine right on the spot that more education is needed on the various quality improvement programs that are implemented or are being implemented. That information alone is worth discovering, but there are other advantages.

Most organizations have studied and used best-of-breed concepts which stress that there are poor, average, and good ways to perform business processes. Management should strive to determine the best ways, and then propagate them across the organization. There is almost no limitation on the use of these concepts. First, it takes a lot of measurement to identify the best practice, and then some persuasion to convince others that some aspects of this best practice may be used in a different area. The concept has been around for many years.

In the 1970s and 1980s, the availability of computer systems was a much bigger issue than it is today. Back then, organizations monitored availability percentages very closely. If a corporation had many computer systems and found that a few were having high availability while others were having low availability, then management would take action. Typically, managers with lower availability studied the disciplines of the centers with higher availability and attempted to propagate the good techniques across all systems. Persuasion was often needed, because managers easily became defensive, and would argue that there were a variety of factors that might make it impossible for the new techniques to work. However, much success has been gained through best-of-breed concepts.

Section 3 provides an ideal setting for best-of-breed studies. The DQ analyst should be able to correlate perceptions of quality with scores on the context assessment. Where the IQ perceptions are low, the analyst looks for context scores that are low. Low perceptions and low context scores reveal areas for developing improvement plans and policies for the organization. These are especially valuable when correlated with the large number of organizations that are submitting their results through the MIT TDQM central system.

Suppose the average organization has a very high awareness of TQM, tools, and accountability, as well as the latest database software, while the organization doing the current study is low on those factors. That information would provide significant input to managers trying to decide if they should begin a study to catch up with the industry. Now combine those results with the dimension assessments found in section 2 of the IQA survey. If perceptions are particularly low for the study but high for the MIT TDQM indices, then the organization knows to follow the best-of-breed techniques.

Section 3: IQ Context	Disagree Agree
1. This firm has tools that identify deficiencies with this information.	1 2 3 4 5 6 7 8 9 10
2. This firm has a specific position or group responsible for IQ.	1 2 3 4 5 6 7 8 9 10
3. Employees are able to take actions to improve IQ.	1 2 3 4 5 6 7 8 9 10
4. It is relatively easy to improve information.	1 2 3 4 5 6 7 8 9 10
5. This firm has adopted a TQM approach.	1 2 3 4 5 6 7 8 9 10
6. Employees view quality improvement as part of their job.	1 2 3 4 5 6 7 8 9 10
7. In this firm, employees participate in quality improvement.	1 2 3 4 5 6 7 8 9 10
8. In this firm, there are tools to ensure the completeness of information.	1 2 3 4 5 6 7 8 9 10
9. This firm is developing a data dictionary to Standardize data definitions across divisions.	1 2 3 4 5 6 7 8 9 10
10. In this firm, there are tools to assure the correctness of data.	1 2 3 4 5 6 7 8 9 10
11. This firm has people whose primary job is to assure IQ.	1 2 3 4 5 6 7 8 9 10
12. This firm has a specific position or group responsible for IQ.	1 2 3 4 5 6 7 8 9 10
13. This firm uses TQM to control process quality.	1 2 3 4 5 6 7 8 9 10
14. This firm solves quality problems using methods developed by Deming, Juran or Crosby.	1 2 3 4 5 6 7 8 9 10
15. This firm has designated people to solve quality problems.	1 2 3 4 5 6 7 8 9 10
16. This firm provides software for aggregating, manipulating, and summarizing information.	1 2 3 4 5 6 7 8 9 10
17. This firm has recently moved its information to a different hardware or software system.	1 2 3 4 5 6 7 8 9 10
18. Our firm has tools to assure the *consistency* of information.	1 2 3 4 5 6 7 8 9 10
19. This firm has a new database for managing the information.	1 2 3 4 5 6 7 8 9 10
20. Users of information are responsible for its quality.	1 2 3 4 5 6 7 8 9 10

Figure 7.3 Section 3 of IQA (note the word firm is a sample and other words such as agency, company, and organization may be used.)

IQA Section 4, Importance of IQ Dimensions

The final section of the IQA asks the participants to rate the importance of each dimension. These ratings will help prioritize potential quality improvement projects. It is possible that one dimension may be ranked as having low quality, but it would be a mistake to spend a lot of time and money fixing an unimportant dimension before fixing the most important dimension.

There was an example in a large company that conducted employee morale or opinion surveys that provide ratings on categories such as "room for advancement on current job" and "satisfied with working conditions." One employee said he ranked the room-for-growth question very low, but he didn't care. He had no desire to advance and start doing other tasks when he was very happy in his current position. It would have been a mistake for management to try to improve that person's ability to advance by moving him into another job for broader training, or assigning him to work in another department for the experience. He was very happy doing what he was doing, and that was his priority.

The analogy to DQ dimensions has similar implications. Suppose a person answered on the IQA that his information was not easily accessible. It would be a mistake to immediately try to make it more accessible. Priorities, costs, and benefits must be understood before DQ projects are implemented [2]. Accessibility may have a lower priority than security. Improving accessibility may reduce security.

Importance ratings may be combined with dimension ratings to produce a set of weighted ratings. Care must be taken to ensure that the scales are in the right direction. Management usually likes to see the quality graphs on a scale from 1 to 10, such that 1 implies low, or no quality, while 10 implies high quality. This is not simply a matter of management desiring to see good news. By showing the ratings with high numbers being good, it is easier to see how much the organization is improving as DQ projects are completed and additional IQA studies are conducted. Note that we must start with 1 and not 0 since we will multiply weights.

However, with the weights following the same convention as the ratings, it is possible to have many mediocre dimensions look like they are the highest priorities. A dimension with a quality rating of 4, but an importance rating of 9, might be more important to fix than a dimension with a quality rating of 5, but an importance rating of 8. Simple arithmetic indicates that the 4 × 9 = 36 is less important than the 5 × 8 = 40 result. Clearly, the dimension with quality rating of 4 has lower quality and higher importance, 9. The fix to this problem is to change the scales on the dimension ratings. Reverse the data ratings so the scale from 1 to 10 means 1 is an excellent quality rating and 10 is a poor quality rating. Dimension 1 is now 6 × 9 = 54, while dimension 2 stays at 5 × 8 = 40, but this time the right dimension gets the highest priority.

Figure 7.4 compares the total organization response to section 2 of the IQA performed in 2002 to a follow-up IQA performed in 2004. This is a subset of an actual, but anonymous, case performed by two DQ classes at Marist College. It is interesting to note that the organization installed a new database about one year after the first survey.

The class expected to see much improved opinions of DQ, but the perceptions decreased by more than a point in five dimensions, and increased by about a point in two dimensions. The other nine dimensions stayed the same. Discussion showed that the reason for the unexpected drop was that expectations were very high when the new database was installed.

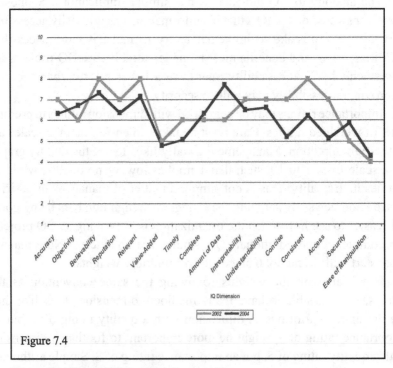

Figure 7.4

Figure 7.4 IQA 2002 to 2004 Comparison

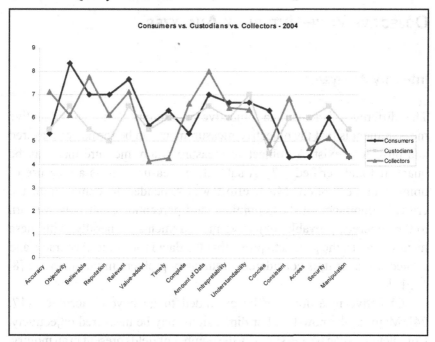

Figure 7.5 Comparison of Three Roles

Figure 7.5 illustrates a comparison of perceptions from three stakeholders. The collectors (triangles) did not recognize the value-added as much as the consumers. Also, the collectors thought that the data was not timely enough. Finally, the collectors thought that there was an over-abundance of data. In essence, the collectors felt that they collected too much data, it didn't have value, and it took too much time. The consumers (diamonds) thought that objectivity and relevance were excellent, but that consistency, accuracy, and access were not up to par. The custodians (squares) were not particularly happy with any one dimension and were unimpressed with the reputation, conciseness, and relevance of the data.

The problems at the end of this chapter ask the student to perform these comparisons for a real client. Note that these are perceptions only, and the true value is realized through frank discussions about why people feel as they do, which leads to areas for improvement.

OBJECTIVE VIEW—INTEGRITY ANALYZER

Integrity Analyzer

The difference between an objective measurement and a subjective measurement is that the objective measurement can be formally measured and proven to exist. An objective measure is any measure that may be quantified and verified [17]. A subjective measurement is a measure of opinion or perception. Much effort was expended to demonstrate the critical importance of those opinions and perceptions, but now we turn to the concrete, provable, objective measurements. Generally, with these measurements, the goal is to prove that the data is accurate. Accuracy, and related forms of it, is considered an integrity problem in the literature [8, 11, 13].

Objective measures can be expanded to go beyond accuracy [17, 24]. Many of the now-familiar dimensions may be measured objectively. Completeness can be measured by the number of fields present in an inquiry, or the number of values for a field present in a database. Consistency can be determined by how many representations there are of the same data in the same or a different format. Timely updating can be proved by its frequency, whether it is done every evening or every minute, as required.

Accuracy, one of the dimensions defined in chapter 3, means that the physical count, or physical reality, must match the data stored and reported through the IS to the users. Integrity is a much broader concept than just counting the parts in a stock room to see if that count matches the database. Dr. E.F. Codd defined five areas of integrity for a relational database system: domain, entity, referential, column, and user-defined integrity [7, 8]. Modern relational database management systems usually require database administrators to define integrity checks that the system must perform every time that there is an update to the database. Those checks follow Codd's five integrity constraints.

- *Domain* integrity requires that all values of an attribute in a relational table must originate from a common domain. This is directly analogous to the concept of data typing that states: the values of a variable are required to be of a given type.

- *Entity* integrity requires that every entity (table) must have a primary key consisting of at least one attribute. The primary key must be unique and have no missing values.

- *Referential* integrity requires that, for each distinct foreign key in a relational database, there must exist in at least one of the tables in the database an equal value of a primary key from the same domain. Simply put, this means that if an attribute in one table refers to a record in another table, then the record in the second table must exist and have a key with equal value to the attribute in the first table. (The foreign key and the primary keys must be equal.) If an employee database contains an attribute to specify the department where each employee works, then that department number must exist as a key of the department database.

- Domain integrity establishes the data type; *column* integrity puts ranges or other limitations on the domain for the attribute in question. The column integrity is a subset of the domain. The domain for the attribute course grade may be letters of the English alphabet, but column integrity may restrict that further by stating that only the letters A-F may be used.

- *User-defined* integrity specifies additional business rules that the column values must follow ([5], p. 72). These rules can be very complex compared to column integrity. One of the main differences is that often attribute values from other tables and remote databases may be involved in the integrity constraint and determination. Examples might include range and format constraints, such as a salary for a particular job code must fall within a specific range.

Although it appears that databases should be in good condition, given the coding of integrity constraints into DBMS rules, we know from chapter 1 that there are numerous errors in databases across the U.S., in both the public and private sectors. One reason for this is that specifying all possible integrity rules is a major task. It has been suggested that the specification of integrity constraints could account for as much as 80% of a typical database definition [11]. Many database administrators do not appreciate the rules, and therefore do not write them all. Estimates for a project do not always take into consideration the time it takes to encode the rules, so if a project is behind schedule, rules are dropped and shortcuts are made. Similarly, many analysts do not know all of the rules that must be, or can be, written. In some cases, users, especially under time pressure, may override the rules. Another cause of poor-quality data is that some legacy databases were built prior to formal implementation of all of Codd's integrity constraints. Also, as the business environment changes, the rules may also need to change, but no one gets around to them.

It is easy to see why there is a need for special software tools to evaluate the objective measurements of a database. Fortunately there is a tool, the Integrity Analyzer (IA), that is based upon the dual theories of TDQM and data integrity. IA has been used in many practical situations. The IA is an outgrowth of research from MIT's TDQM program and the Cambridge Research Group (CRG). It combines the principles of the TDQM cycle with principles of integrity constraints in relational databases ([17], p. 72). The IA covers the five basic integrity constraints defined by Dr. E.F. Codd [8].

The following brief description of the IA is based on the work by the CRG [10, 24] and work by Dr. Richard Wang, MIT's TDQM Program chair, and his colleagues [17]. The two main sections in the IA are the tools and data integrity menus. Both menus have three or four options that guide the user through a set of screens to analyze and improve the quality of the data in the database. The IA follows the TDQM process, and uses a GUI menu with a breadth of five items. The tools and data integrity menus include the IA specific functions. Data integrity contains the five integrity constraints that IA analyzes. The system is very easy to use and has been used in DQ classes at Marist College. Students are able to pick up the user guide and run a basic analysis of example relational tables an hour or so after their first exposure to the package. No attempt is made here to teach or demonstrate the entire package, but some screens are shown to illustrate the type of menu approach that is implemented. Figure 7.6 shows the first screen. If file is selected, the user can start a new project or select from a list of files.

Figure 7.6 IA First Screen

Once a project is started and a file is selected, the user can decide which fields to examine for the study. Figure 7.7 shows an example screen listing fields for the customer table.

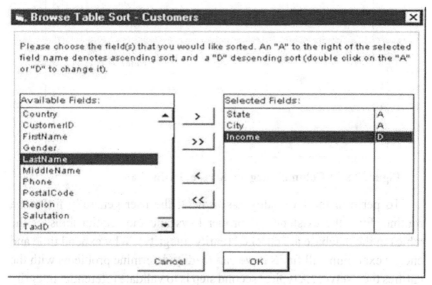

Figure 7.7 IA Customer Table Screen

Once file is selected, the user usually selects data integrity or tools. If data integrity is selected, the user can choose from among the various types of integrity. An example of the column integrity screen is shown in figure 7.8. The screen for each of the integrity checks within the IA is divided into four sections that are consistent with the TDQM cycle: define, measure, analyze, and improve. Note that those names are in the tabs at the top of the screen in figure 7.8. Each tab points to one control dialog box for each step in the TDQM cycle. Using the tabbed interface, the user can easily navigate from one cycle to the other while doing a particular analysis. As a result, only the relevant data that the user needs is visible. If the user needs to reference something already chosen or filled in, it is easy to go back to it using the tabs.

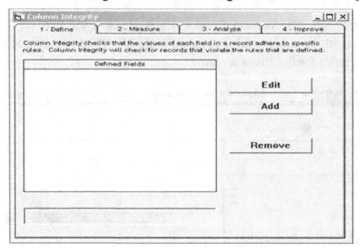

Figure 7.8 IA Column Integrity Screen, Define Tab

To perform the IA quality assessment, the user generally follows a routine. First the existence of proper keys and the relationships of the tables in the database are checked (entity integrity). Why expend time and energy examining all fields if we can readily determine problems with the entities themselves? A typical second step is to validate referential integrity by ensuring that all foreign keys point to a primary key in one or more of the other tables. Thirdly, the domain and column integrity is checked for all fields. Lastly, all business rules are examined. In addition to the data integrity checks, the user can run frequency checks using the tools menu.

The entity integrity function checks that the primary keys for every table are unique and not null. The referential integrity function checks that all foreign keys have corresponding key values.

To check entity integrity, the user selects entity integrity from the data integrity pull-down menu and selects the define tab. In the define list box, the user selects the fields that are primary keys for each table. Next the user selects the measure tab and asks the system to measure the number of violations to entity integrity. After the assessment has been completed, the user moves to the analyze tab. In the analyze section of any of the data integrity options, the user has a choice of viewing the results of the measurement in numerical, graphical or report form, figure 7.9. Depending on the choice that the user makes, the appropriate information appears. Choosing report results in a complete detailed analysis. Choosing graph gives a visual representation of the analysis, allowing the user to make comparisons between results. The report or the graph may be printed and distributed to others so they can continue the analysis or improvement as necessary. Selecting the improve tab produces a data object that displays the actual violation instances. Examination of these instances allows the user to take corrective action. The referential integrity check works in a similar fashion [17].

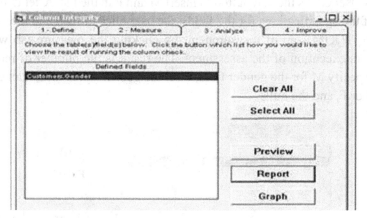

Figure 7.9 IA Customer Integrity Screen, Analyze Tab

Databases that deal with people usually contain a gender attribute, and gender provides a straightforward example of column integrity. The domain may be equal to the text data type. Further column integrity restriction may be established such that the acceptable values are only M or F and not null. After choosing column integrity the user specifies the table, the column, the type of data, and one or more checks by using the define function. Figure 7.10 shows the column integrity screen.

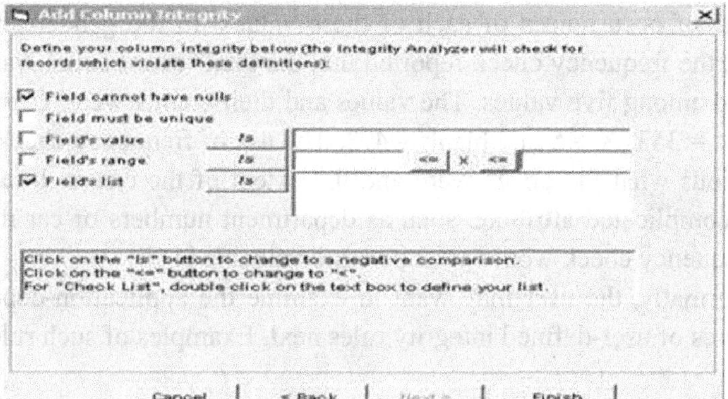

Figure 7.10 IA Add Column Integrity Screen

The user proceeds to check the rules, in this case, to disallow nulls (first check box in list at the left of the screen), and then the list to specify the values allowable for the field (last check box in list at the left of the screen). Figure 7.11 shows the screen displayed when the *is* button to the right of field's list is clicked. In figure 7.11 we illustrate the entry of M and F; the user clicks the add button to insert M and F in the list. After defining all of the specifications for the fields, the user clicks finish and then goes to the TDQM step of measurement by clicking the measure tab which triggers execution of the assessment. The result is the number of records that specify M for the gender field, F for the gender field, values not equal to M or F, and the nulls.

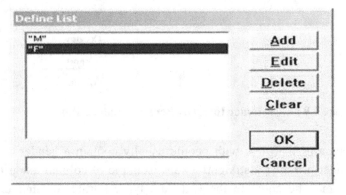

Figure 7.11 IA Define List Screen

There are additional tools available with IA to allow further analysis of column data. For example, frequency check reports the values that actually occur for each attribute in the column. It also tells the exact number of occurrences of each of these values. In the gender example above, the frequency check reported that the total record count was 1180 divided among five values. The values and their counts were: C = 9; F = 320; M = 353; X = 5 and blank = 493. The use of frequency check made it obvious what the errors were and the extent of the errors. In a much more complicated attribute, such as department numbers or car models, the frequency check would even be more valuable [17].

Normally, the user may want to examine the application-dependent measures of user-defined integrity rules next. Examples of such rules are:

- A student does not accrue interest.
- ATM transactions incur a fee beginning January 1, 1997.
- A senior is defined as being at least 65 years old.
- A customer with a balance greater than $1,000,000 should be flagged for new business opportunities.

Consider the example that a student does not accrue interest. The user selects user-defined integrity and is presented with a display of pre-defined conditions. The user may enter a new rule or modify an existing rule. If the user selects "Add" then the system displays a window for defining the condition. This rule may be specified: IF Account type = Student, THEN interest rate = 0. The user then proceeds to select the measurement tab as in the previous example. Measurement evaluates the database for violations of the rule. Selecting analysis allows numerical, graphical, or report formatting of the results. Finally, selecting improvement displays the actual records that violate the condition [17].

Since a database may change at any moment, the exact time a particular measurement is made is stored and displayed. This can be useful in keeping track of what discrepancies have shown up at what time, and for checking if they have been fixed. It is also important to know how much time has passed since the last data audit. If it was audited one day ago in a volatile environment, then the user may not want to depend on the data. However, if it is a nonvolatile environment, then the user may want to use the data even if last audit was a month ago.

In summary, the IA software package supports both Codd's formally defined integrity constraints and locally-tailored user-defined constraints. The integrity constraints are objective application-independent rules, while the user-defined constraints are objective application-dependent rules. IA functions within the TDQM framework of define, measure, analyze, and improve. Following the spirit of continuous improvement found in TQM programs, the IA may be run on a regular basis to ensure that the quality of the data is being maintained. IA delivers a specific statement of the quality of the data and indicates where improvements may be made. When IQA and IA are used together, the user may build a picture of both the subjective and objective measurements of the organization's database to form the basis for comprehensive DQ improvement programs.

Prioritizing DQ Improvement Projects

The DQ analyst works closely with the stakeholders in all roles to develop meaningful projects to improve the quality in a way that balances the needs of the users along as many dimensions as possible. "Depending on the organizational context, the technical solutions can range from data scrubbing to integrity enforcement to dummy record tracing to data dictionary standardization to a complete information systems rewrite or a completely new system" ([17], p. 81). Given the range of possible actions, it may not be possible to correct everything on a timely and cost-effective basis. The organization needs a methodology to systematically incorporate the number and diversity of tradeoffs to select the optimal DQ enhancement projects to maximize value. The tradeoffs to consider when selecting DQ projects to pursue include [2]:

- Current levels of DQ by database
- Required levels of DQ by database
- Anticipated levels of DQ by database
- Costs of projects to clean a DB
- Benefits of DQ Projects
- Organizational Priorities

Dr. Ballou developed a mathematical model that incorporates these factors when deciding upon which projects to pursue in order to achieve an efficient use of resources with the most payback of benefits [2]. The model helps answer a number of questions. Is it worth it to fix a database even if it is inexpensive to fix but is seldom used? Why clean a database if it is of low value? Can a project that appears to be of low value for one database be of high value for another if it incorporates many low-level activities? Alternatively, suppose a project appears to be very expensive, but it supports one of the major activities in the organization; should it be pursued? Considering our work in chapter 3 on the 16 DQ dimensions, should an organization pursue the optimization of a single dimension independent of the other dimensions? For example, should the organization improve timeliness at expense of completeness or accuracy? Consider pairing off all other dimensions, security versus accessibility and timeliness versus accuracy, to name just two.

Ballou and Tayi suggest a systematic methodology in which the analyst identifies the organization activities, prioritizes these activities, and sets weights for each activity. Next the analyst should build a matrix illustrating which databases are linked to which activities. Once the problems are identified for each of the 16 dimensions for each database and organizational activity, then a portfolio of potential projects may be developed to address each. (We suggest the use of IQA and IA for this purpose as well as any means available.) Finally, a utility function may be developed to compare the various projects weighted by the considerations just listed. The goal is to identify the projects that maximize the benefits of improving DQ, while assisting the organization with its main priorities [2].

Improvement projects are easier to suggest than implement. Specialized knowledge and skill are often required, especially in today's world of large databases and data warehouses that were built by merging many legacy databases. As stated earlier, many legacy databases did not confirm to Codd's integrity rules. Suppose one believes, after using IA to perform column integrity, that there are many duplicates in an attribute. This can be substantiated, since consumers expressed in IQA that they do not believe the data and gave specific feedback related to expected duplicates. It is not trivial to simply say "OK, let's correct all duplicates." A major task is to clearly and safely identify the duplicates. Usually, this involves writing and running many programs to compare a variety of similar values in a variety of attribute entries. Fortunately, ChoiceMaker Technologies, Inc. has developed tools for this purpose. Below is an example of using ChoiceMaker and ClueMaker software on very large projects [3-5, 15].

RECORD MATCHING

Andrew Borthwick and his colleagues have developed methods and software to address one of the most common and often difficult problems within databases. The problem of *record-matching* is discussed in this section and is largely based upon the four referenced papers. The New York City Department of Health and Mental Hygiene had a pressing need to accurately identify individuals for a variety of public health purposes. This led to the construction of the Master Client Index (MCI), which offers a department-wide service that provides fast, real-time processing of incoming medical records to determine whether the individual is already in the database, needs to be added to the database, or requires human intervention to determine whether the person is present. There are hundreds of thousands of records. It was clear that simple or traditional tools would not suffice. ChoiceMaker uses machine-learning-based software to provide MCI's matching capabilities [19-22].

ChoiceMaker was specifically used to de-duplicate the Citywide Immunization Registry (CIR), a children's vaccination database which tracks every vaccination of every child in New York City. CIR matching requires exact matches on first and last name, gender, and birthday. It is critical to have accurate data in the CIR because of the potential medical consequences. Allergies, under—or over-vaccination, and other concerns are crucial. One of the difficulties is that children move from one doctor to another, some children fall behind on vaccinations and the city must remind them, and the data is transmitted to schools.

There are additional problems. Names change frequently because of nicknames and mothers remarrying. Data is often missing including first names, parents' names, and addresses. Data is often inaccurate. CIR receives inaccurate data from billing (here the billing data has a less stringent need for accuracy), and there are clerical errors from poorly filled out forms.

The history of CIR was not good. When ChoiceMaker arrived, the CIR was nearly useless because of duplicates. There were approximately three records for every two children. A make-shift programming technique from CIR pumped out 260,000 pairs of records for human review. Clerks spent 1,700 hours manually examining records for possible true duplicates and missed thousands of them. ChoiceMaker removed over 600,000 duplicates with an estimated 99.7 % accuracy.

Although there are still process problems that allow new duplicates to enter the system, ChoiceMaker made CIR usable, and it can be rerun to catch future errors. ChoiceMaker uses patented artificial intelligence techniques to solve the problem of record matching. This is a multi-pass approach, since it is currently impossible to do a complete pair-wise scan of all 2 million records in the database. Each pass reduces the total number of candidates to examine with clues.

The first pass uses a frequency-based approach. It considers the frequency of values in the database. For example:

last_name = "Borthwick"
last_name = "Smith" & zip ="12345"

The user must encode business rules for matching; the rules take pairs of records and suggest whether they match or differ. The importance of each clue is determined by a machine learning technique called *maximum entropy modeling*. Typical clues include: first name match, match approximately based on various techniques such as soundex, edit-distance, NYSIIS or Jaro-Winkler; uncommon first names match, birthdays match, transposed digits examination, and any number of corresponding attributes (e.g., immunizations) matches. Another clue is that HMOs may have certain identifying idiosyncrasies in their reporting techniques.

In a test on a database of 120,000 records that had not been de-duplicated using conventional means, ChoiceMaker found 35,000 duplicates at 99.8% accuracy. Improved data accuracy will enable better data sharing of immunizations with NYC schools and physicians. Thanks to the improved DQ, there is a significantly less chance of over—or under-vaccinating [3, 4].

While there has been a lot written about record-matching of records for entities with name as the primary identifier, there has been less written about identifying consumers' addresses. Researchers at Acxiom, Inc. have identified that major problems in customer relations management systems stem from difficulties in matching consumer addresses [16, 20, 21]. They showed that while corporations "maintain many pieces of data about a consumer, the foundational elements of the consumer's address often times are the road blocks to successful matching, and successful matching is needed for cost-effective data integration" [16].

In pre-data warehouse days, lists of mailing addresses could be easily validated through U. S. Postal delivery point validation, cleaning and correction. The U.S. Post Office fine tuned the addresses but ignored the name. To them it made no difference if the name said, resident or Mr. Smith. But with advanced database dependent systems of Customer Relationship Management (CRM) systems with their need for highly accurate Customer Data Integration (CDI), the situation has changed. [16] Now the systems must use methods for name validation that are as accurate as the address schemes used by the U. S. Post Office. However, "assessing name quality is a more difficult process that requires collecting and cross-referencing name knowledge from a variety of sources, and properly applying that knowledge in the context of user needs [16]."

Acxiom suggests data mining of best practices throughout a corporation and then applying those best practices across the board. In large companies there are often a large number of similar validation rules for name quality. The astute reader should see the value of coding validation rules in the Integrity Analyzer mentioned earlier. The data quality analyst may collect information through surveys, interviews, examination of database rules, etc. about those rules. The DQ analyst would study and using concept of 'best-of-breed" create a set of name validation rules that have the most promise and become available for the entire corporation.

Acxiom also suggests that "several methods exist for gathering data and driving name assessments." They make use of established databases such as the U. S. Census, Social Security Death Index, Fortune 500 Business List and USPS standard business abbreviations. It is easier and faster to match for valid names against an existing valid list than it is to perform extensive computation. So Acxiom has made a very valuable contribution in improving name quality while reducing expenses of doing so. However, they do not stop there. There may be a number of names that are still not validated and Acxiom provides techniques for more complex and time-consuming analysis. They developed the "NameCheck" system. "NameCheck's primary focus is on patterns. It assumes that names presented to it are valid unless it detects a specific pattern indicating otherwise. NameCheck is a general purpose system. It is comprehensive enough for corporate-wide use and allows a variety of input options. The NameCheck report allows users to determine overall quality of their file with summary statistics and examples for all reasons codes" [16].

There is an old cliché that says if garbage comes into the database then only garbage will be produced by the system that uses the database. Colloquially this seemed to carry a lot of meaning. It became shortened to Garbage-In, Garbage-out and even GIGO. The implication is that cleaning the inputs should provide a clean database and hence clean results. Earlier in this text we posed a question that asked if the input data was correct would the database be correct. The answer to that question is not necessarily, especially when combining several inputs to create one larger database or warehouse. Acxiom has realized this fact, have begun addressing it through research and developed "An Algebraic Approach to Quality Metrics for Customer Recognition Systems" [20]. The reader is encouraged to obtain a copy of this paper and perform independent study of this fascinating topic.

SUMMARY

The primary message of chapter 7 is that it is important to use both subjective and objective measurements of IQ. Until the Wang and colleagues study on consumers' of IQ, few organizations systematically measured user perceptions on all 16 dimensions of IQ. More tools are now available for objective measurements of accuracy, completeness, redundancy, and Codd's rules of integrity. We have the IA. Quality analysts are encouraged to use both the IQA and the IA to form a comprehensive picture of the IQ within an organization. Finally, advances such as those made by Acxiom and Borthwick in the areas of record-matching techniques and software provide a sound foundation for studying and fixing databases when the potential for duplicate entity identifiers, such as names, are involved. These techniques, when combined with the techniques covered earlier in the text that are focused on IP (IP-MAPs, TQM, and TDQM programs), promise significant improvement in data and information quality. The student is encouraged to study the current IQ literature as it unfolds, since new tools will certainly be forthcoming as more people realize the value of improving IQ.

CHAPTER SEVEN QUESTIONS

Review Questions

1. Explain why delivering a product to a customer earlier than scheduled is not always better.
2. Explain in understandable terms the two primary reasons that benchmarks are performed. Give an example.
3. What are the purposes of the 3 different sections of the Information Quality Assessment (IQA)?
4. Give the purposes and benefits of each individual question in Section 1 of the IQA. Note an explanation for all five questions is expected here.
5. If there are only [only?] 16 dimensions then why did Dr. Wang create over 60 questions in his survey? For the modified questionnaire

given in Figure 7.2 of the text state which dimension is examined by which question.

6. Explain the purpose and benefits of CHOICEMAKER.
7. How is the IQA used to make comparisons between groups? How is the IQA used to make comparison within one group but at different times? State how such comparisons could be useful.
8. What are E. F. Codd's Integrity constraints?
9. What are some difficulties in ensuring conformance to Codd's rules?
10. What considerations must be made when trying to select among a group of possible projects to improve the quality of databases?

Projects

PROJECT 1: IQ Assessment

Objective: Perform an assessment of IQ at a local organization.
Systems: Choose a containable system that is important to the users. (Avoid an ERP with a global nature.)
Personnel: Identify Management and staff TBD.
General Statement:
    Study and apply IQ Assessment concepts; references are below. Text: *Quality Information and Knowledge* (Huang, Lee, and Wang; 1999); and article: "Data Quality in Context" (Strong, Lee, & Wang; 1996).
Teams: Work in teams of four or five. Determine the details of the general steps listed below, and divide the work accordingly.

General Steps to be modified as needed by each team:
1. Prepare and administer an IQA survey. Obtain permission from Professor Richard Wang of MIT.
2. Note the IQA in this chapter. Use a subset of questions. Note the direction of responses for good and bad (does 1 = good or does 1 = bad?).
3. Discuss with the client and persuade them as to the value of IQA. In "real life" a data quality analyst would have to convince the client of the benefit of the study prior to conducting the study.

4. Conduct the data collection process; assure the participants of their confidentiality and of your commitment to use your results only for this study.
5. Design an Excel or Access database to store the data.
6. Populate your data storage with the actual data results.
7. Group data in a variety of ways including:
    *   the entire population of the organization
    *   by job title
    *   by department
    *   by database
    *   by roles (custodians, providers, consumers, managers)
8. Design and apply statistical evaluations of the data; these can include, but are not limited to:
    *   averages, ranges etc for entire population on the 16 DQ dimensions
    *   rank the dimensions
    *   averages, ranges by the groups you established above on the 16 DQ dimen-sions
    *   rank the dimensions by groups
    *   statistically compare various groups (t-tests)
    *   use correlations to determine strength of relationships
    *   perform IQ context assessment (section 3 of IQA Survey)
9. Develop a wide variety graphs to illustrate your findings.
10. Reach conclusions.
11. Develop recommendations.
12. Develop and deliver formal presentations to the stakeholder groups.

PROJECT 2: IA Assignment[10]

The purpose of this assignment is to expose the student to a software tool for analyzing the integrity of a relational database. Although the assignment is not exhaustive, the basic concepts are introduced. The successful student will try to understand the concepts behind the integrity

---

[10] This assignment assumes that your organization obtains the Integrity Analyzer package from Dr. Richard Wang of MIT [13].

tests such as frequency checks, dataset builder, column, entity, referential and user-defined constraints.

Tasks:
1. Write a two-page summary of Codd's integrity rules.
2. Run frequency checks on at least three fields in each of the three main tables provided by IA: accounts, customers, and transactions. Use your judgment to determine which fields you think are important, and explain why you picked those fields.
3. Run column integrity for five fields.
4. Run entity integrity for the three tables given.
5. Run referential integrity checks on the databases as appropriate.
6. For user defined integrity, please suggest at least two user-defined rules, and run user defined integrity tests for those rules.

Hand in: Your summary of Codd's rules, your explanation of the tests you performed, your analysis of the results, and your conclusions. Your paper should demonstrate that you understood the tool, the tests, and the results.

REFERENCES

1. Bailey, K.D., *Methods of Social Research*. 3 ed. 1987, NY, NY: The Free Press.
2. Ballou, D.P. and G.K. Tayi, *Enhancing Data Quality in Data Warehouse Environments*. Communications of the ACM, 1999. 42(1): p. 73-78.
3. Borthwick, A. *Record Matching for a Large Master Client Index at the New York City Health Department*. in *Eighth International Conference on Information Quality*. 2003. Cambridge, MA.
4. Borthwick, A. and M. Soffer. *Business Requirements of a Record Matching System*. in *Ninth International Conference on Information Quality*. 2004. Cambridge, MA: MIT TDQM Program.
5. Buechi, M., A. Borthwick, A. Winkel, and A. Goldberg. *ClueMaker: A Language for Approximate Record Matching*. in *Eighth International Conference on Information Quality*. 2003. Cambridge, MA.

6. Cappiello, C., C. Francalanci, and B. Pernici, *Data Quality Assessment from the User's Perspective.* IQIS 2004 ACM, 2004: p. 68-73.

7. Codd, E.F., *A Relational Model of Data for Large Shared Data Banks. Communications of the ACM*, 1970. 13(6): p. 377-387.

8. Codd, E.F., *Relational Database: A Practical Foundation for Productivity.* Communications of the ACM, 1982. 25(2): p. 109-117.

9. CRG, *Information Quality Assessment Survey: Administrators Guide.* 1997, MIT: Cambridge, MA.

10. CRG, *Integrity Analyzer: A Software Tool for TDQM.* 1997, MIT: Cambridge, MA.

11. Date, C.J., *An Introduction To Database Systems.* 7 ed. 2000, Reading, MA: Addison-Wesley Publishing Company.

12. Deming, W.E., *Out of the Crisis.* 1986, Cambridge, MA: MIT, Center for Advanced Engineering Study.

13. Elmasri, R.a.N., S., *Fundamentals of Database Systems.* 2 ed. 1994, Redwood City, CA: The Benjamin/Cummings Publishing Company, Inc.

14. Eppler, M.J. and D. Wittig. *Conceptualizing Information Quality: A Review of Information Quality Frameworks from the Last Ten Years.* in *The 2000 Conference on Information Quality.* 2000. Cambridge, MA.

15. Goldberg, A. and A. Borthwick. *An Approximate Matching Technology for Database Searching, Linking, and De-Duplicating.* in *Sixth International Conference on Information Quality.* 2001. Cambridge, MA: MIT TDQM Program.

16. Hess, K. and J. Talburt. *Applying Name Knowledge to Name Quality Assessment.* in *The Ninth International Conference on Information Quality.* 2004. Cambridge, MA: MIT TDQM Program.

17. Huang, K.-T., Y.W. Lee, and R.Y. Wang, *Quality Information and Knowledge.* 1999, Englewood Cliffs, NJ: Prentice Hall. 209.

18. Pipino, L.L., Y.W. Lee, and R.Y. Wang, *Data Quality Assessment.* Communications of the ACM, 2002. 45(4): p. 211-218.

19. Strong, D.M., Y.W. Lee, and R.Y. Wang, *Data Quality in Context.* Communications of the ACM, 1997. 40(5).

20. Talburt, J., E. Kuo, R. Wang, and K. Hess. *An Algebraic Approach to Quality Metrics for Customer Recognition Systems.* in *The Ninth International Conference on Information Quality.* 2004. Cambridge, MA: MIT TDQM.

21. Talburt, J., C. Morgan, T. Talley, and K. Archer. *Using Commercial Data Integration Technologies to Improve the Quality of Anonymous Entity Resolution in the Public Sector.* in *International Conference on Information Quality.* 2005. Cambridge, MA: MIT TDQM.

22. Tayi, G. and D.P. Ballou, *Examining Data Quality.* Communications of the ACM, 1998. 41(2): p. 54-57.

23. Wang, R.Y., *A Product Perspective on Total Data Quality Management.* Communications of the ACM, 1998. 41(2): p. 58-65.

24. Wang, R.Y. and Y.W. Lee, *Integrity Analyzer: A Software Tool for Total Data Quality Management.* 1998, MIT: Cambridge, MA.

25. Wang, R.Y. and D. Strong, *Beyond Accuracy: What Data Quality Means to Data Consumers.* Journal of Management Information Systems, 1996. 12(4): p. 5-34.

CHAPTER **8**

Decision Support and Business Intelligence

*T*he *American Heritage Dictionary* defines management as the act, manner, or practice of managing, or handling, supervision or control. To accomplish their work and attain organizational goals, managers engage in a continuous process of decision making. Turban and Aronson [1] call attention to the fact that managers have generally regarded decision making as a pure art, a talent developed over time as a consequence of accumulated job experience. Different management styles, usually based on a mixture of experience, good judgment, and intuition, can bring forth alternative successful solutions to a problem. However, the increasing complexity of the business environment requires that decision making be dealt with systematically, instead of using the trial-and-error approach. Managers require more sophistication and better analysis, specifically, better computer-based decision support tools. Some of these tools and techniques, the quality of the data they process and the information they deliver, are the subject of this chapter.

INTRODUCTION

We know that the use of best practices[11] embedded in current business processes provide significant efficiency gains. But in many organizations, the information infrastructure is not designed to support the development of new paradigms and new business models through experimentation or what-if analytical scenarios, a feature critical to any modern organization. This requires an agile and responsive information infrastructure. According to Prahalad [29], the core capabilities of an agile information infrastructure should include:

- The ability to produce information by integrating data from multiple, heterogeneous sources.

- The capacity to present information to decision makers in a meaningful manner that is relevant in a particular decision context.

- Decision making does not follow a homogeneous rationale. Decision makers use information in their own unique ways, raising questions to attain knowledge on the specific business problem. Their effectiveness requires that they think independently of the information infrastructure. An agile information infrastructure should help decision makers attain such a level of independence.

- Achieving standardization in the language, concepts, and norms that govern inter-organizational business processes is a critical feature of an agile information infrastructure, without which decision makers cannot accrue the potential benefits of synergies across a value network.

---

[11]   Best practices are the collection of template methodologies, policies, and procedures put in place for consistently and effectively attaining a business goal. Best practices typically derive from experience in the business arena. Managers and consultants review those business processes that were deemed successful and eventually assign them best practices status. Whereas a business process is the series of tasks organized to fulfill a specific business goal, a best practice is a business process for which there is enough evidence that the best possible results can be attained.

DATA, INFORMATION, AND KNOWLEDGE

Data, information, and knowledge are closely related concepts that, although they have distinct meaning, are often used interchangeably. These three concepts are described as follows.

- According to Kock, McQueen, and Corner, data is a carrier of knowledge and information, a way through which knowledge and information can be stored and transferred [19].

- Information is data that has been processed and organized so that it is meaningful to the receiver.

- Knowledge fuels results [32]. It leads to understanding and expertise on the problem or domain at issue. While information is typically related to the past and the present, knowledge provides the basis for predicting events with a degree of certainty, based on information about the past. Drucker contends that in that sense, knowledge is the basis for effective action [5].

A manager requires knowledge to make proper decisions. How does a manager acquire knowledge? As noted by **Lauría and Tayi**, modern organizations lay out strategies through which business processes are implemented [22]. These business processes handle the interaction among actors—management, employees, customers, business partners, vendors—generating large amounts of data. This data is collected, stored, and processed, giving way to information from which knowledge is elicited and acted upon, figure 8.1.

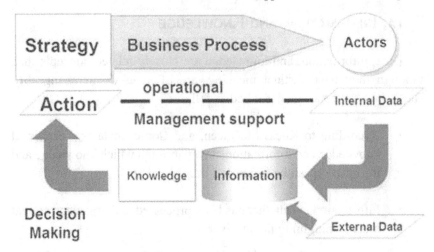

Figure 8.1 Knowledge Platform for Decision Making (Extracted from Lauría & Tayi [22])

SEEKING BUSINESS INTELLIGENCE

During the last decade, organizational strategies have focused on concepts such as e-business, virtual business models, customer orientation, one-to-one marketing, shrinking time to market, increasing competition, globalization, and high workforce turnover. Facing these challenges, organizations have come to recognize the importance of having actionable data to support their business strategies and processes. Decision makers need real-time access to this business-critical information. Are there systems in place to deliver this basic resource? According to Gaurav Dhillon, CEO of Informatica, in this challenging economy, every IT dollar must have an explicit effect on a company's bottom line. In Dhillon's words, "enterprise analytics—which help companies translate data into intelligence by measuring ROI, providing a total business view, and analyzing underlying relationships between customers, suppliers, distributors and customers—are becoming mission critical." [15]

The convergence of management decision modeling and data management systems cannot be overlooked. Following Lauría and Tayi, data management and managerial decision modeling should be regarded as complementary disciplines with a vital role in rational business decision making [22]. A description of each of them follows.

- Data management systems are concerned with recording, extracting, organizing, finding patterns, and displaying data, internal or external, which provides the decision maker with the facts about the problem they are facing.

- Managerial decision modeling systems deal with the creation of models that provide a simplified representation of a decision-making problem. These are used to assess possible actions and estimate the probable outcomes of these actions. In particular, a series of scenarios are used in the analysis phase to evaluate the decision maker's understanding of the problem by changing model parameters. As the future is uncertain, what-if type analyses assist the decision maker to evaluate potential scenarios [20]. These applications typically include decision support systems (DSS), executive information systems (EIS), and expert systems (ES).

The evolution and convergence of these sets of tools, techniques and technologies can be summarized in two words: *business intelligence* (BI). This term has been widely used in the last decade. It was initially applied by the Gartner Group to describe obtaining strategic business value from the data warehouse (DW) [26]. Vendors like IBM and Microsoft have used the term broadly when referring to their data management tools.

BI was originally used to describe a set of three complementary data management technologies.

- Data warehousing: integration of data from multiple sources, and support of online analytical processing, data mining, and managerial decision modeling [23].

- Online analytical processing (OLAP): complex queries applied on data organized dimensionally and displayed from different perspectives of analysis. Query operations include slicing and dicing, drilling and aggregating, pivoting, and filtering of data.

- Data mining and knowledge discovery: extraction of patterns and regularities in the data from large databases or other data sources.

Marakas argues that if the right mix of data warehousing and data mining is used, it is possible to unveil the secrets deeply embedded in business data, which can, in turn, help an organization gain a competitive advantage in any data-driven industry or environment [23].

BI is actually an overarching concept that extends beyond data-driven technologies such as data warehousing, data mining, and enterprise analysis; it becomes an integral part of the overall strategy of a firm. It is the interaction of data management systems and decision modeling systems that helps improve management decision making through which a competitive advantage can be attained. This goal is not optional; it may lead to survival. These are the two technological pillars that can help an organization attain true BI.[12]

Data management systems and managerial decision modeling systems interact closely. DSS and EIS were born at a time where the concepts of data warehousing and OLAP had not been developed, but today it is unthinkable to consider a DSS without a data repository based on a data warehouse or data mart [6].[13] The dimensional approach provided by OLAP has added an appealing flexibility to DSS and EIS interface design. This is especially relevant in the case of EIS. In addition, the useful application of data mining techniques is naturally facilitated by an adequate DW infrastructure. The again, a data management systems approach by itself is not enough. Peter Keen [17] has asked, "If a magic fairy instantly gave you absolutely all the information resources the company would ever need, do you think people would instantly know what to do with it and how to use it well?" Managers ask for analysis, not just retrieval of information. In that sense, DSS and EIS, at the managerial or executive level, provide a goal-oriented approach to decision making [22].

Implementing data marts and data warehouses increases the decision-making capabilities. But in order to achieve the goals articulated in the corporate, business, and functional strategies, data must be gathered from internal and external sources, and a comprehensive BI system must

---

[12]   This approach is not complete without a reference to knowledge management. If knowledge is the basic asset that drives successful decision making, management of knowledge cannot be overlooked. The topic is broad and critical enough to deserve a full treatment that goes beyond the scope of this chapter.

[13]   A data mart is a reduced version of a data warehouse, defined later in this chapter.

be in place to process and share the information and knowledge that is garnered from that data.

Artificial intelligence (AI) and ES deserve a separate analysis, since they are among the least understood and, therefore, most feared technologies in the domain of BI. An ES can be broadly described as a computer program that attempts to mimic human experts by giving advice, teaching, and executing intelligent tasks. A thought-provoking definition of artificial intelligence is given by Rich and Knight [30], "AI is the study of how to make computers do things at which, at the moment, people are better."[14] Some signs of intelligence are: learning from experience, using reasoning in solving problems, understanding and inferring, and making sense of ambiguous situations. State of the art AI still has a long way to go in being able to perform the tasks that comprise the distinguishing qualities of human intelligence, but AI development has continuously improved in terms of productivity and quality.

Of special interest for business applications are tasks such as symbolic processing, heuristics, pattern matching, knowledge bases, machine learning and inference. Data mining and knowledge discovery should receive special mention in this analysis. It is a multidisciplinary set of technologies based on research drawn from inferential statistics, machine learning, knowledge based AI, and theory of control.

ES deliver increased productivity and decrease the time it takes human decision makers to make decisions. ES can work with inaccurate, incomplete, or uncertain data, information, or knowledge, and have the potential for improved decision making and decision quality by providing consistent recommendations and reducing the rate of errors.

Consider, for example, the extensive use of Bayesian networks as probabilistic ES within Microsoft. A Bayesian network is a machine learning technology that constitutes a marriage between graph theory and Bayesian statistics. Leslie Helm [13] has reported that, according to Bill Gates, one of Microsoft's competitive advantages was its expertise in Bayesian networks. According to Helm, Microsoft has been very aggressive in pursuing this new approach. Microsoft offers a free web service that

---

[14]   An alternate definition by Wallace Marshal states that "Artificial stupidity (AS) may be defined as the attempt by computer scientists to create computer programs capable of causing problems of a type normally associated with human thought." (cited by Kurzweil, R., *The Age of Spiritual Machines*, Penguin Books, 1999, p 66).

helps customers troubleshoot problems with the printers connected to their computers. The help wizard in Microsoft Office, one of Microsoft's most profitable cash-cow applications, is actually a Bayesian network. An article in *The Economist* [6] explains that future Microsoft products will try to determine users' intentions more broadly to speed interaction. For instance, having determined which hyperlink on a web page a user is most likely to click, the software could retrieve the corresponding article in advance, so that it comes up on the user's screen faster.

In spite of these virtues, ES exhibit some limitations. The underlying complex, obscure models are not trusted by end users, and this could be a barrier for the adoption of ES. Additionally, ES work well only in a narrow domain of knowledge. Expertise can be hard to extract from humans, and each expert's approach to diagnosis, assessment, and problem solving may be different, yet correct. In that sense, the machine learning approach of learning from data can provide more objective, unbiased, advice; but this means that enough data should be available. Finally, expert knowledge, or historical, accurate data used for machine learning purposes, is not always readily available.

DATA WAREHOUSING

Data warehousing has swiftly unfolded into one of the most popular and demanded business applications. What is a DW? Bill Inmon [16], recognized as the father of the DW concept, defines a DW as a subject-oriented, integrated, time-variant, nonvolatile collection of data supporting the decision-making process.

- Subject-oriented: in the sense that it is organized by major subject areas, identifiable by the user.

- Integrated: not simply a combination of data from a variety of sources, or linked applications. It is the process of mapping dissimilar codes to a common base, developing consistent data element presentations, and delivering this standardized data as broadly as possible [11]. As data from different systems is entered into the DW, entities and attributes are encoded using a consistent nomenclature.

- Time-variant: the structure of a DW always contains a time dimension. A DW can be viewed as a well-organized time-series of snapshots of operational data.

- Nonvolatile: after the data is stored in the DW, it remains unchangeable. This is a basic prerequisite to be able to retrieve data belonging to any point in time. As Haisten [11] points out, maintaining institutional memory is one of the higher goals of data warehousing.

Table 8.1

Operational Data Versus Analytical Data (Extracted from Ewen[8])

Characteristic	Operational Data	Managerial Decision Support Data
Business Goal	Tactical	Strategic
Purpose	Business operations, customer service	Strategic planning, business reorganization
Users/audience	Front line employees, customers	Managers, executives, analysts
Focus	Specific customer, department	Product, line of business, customer profiles
Outputs	Orders, reports	Graph, stats, models, forecasts
Grain	Individual transactions	Aggregates of transactions
Items	Fixed structure, variable contents	Flexible structure, multidimensional
Data structures	Normalized tables	Single flat data sets, star schema
Data needs	Small sets of rows and tables	All records from multi-table joins
Data coding	Mostly require numeric data coding	Textual descriptions preferred
Data manipulations	Insert, edit, delete, retrieve individual records or small sets	Summarize, aggregate, cross-tab

Analytical and Operational Databases

Operational systems are designed for the efficient storage of data and the rapid processing of individual transactions or small sets of records, and as such are performance oriented. Conversely, managerial decision support systems need to be flexible and analytical.

In operational systems, transactions are typically predefined and require the database to provide fast access to a relatively small number of records. Analytical systems, used for decision support, require data to be combined from multiple sources to answer ad hoc queries. In the past, business data was usually stored in operational databases, usually described as online transaction processing (OLTP) systems. It is only recently that data management specialists have realized the advantages of storing analytical data in a form that is much easier to use for decision-making purposes [20]. Codd's work [4] has led to a distinction between analytic databases and operational databases. The characteristics of operational data versus analytical data for decision support are outlined in table 8.1.

In contrast to the familiar OLTP systems used to handle operational data, OLAP describes technology that is designed for real-time, ad hoc querying, by creating multidimensional views of business data. These views are supported by multidimensional database technology. OLAP is based on a cross-tabulation summarization approach. A standard data analysis can include many individual cross-tabs as part of the process of understanding relationships in the data [8].

OLAP can be implemented on relational DBMS, called relational OLAP (ROLAP) servers. These servers usually support extensions to SQL to efficiently implement the multidimensional data model and related operations. In contrast, multidimensional OLAP (MOLAP) servers use data structures specially tailored to accommodate the multidimensional, sparse nature of the data, and implement the OLAP operations over these special data structures. A more detailed explanation of MOLAP and ROLAP architectures can be found in Pendse [27].

Data Warehouse Architecture

Following Ponniah, a standard architecture of a DW should include a source data module, a data staging area, a data storage module, a metadata module, and an information delivery module, figure 8.2 [28].

- Source data module: The DW integrates data from a variety of sources—internal data, including operational data coming from the transactional applications; confidential data, stored on spreadsheets and desktop databases; and external data from sources outside the organization, such as market share data from competitors and financial indicators. Dealing with this wide range of sources, platforms, and formats, and combining them into useful data for integrated storage, is one of the most important challenges in a DW implementation.

- Data staging module: Data coming from different sources has to be extracted, transformed (organized, cleansed, and formatted), and then loaded into the DW. These operations are generically referred to as ETL (extraction, transformation, and loading). The extraction process has to deal with data from multiple sources, platforms, and formats. Given the complexity of the task, organizations often have to resort to in-house development to fulfill the extraction process.

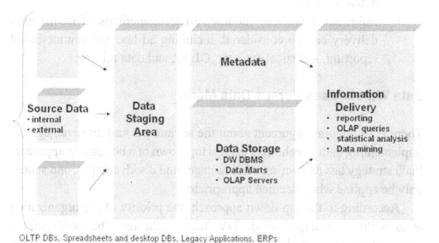

OLTP DBs, Spreadsheets and desktop DBs, Legacy Applications, ERPs

Figure 8.2 DW Architecture (Adapted from Ponniah [28])

The extracted data is usually stored in an intermediate area, known as the staging area, to be used for the transformation process, before moving it to the DW. The transformation process is a critical aspect in the success of a DW project. There are many factors to consider such as the heterogeneous nature of data sources, the quality of the data being fed, and the fact that ETL is an ongoing process, with data being continuously fed from the data sources. The challenge is to preserve the DW as the institutional memory of the organization while accepting the fact that it is a time-variant, nonvolatile, database environment.

- Data storage module: DW data is stored in a separate repository from operational data, typically in the form of relational databases or multidimensional data structures.

- Metadata module: the metadata module provides support to handle the data describing the data in the DW, similar in concept to the data catalog in an operational database, but more relevant. It should, ideally, encompass data from all the key components of the DW architecture, including: information on the sources that feed the DW and the frequency of update; the procedures, business rules, and methods used in ETL processes; a description of the tables, indexes and/or data structures that comprise the DW's data repository; and detailed information on the available information delivery tools.

- Information delivery module: different methods of information delivery can be considered, including ad hoc and routine-based reporting, statistical analysis, OLAP, and data mining.

Data Warehouses Versus Data Marts

There is an ongoing argument about the advantages and disadvantages of implementing data warehouses using a top-down or a bottom-up approach. Each strategy has its own set of advantages and disadvantages, and should only be applied when deemed appropriate.

According to the top-down approach, the priority of the organization is to build an enterprise-wide DW that synthesizes the needs of the organization as a whole. Centralized processing rules and a common metadata repository, located at the corporate DW, simplify the task of integrating data from multiple sources and ensure data consistency across the set of smaller data repositories (data marts) derived from the centralized repository. In other words, this strategy, if successfully attained, guarantees one version of the truth. But this ambitious approach is not free. Top-down DW projects are high-risk undertakings that can take a long time to implement and can easily upset the community of users. Typically, projects can take one or two years to be delivered, which is a long time to maintain user expectations, management commitment, and budget support. Given these issues, top management (CEO) sponsorship becomes a critical factor in the success of enterprise DW implementation. Although the top-down approach was the strategy of choice of most of the early DW projects, the failure rate led the majority of current DW projects to settle for the safer alternative of structuring the DW from the bottom up.

The bottom-up approach posits the advantage of organizing the DW as a collection of incremental, conformed data marts. A data mart is a small, narrowly focused DW that contains data of a specific sector of the organization such as a department or a business unit. This allows faster implementation; a data mart can typically be brought to production status in less than a year. Faster implementation can, in turn, show results faster, which considerably reduces end user dissatisfaction and management anxiety, and consequently, the overall risk of the project. Obviously, this approach is less ambitious and easier to implement, but it does pose the challenge of having to integrate heterogeneous data. Data marts are sometimes built to suit short-term business needs, disregarding the overall corporate environment. This can lead to inconsistent and irreconcilable DW architectures.

Dimensional Modeling

Operational database systems have two basic goals:

- Enhance performance of transaction processing and individual record retrieval and update.
- Minimize data redundancy in order to maximize consistency and overall throughput.

In the last 20 years, the database market has been driven by the relational model: normalized tables with atomic field values (no multi-valued items or repeating groups) linked through foreign keys representing 1:N relationships, and query languages based on first order logic predicates. SQL has become the standard query language for relational DBMS. Although appropriate for the design of transaction processing systems, the relational model has failed to provide an adequate framework for decision support and ad hoc business querying. Normalization yields a large number of tables, even in simple applications. The data model is often difficult to grasp by business users, who find it difficult to develop queries spanning several tables.

With data warehousing, a new model has emerged, the dimensional model [18]. This model is designed around subject categories, referred to as dimensions of analysis, which provide the business user with the ability to view the data from a multidimensional perspective and aggregate data or drill into the details. As a result, it is much easier for the business user to comprehend the data model. Moreover, the geometrical, dimensional approach provided by OLAP has added an appealing flexibility to user interface design and eliminated the threatening first order logic, SQL-based approach that dominated the ad hoc querying arena before the inception of OLAP.

Dimensions may be described as qualifying properties that confer additional perspectives to a given fact. If, for example, the subject area was sales, the dimensions of analysis could be customers and products, if the requirement is to analyze sales by customer and by product. Note that time was not mentioned in the example, but it is an implicit dimension of analysis, given the time-variant characteristic of any DW.

The dimensional concept defines the following business aspects: the subject area, the dimensions of analysis, their levels or hierarchies of aggregation, and the facts (measures or metrics) to be analyzed according to these multiple dimensions.

The most typical dimensional model is the *star schema*. In the star schema, a single fact table containing the set of measures is linked to a number of dimension tables radially. The name comes from the fact that its ERD loosely resembles a star. The subject area (fact table) is the center of the star and the dimensions of analysis (dimension tables) form the points. The link between each dimension table and the fact table is a one-to-many relationship. The classic star schema has a single fact table containing a compound primary key, with one segment for each dimension and additional columns of numeric facts. There is a single table for each dimension, a generated key, and the set of attributes that characterize the dimension.

Star schemas do not provide explicit support for dimension hierarchies, which means that dimension tables are typically not normalized. *Snowflake schemas* provide an additional refinement by further normalizing the dimension tables. Its main advantage is making explicit the dimensional hierarchy, which is hidden in the dimension table in the case of the star schema. But the snowflake schema adds complexity to the dimensional model. It can lead to additional complications in handling multiple tables and introduce a burden on performance. Kimball, as a matter of fact, proscribes the use of snowflake schemas.

Data granularity refers to the level of detail with which data is stored in the DW. The more detail there is in the fact table, the higher its granularity, and the more rows it will have. The level of granularity has to be decided based on the types of queries and the expected performance of those queries. In an operational database, data is typically stored with the lowest level of detail. A query requiring summarization aggregates individual records. Summarized data is not usually kept in an operational database. Instead, a DW usually keeps pre-aggregated data at different levels, given the fact that most queries launched by users require some kind of aggregation. These higher levels of aggregations are generally referred to as materialized views. These materialized views correspond in the simplest cases to aggregating the fact table on one or more selected dimensions. Materializing summary data can significantly speed up query processing, but has the disadvantage of having to load and refresh them periodically [2]. With regard to identifying which views to materialize, there are three alternatives to consider: physically generate all possible materialized views, which would yield the best query performance, but could be very expensive in terms of computation and storage; materialize nothing, in which case computation is performed on demand; or materialize only part of the data cube, balancing each tradeoff [12].

Consider a supermarket chain with stores in many cities and many states. The sales department wants to analyze all the point-of-sale (POS) transactions by product, region, and time. Create a dimensional model to structure a sales data mart that can help the sales analysts query the data.

Following Kimball's approach to dimensional modeling [18], we should follow these steps:

- Identify the process being modeled.
- Choose the dimensions.
- Determine the granularity at which facts will be stored.
- Identify the numeric measures for the facts.

We start by identifying the subject of the data mart, which in this case is centered around the retail sales of the supermarket chain. The dimensions of analysis are product, region, and time. We may want to add the POS transaction number so we can track each one.

Next, we determine the granularity of each dimension. For region, we consider state, county, city, and store name. For product, we include product category, product brand, product name, and the name of the department with the product. The time dimension includes year, quarter, month, date, day, and indicator flags for holiday or non-holiday, weekday or weekend day.

Finally, we determine the numeric measures for the facts. In this case, we consider number of units sold and sales in dollars.

The set of dimension hierarchies and measures are summarized in figure 8.3.[15]

Subject: Sales			
REGION	PRODUCT	TIME	TRANSACTION
State	Department	Year	Transaction ID
County	Product Category	Quarter	
City	Brand	Month	
Store Name	Product Name	Week	
		Date	
		Day	
		HolidayFlag	
		WeekdayFlag	
Fact measures: Units Sold, Dollars Sold			

Figure 8.3 Dimensions and Measures for Sales Analysis

The diagram in figure 8.3 can be used to structure the star schema that implements the dimensional data mart. Each dimension hierarchy is converted into a dimension table. Note that an exception is made with the transaction dimension since it has no associated dimension table; for this reason it is known as a degenerate dimension.

Every dimension table carries a primary key, automatically generated, that is not semantically related to the dimension hierarchy. The fact table,

---

[15]   Ponniah calls this diagram an *information package* [20].

in turn, contains the fact measures and has a primary key formed by compounding the primary keys of all the dimension tables together with any degenerate dimensions included in the model (the transaction ID in this case). The primary key in each dimension table is, therefore, the foreign key in the fact table. Figure 8.4 displays the resulting star schema.

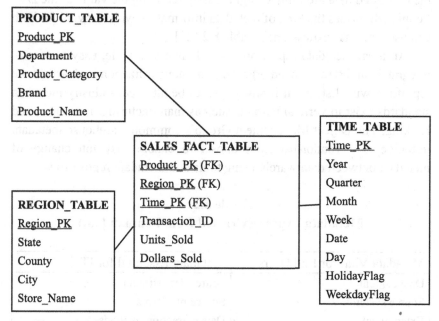

Figure 8.4 Star Schema of the Sales Data Mart

Data Warehouse Metadata

Metadata is one of the most neglected components of DW architecture. At the same time, it is a key ingredient for the success of a DW project in terms of its implementation, use, and administration. The complexity of modern information decision systems, with huge inventories of data elements and objects, makes it impossible for it to be handled by human resources without the assistance of computer-based knowledge repositories that describe what data, processes, and systems mean and do. The gap in the knowledge is filled by metadata, which is, by definition, data about data. In terms of information technology, it is the set of data structures, files, or tables with information describing other attributes. There are many kinds of metadata that can be associated with a DW. There is metadata to describe the data that is extracted, transformed, and loaded into the DW; metadata to characterize the data storage and underlying data structures; and metadata to identify the resources for information delivery. Metadata acts as a roadmap of the DW; without metadata, the chances of locating the requested data are limited, significantly reducing the value of the DW. Ponniah describes the kind of metadata information which is vital for both end users and IT professionals, table 8.2 [28].

An ideal metadata repository should have a flexible, easy-to-access, integrated, and standardized organization. Standardization is clearly at the top of the wish list, but it is still a goal to be attained. Industry metadata standards exist in vertical markets such as manufacturing, insurance, and banking. The Object Management Group's common warehouse metadata initiative is a vendor-backed proposal to enable easy interchange of metadata between data warehousing tools and metadata repositories.

Table 8.2
Metadata Types (Extracted from Ponniah [28])

Metadata Vital for End Users	Metadata Essential for IT
Data content	Source data structures
Source systems	Source platforms
External data	Data extraction methods
Data transformation rules	External data
Last update dates	Data transformation rules
Data load/update cycles	Data cleansing rules
Business dimensions	Staging area structures
Business metrics	Initial loads
Summary data	Incremental loads
Navigation paths	Dimensional models
Query templates	Data summarization
Report formats	Web-enabling platforms
Predefined query reports	Query/report design
OLAP data	OLAP systems
Data mining models	Data mining algorithms and tools

QUALITY ISSUES OF DATA WAREHOUSING

The quality of the data in a DW represents one of the major elements that must be managed when designing, implementing, and administering a DW. End users, who blame a DW implementation for shortcomings in the quality of the data, easily lose confidence in the technology. This usually results in a major project failure. The following examples, extracted from Hufford [14], table 8.3, illustrate this.

Table 8.3
Examples of DW Quality Issues (Hufford [14])

Inaccurate data related to categorization of bank customers resulted in erroneous risk exposure estimates, leading the bank to believe it was more diversified than it was. When the oil market softened in Texas, banks having a large number of Texan accounts suffered a major loss because of the inaccurate representation of risk.
A downsized manufacturing firm took action to rid itself of excess items of expensive equipment. Three months after the equipment was sold as excess or distributed to plants showing a shortage, inter-departmental equipment loan information surfaced showing that transferred equipment was double counted. The firm had overestimated its excess inventory.
A senior-level military officer was defending the defense budget before the U.S. Senate. When questioned about a discrepancy in the number of authorized officers shown in the proposed budget vs. the congressional numbers, no one could explain the discrepancy. That day the military lost 2,500 authorized officers it needed because Congress liked the lower number. It turned out that a data timeliness problem within one of the DW source systems caused the discrepancy. Based on the congressional action, this launched an extensive effort to review and scrub the budget data's consistency as part of the budget preparation process.

DW quality can be defined in terms of the DQ dimensions defined in chapter 3. Of these, we chose the degree of accuracy, relevancy, completeness, consistency, and timeliness that make a DW suitable to answer user queries.

DQ is a quality measure of the relative amount of erroneous data stored in the database [25]. Users' expectations demand that only the right data be retrieved when querying the DW. A sales record retrieved from the DW should contain accurate data associated with the queried sales transaction. *Accuracy* implies validity. The value of each DW attribute conforms to prescribed business rules and should fall within the domain of allowable values, that is, the quantity on hand of a product in inventory must be greater than or equal to zero.

Relevancy is the degree to which the provided information matches the users' needs [25]. A data element must be accurate, but if it is not relevant to any of the DW users, it should not be included in the DW. If the result of a user query is not relevant, it should be because the query was not specific enough or that it was incorrectly formulated.

Completeness is the degree to which values are present in the attributes that require them [14]. The assumption is that there are no missing (or null) values for a given attribute or field in the DW. For example, end users of a sales database assume that all transaction data is correct, and that it is actually stored in the database.

Consistency is the degree of coherence among data integrated across multiple sources that rules out the chance of variation or contradiction. For instance, customer information should be coded in a homogeneous way, whether it comes from a sales database or from the accounting system.

Timeliness describes whether the requested data items are updated when specified. This is typically determined by the users' requirements and has to do with the periodicity of the updates and the granularity of the data (more on this later). Timeliness refers to the age of the data. If the users expect data updated daily, the ETL process must be applied daily. Timeliness should not be confused with response time. Traditionally, the quality of an operational database is determined by its ability to respond quickly to queries. This is not the case with DW, where the business user is much more concerned about the results than the time it takes to produce them, within reasonable limits.

The Issue of Integration

An irritant of our database-driven society is the fact that, because of data integration issues, we, as customers, may have more than one identity. We may receive a call from a telemarketer, on behalf of a financial institution of which we are long-time customers, offering us services we already have. Integrating data from multiple sources on an ongoing basis is probably the most critical and challenging issue to be faced by a DW implementation. Most of these problems arise from the disparities among the source systems that feed the DW.

- Different platforms and operating systems.

- Evolving structure of programs and data models in operational systems because changing business rules affect ETL operations.

- Lack of consistency among source systems that may exhibit different results of the same data.

- Lack of means for resolving detected inconsistencies.

Larry English pointed out that "assuming the source data is OK because the operational systems seem to work just fine" should be avoided if the DW is to deliver quality information [7]. According to English, operational DQ can be sufficient to support the operational processes within the performance measures of the information producers, but is not necessarily of acceptable quality to satisfy decision support processes. This misconception points to the complete denial most organizations exhibit as to the extent of their information quality problems.

The issue of integration is starting to move beyond the boundaries of the enterprise itself. The requirement to integrate people and organizations external to a business entity is on the rise.

Wixom and Watson investigated the critical implementation factors in a data warehousing implementation [34]. They identified significant relationships between the system quality and DQ factors, and perceived net benefits, figure 8.5. Wixom and Watson question whether a DW can even exist without DQ.

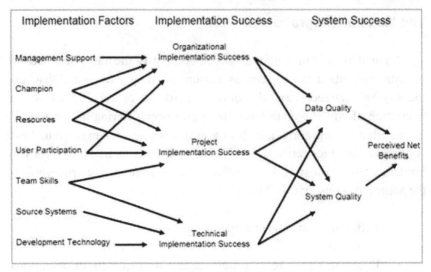

Figure 8.5 Wixom and Watson's Research Model for DW Success

According to Wixom and Watson's study, management support and resources help address organizational issues during DW implementations [34]. Resources, user participation, and highly-skilled project team members increase the chances of timely, within-budget data warehousing projects that render adequate functionality. The heterogeneous nature of data sources adds complexity to the ETL processes. The project's success, together with organizational and project implementation issues, in turn, influences the system quality of the DW. However, other factors not present in the research model are required to explain the impact on DQ.

Data Quality Enhancement

Poor-quality data (dirty data) is a widespread problem in all companies. The problem has gotten worse with the inception of DW, with its promise of delivering accurate, integrated, historical data in support of decision making, all at a reasonable cost. Typical DQ problems faced by organizations when implementing/operating DW are:

- Incorrect values: values fed into the DW may be wrong.

- Missing values: data may not exist in some of the data sources that feed the DW.

- Dummy values in data fields: default values may be used to replace or compensate for missing values.

- Reused primary keys: inadequate coding may lead to a shortage in the number of feasible primary keys and require the reuse of keys that identified archived data. This has the potential of introducing misleading interpretations about the identity of data recorded in the DW.

- Multipurpose fields: data from several fields may be consolidated into one; for instance, the different components of an address.

- Noncompliance of business rules: lack of validation may lead to attribute values that fall out of the scope of the attribute domain.

- Conflicting data from different sources: different sources may have conflicting data; for instance, two addresses for the same customer.

According to Moss, four questions need to be answered regarding dirty data: can it be cleansed, should it be cleansed, where do we cleanse it, and how do we cleanse it [1].

Following Moss [24], the answer to the first question is: not always. There are situations where it is not possible to cleanse the data, regardless of the effort expended. The data could be dispersed, lost, or never existed. Changes in business processes introduce different coding terminologies in data records. If these changes are not well documented, and the documentation is not properly stored and classified, applications become black boxes, only known in detail by those who developed them or maintained them at some point in their life cycle. If these veteran members of the organization are no longer around to accomplish the task, it would require extensive research to extricate the meaning of the data. Sometimes, any attempt to decipher such data produces even more errors due to inaccurate interpretations. Therefore, it may be best to abandon the task altogether.

The answer to should it be cleansed is typically cost dependent. Data cleansing is a time-consuming and therefore expensive activity, and must be cost-justified. In most cases the answer is yes, and to a certain extent, there is always some kind of data cleansing. However, for some worst-case scenarios, the time, money, and effort required to complete the task is prohibitive and outweighs the benefits. If the cost of cleansing exceeds the business loss being incurred by leaving the data dirty, it may be better not to clean it. Ballou and Tayi note the importance of assigning priorities to efforts to improve DQ, such as data cleansing, and propose models for determining those priorities based on a cost-benefit analysis [1]. They identify factors that influence DQ enhancement projects: current quality of data, required quality of data, priority of organizational activity linked to data, cost of DQ enhancement, and change in value (utility) for organizational activity if a DQ enhancement project is undertaken. With this set of factors, they set up an optimization (integer linear programming) model that maximizes the total value from all projects, given a set of resource allocation constraints.

Where do we cleanse it is a good question. Should we focus on the operational data, or do we perform the cleansing operations as part of the ETL process at the staging area of the DW? Cleansing the operational data is probably the ideal scenario, since that is the source of the errors. Standard QC practice suggests that it is usually cheaper to control the errors where they originate. However, attempting to cleanse operational data in multiple heterogeneous source platforms can be complex and expensive. Cleansing the data at the staging area may be easier.

The final question, how to cleanse dirty data, requires organizations to establish an adequate balance between in-house programming and the use of third-party tools. Many tools are available for several types of data cleansing tasks, but reality dictates that even the most sophisticated products are not capable of dealing with all possible data-cleansing issues. This means that custom programming will certainly be required to complete the data cleansing process.

Data Quality Information and Data Tagging

As mentioned, when the DQ is compromised, incorrect interpretation and use of information from the DW can drastically affect the confidence of the users. Data quality information can be used as a way of preventing or limiting these DQ issues. Information about the quality of stored data can be thought of as metadata. Chengalur-Smith, Ballou, and Pazer explain that there are levels of granularity for which the metadata should apply [3]. It is possible to have information at a number of levels of granularity including entire files, data fields, and individual data items. This could be done by including relevant DQ dimensions, such as accuracy and timeliness, in the form of data tags, as proposed by Wang and Madnick [33]. Data tagging is the process of attaching quality indicators to data in a DW as a way of raising awareness of the level of DQ among end users. Empirical studies have shown that the data field level of granularity provides a reasonable compromise between sufficient detail and cost effectiveness [3]. Note, however, that most, if not all, current data dictionary implementations still lack this kind of DQ information.

An important consideration is how DQ information is recorded and presented. DQ tagging may be represented in several ways, including interval and ordinal scales. But it must be completely understood in order to be used and affect decisions.

Can data tagging eliminate DQ problems? Fisher, Chengalur-Smith and Ballou contend that since users are increasingly removed from any personal experience with data, knowledge that would be beneficial in judging the appropriateness of the data for the decision to be made has been lost [9]. Data tags could provide this missing information. However, as it is generally expensive to generate and maintain such information, doing so would be worthwhile only if DQ information effectively enhances decision making.

Data Mining and Knowledge Discovery

Aristotle Onassis said once, "The secret of success is to know something that nobody else knows". We live in a world that feeds on information, available from multiple and heterogeneous sources. Unfortunately, information is not always organized in a standard easy-to-retrieve format [21]. It is a subtle and slippery concept buried in massive amounts of raw data. Organizations must find ways to automatically analyze, summarize, and classify data, as well as discover hidden trends, patterns, and anomalies [21]. This is the goal of data mining and knowledge discovery, a set of methods, technologies, and tools used to make critical business decisions. Data mining is an interdisciplinary area. It feeds off of statistics, database technology, computer science, AI, and machine learning. The data mining process is sometimes referred to as knowledge discovery, or knowledge discovery in databases (KDD).

An essential aspect of data mining is the exploration of data and the application of algorithms to identify patterns and regularities in the data. Once these regularities are identified, they can be generalized, for prediction purposes, to incoming data sets, assuming that the incoming data elements have a statistical distribution similar to the sample data used for mining.

How does data mining differ from statistics? Although the disciplines are similar and share many techniques, statistics has developed over the last 300 years to help scientists collect, organize, and analyze data, test hypotheses, and measure the accuracy of experimental results. In almost all of these situations, the scarcity of available data was the main issue. The challenge of data mining takes the opposite path—finding ways to make sense of masses of data that modern organizations and businesses generate daily.

Choosing a data mining technique depends on the nature of the analysis and the kind of data available. A very broad grouping of data mining algorithms should include the following categories.

- Classification: mapping a data item into one of several predefined categories [21]. Stored data is used to locate data in predetermined groups. For example, a retail store chain could mine customer purchase data to determine what customers typically buy. In a different application, a classifier can be built to assess the risk of potential intrusions (hacker attacks) in a computer network.

- Prediction: predicting a continuous dependent variable given a data set containing a group of continuous and/or discrete (categorical) attributes.

- Clustering: finding groups of unlabeled instances within a dataset with certain commonalities. For example, data can be mined to identify market segments or consumer affinity groups.

- Associations: determining relations between fields in the database/dataset [21]. The beer and diaper purchase combination is an example of associative mining. A large supermarket chain, analyzing consumer behavior, found a statistically significant association between purchases of beer and diapers on Fridays. The hypothesis was that fathers were stopping at the supermarket to buy diapers and beer. So the supermarket put together a promotion of both diapers and beer, resulting in increased sales of both.[16]

- Sequential patterns: data is mined to anticipate behavior patterns and trends. These algorithms can help organizations understand what (time-based) sequences of events are frequently encountered together and detect anomalies or outliers [21]. This approach is followed by most credit card companies to detect a succession of fraudulent purchases.

From a statistical perspective, many data mining tools can be described as methods for exploratory data analysis and multivariate data analysis. From the point of view of AI, data mining is closely related to machine learning, a process through which a computer algorithm learns from experience (the training data set) and builds a model that is then used to predict behavior.

There are very good reasons for businesses to invest in data mining. Organizations of all sizes have become customer-oriented, and they are learning the need to understand individual needs as well as look at the lifetime value of each customer. An organization that reaches out to customers considers every interaction with a client or prospect as a learning opportunity, and data warehousing can provide organizations with a record of every transaction. However, learning goes beyond simply gathering, storing, and structuring data adequately. Learning is about eliciting knowledge from meaningful, actionable data/information. While data warehousing provides the means of creating an institutional memory for the organization, data mining delivers intelligence. Table 8.4, extracted from Groth, describes several areas in business where data mining can directly affect a company's profitability and competitive advantage [10].

Table 8.4
How Data Mining Affects Various Industries (Groth [10])

---

[16] Although this story is a good example and is often used to exemplify the use of data mining in retail marketing, it has never been confirmed, and could be an urban myth. A compilation of versions of this story can be found in http://dssresources.com/newsletters/66.php.

Data Mining in Retail	
Business problem	Increase response rates on direct-mail campaign
Solution	Through data mining, marketers build predictive models that indicate who will most likely respond to a direct-mail campaign
Benefit	Increase revenues by targeting campaigns to the right audience
Data Mining in Insurance	
Business problem	Decrease number of fraudulent claims
Solution	Through data mining, marketers build predictive models that identify those claims that are most likely fraudulent
Benefit	Increase profits by reducing costs
Data Mining in Financial Markets	
Business problem	Improve ability to predict the likely fluctuations in the market
Solution	Through data mining, financial analysts build predictive models that identify patterns that have historically caused market fluctuations
Benefit	Increase revenues by investing more intelligently

Data warehousing and data mining are complementary technologies and natural allies. Knowledge discovery is, by definition, the process of identifying regularities in the data through application of data mining techniques. The natural prerequisite of this task is to have good-quality data. Much of the effort behind a data-mining project deals with acquiring clean and consistent data, a similar concern of any well-designed DW architecture.

A major result of implementing a DW is that an organization has the opportunity to use data mining techniques on existing data to "discover hidden truths within the data" [31]. Without a central repository, an organization would have to access each transactional system and collect data from them separately in order to mine data.

The application of data mining techniques allows the organization to identify patterns and relationships in the data stored in the DW. The patterns discovered lead to an increase in knowledge and a strategic competitive advantage. By using data mining techniques on a DW, organizations have the opportunity of detecting patterns in the data and can react accordingly. For example, a company could notice a relationship between two products in sales data and consequently place them together as part of a promotional package to get the customers to purchase both products. In this way data mining fulfills the promise of converting data into actionable information.

As useful as a DW may seem for any data-mining endeavor, it should not be considered a prerequisite. Many data mining applications are done on data which does not have the benefit of being stored and structured in a central DW repository.

Data Quality and Data Mining

Data mining, like other data management disciplines, faces the challenge of dealing with real-world data of diverse quality. This means that the overall performance of a data mining technique is tied to the quality of data available to an organization. We know by now that organizational databases and data sources have persistent DQ problems [10]. Users view DQ to be a combination of several dimensions. So a database containing complete data may, in fact, be of poor quality because of errors in the data. Generally speaking, any successful data-mining task has as a prerequisite a DQ enhancement activity. Lauría & Tayi contend that determining which dimension of DQ should be improved, and to what extent, is not straightforward [21]. It requires understanding the interaction between the problem domain, the nature of data errors in that domain, and the characteristics of the proposed data mining technique.

A careful choice of data mining algorithms can sometimes mitigate the poor quality of the data to be mined. Many current data mining algorithms are quite resilient to quality issues. The algorithms are able to learn predictive models which are reasonably accurate, even in the presence of dirty data. As shown by Lauría and Tayi, totally clean data may not be required to train a classifier that performs acceptably [21]. By analyzing the algorithms' performance when applied on training data of varying quality, thresholds can be established beyond which derived predictions are no longer reliable. This means that the tradeoff between the quality of the training data and the cost of attaining such quality may be improved if adequate data mining tools are put in place [21].

SUMMARY

In the information era, BI means developing a vision of how an organization can be more efficient and realize a better return on their information assets, based on a thorough application of data management systems and managerial decision modeling. Data warehousing has become a top priority in the IT departments of large organizations, because there are increasing amounts of data and of data storage available which can be used to gain a competitive advantage. Organizations are mining their historical data looking for patterns to support decisions. End users are seeking more sophisticated ways of analyzing data, eliciting knowledge, and enhancing decision support. BI has become a key component of any modern organization that seeks to attain market leadership and propel itself beyond its competition. But BI technologies require a basic ingredient to achieve successful implementation, and its name is data quality.

CHAPTER EIGHT QUESTIONS

Review Questions

1. What are the main features of an agile information infrastructure?
2. Differentiate the concepts of data, information, and knowledge.
3. What kinds of technologies underlie the current meaning of BI?
4. What is a DW, according to Bill Inmon?
5. Why are operational databases not especially suited for decision support applications?
6. What are the basic components of a standard DW architecture?
7. What is a star schema?
8. What are the challenges faced when integrating data from multiple sources?

9. What are some of the typical DQ problems faced by organizations when implementing DW projects?
10. What is data tagging? How does it affect DQ?
11. How would you classify data mining tasks?
12. What is the advantage of mining data out of the DW?

Discussion Questions

1. Find a local organization that has implemented a DW. Try to contact the project manager/DW administrator and ask them about the critical challenges faced when designing and implementing the DW. How did they deal with the DQ issues?
2. You are the vice president of marketing for a nation-wide car manufacturer. List the dimensions and business metrics that you would choose for your analysis.
3. Analyze a data-mining product in the market; identify its features and the kind of data-mining tasks that can be performed with it.
4. Explain why dimension tables are usually not normalized.
5. Discuss the relevance of metadata in a DW. What is the link to DQ?
6. Design a dimensional DW for an airline. The DW should allow the business to study and analyze the units sold (dollars, seats), passengers flown, costs (fuel, catering, airport, HR) opened up by time, route, region, customer class, and fleet. Define dimensions and measures, and draw a star schema. What is the fact table and what are the essential dimension tables? List the primary keys and associated attributes for each table. What kind of data tags would you recommend to enhance DQ in the DW?
7. Should data always be cleansed? Explain.
8. You are the CIO of a large, multinational company. You must make a presentation to persuade the board to invest in a DQ program that will help enhance the current BI platform of the organization. What key points do you need to make in favor of this investment?
9. As a data mining expert working for a retail company, you are asked to find products that are frequently purchased together, potential candidates for a new promotion. What kind of data mining approach would you apply? Explain your reasons.
10. Discuss the effect of DQ on data mining. Cite three examples.

REFERENCES

1. Ballou, D.P. and G.K. Tayi, *Enhancing Data Quality in Data Warehouse Environments.* Communications of the ACM, 1999. 42(1): p. 73-78.
2. Chaudhuri, S. and U. Dayal, *An Overview of Data Warehousing and OLAP Technology.* ACM SIGMOD, 1997. 26(1): p. 67-74.
3. Chengalur-Smith, I., D.P. Ballou, and H. Pazer, *The Impact of Data Quality Information on Decision Making: an Exploratory Analysis.* IEEE Transactions on Knowledge and Data Engineering, 1999. 11(6): p. 853-864.
4. Codd, E.F., S.B. Codd, and C.T. Salley, *Providing Online Analytical Processing to User-Analysts: An IT Mandate.* E. F. Codd and Associates, 1993.
5. Drucker, P.F., *The New Realities.* 1989, New York, NY: Harper & Row.
6. Economist, T., *In Praise of Bayes.* 2000: Berkeley, CA.
7. English, L., *Mistakes to Avoid if Your Data Warehouse is to Deliver Quality Information.* The Data Administration Newsletter, 2002.
8. Ewen, E.F., C.E. Medsker, R.N. Dusterhof, R.N. LevanShultz, and J.L. Smith, *Data Warehousing in an Integrated Health System: Building the Business Case*, in *DOLAP '98.* 1998: Washington DC, USA.
9. Fisher, C.W., I. Chengalur-Smith, and D.P. Ballou, *The Impact of Experience and Time on the Use of Data Quality Information in Decision Making.* Information Systems Research, 2003. 14(2): p. 170-188.
10. Groth, R., *Data Mining: Building Competitive Advantage.* 2 ed. 2002, Upper Saddle River, NJ: Prentice Hall.
11. Haisten, M., *Real-Time Data Warehouse: The Next Stage in Data Warehouse Evolution.* DM Review, 1999.
12. Harinarayan, V., A. Rajaraman, and J. Ullman. *Implementing Data Cubes Efficiently.* in *ACM SIGMOD '96.* 1996.
13. Helm, L., *Improbable Inspiration: The Future of Software May Lie in Obscure Theories of an 18th Century Cleric Named Thomas Bayes*, in *Los Angeles Times.* 1996.
14. Hufford, D., *Data Warehouse Quality*, in *DM Review.* 1996.

15. Informatica, *Enterprise Analytics and Collaborative Commerce Cited as Highest Priorities for 2002 Among IT Executives Surveyed.* 2001.

16. Inmon, W., *What is a Data Warehouse?* Tech Topic Prism Solutions, Inc, 1995. 1(1).

17. Keen, P., *Let's Focus on Action, Not Information*, in *Computer World*. 1997.

18. Kimball, R., *The Data Warehouse Toolkit: Practical Techniques for Building Dimensional Warehouses.* 1996, New York, NY: John Wiley & Sons.

19. Kock Jr., N.F., R.J. McQueen, and J.L. Corner, *The Nature of Data, Information and Knowledge Exchanges in Business Processes: Implications for Process Improvement and Organizational Learning.* The Learning Organization, 1997. 4(2).

20. Koutsoukis, N., G. Mitra, and C. Lucas, *Adapting Online Analytical Processing for Decision-Modeling: the Interaction of Information and Decision Technologies.* Decision Support Systems, 1999. 26: p. 1-30.

21. Lauría, E. and G. Tayi. *A Comparative Study of Data Mining Algorithms for Network Intrusion Detection in the Presence of Poor Quality Data.* in *International Conference on Information Quality.* 2003. Cambridge, MA: MIT TDQM Program.

22. Lauría, E. and G. Tayi, *The Quest for Business Intelligence*, in *Annual Reader on Management*, R. Brendt, Editor. 2005, Zurich Graduate School of Business Administration: Heidelberg, Germany.

23. Marakas, G., *Modern Data Warehousing, Mining and Visualization: Core Concepts.* 2003, New Jersey: Prentice Hall.

24. Moss, L., *Data Cleansing: A Dichotomy of Data Warehousing?* DM Review, 1998.

25. Naumann, F. *From Databases to Information Systems—Information Quality Makes the Difference.* in *Sixth International Conference on Information Quality.* 2001. Cambridge, MA: MIT TDQM Program.

26. Osterfielt, S., *Business intelligence: Tactical Intelligence.* DM Review, 1999.

27. Pendse, N., *OLAP Architectures.* The OLAP Report, 2004.

28. Ponniah, P., *Data Warehousing Fundamentals*. 2001, New York, NY: John Wiley & Sons, Inc.

29. Prahalad, C.K., M.S. Krishnan, and V. Ramaswamy, *The Essence of Business Agility: Looking at the Line Manager as a Consumer of Business Technology Will Yield a Nimbler Company*. OPTIMIZE, 2002. 11.

30. Rich, E. and K. Knight, *Artificial Intelligence*. 1991, New York, NY: McGraw-Hill.

31. Turban, E. and J. Aronson, *Decision Support Systems and Intelligent Systems*. 7 ed. 2004: Prentice Hall.

32. Turban, E., McLean, E. and Wetherbe, J., *Information Technology for Management*. 2 ed. 1999, NY: John Wiley & Sons, Inc.

33. Wang, R.Y. and S.E. Madnick. *A Polygon Model for Heterogeneous Database Systems: The Source Tagging Perspective*. in *16th International Conference on Very Large Databases*. 1990. Brisbane, Australia.

34. Wixom, B. and H. Watson, *An Empirical Investigation of the Factors Affecting Data Warehousing Success*. MIS Quarterly, 2001. 25(1): p. 17-4

INDEX